IRAQI REFUGEES IN THE UNITED STATES

Iraqi Refugees in the United States

The Enduring Effects of the War on Terror

Ken R. Crane

NEW YORK UNIVERSITY PRESS

New York

NEW YORK UNIVERSITY PRESS
New York
www.nyupress.org
© 2021 by New York University
All rights reserved

Library of Congress Cataloging-in-Publication Data
Names: Crane, Ken R., 1957–   author.
Title: Iraqi refugees in the United States : the enduring effects of the War on Terror / Ken R. Crane.
Description: New York : New York University Press, [2021] | Includes bibliographical references and index.
Identifiers: LCCN 2020015852 (print) | LCCN 2020015853 (ebook) | ISBN 9781479873944 (cloth) | ISBN 9781479886906 (paperback) | ISBN 9781479849611 (ebook) | ISBN 9781479812448 (ebook)
Subjects: LCSH: Refugees—Iraq. | Iraqis—United States—Social conditions. | Immigrants—Cultural assimilation—United States. | Islamophobia—United States. | United States—Emigration and immigration—Social aspects.
Classification: LCC HV640.5.I76 C73 2021 (print) | LCC HV640.5.I76 (ebook) | DDC 305.892/7567073—dc23
LC record available at https://lccn.loc.gov/2020015852
LC ebook record available at https://lccn.loc.gov/2020015853

For Rebecca, Justin, and Graeme

Astonishingly, I was born
With a passionate tendency for kissing the sky
In the mirrors of lakes;
An obstructive heart for nostalgia;
An ironic sense of the sanity of penitents.

In the depth of my soul there is a vaporous window
Of oblivion to patience that awaits
The arrival of turtle's death.

In my savage determination
I feel a lust to thrash the weakness
Of these cowards which they call "postponement."

In this beautiful hell where flitting is my way of life
Every night (oh, life!)
In my imagination

With a sense full of sleepy lightning
I draw the sketch of your abstract face
on the pale and shadowy wall of my grave room
By the smoke of my only cigarette.

The nausea of normality
Embodies a madness inside me
Which I cannot recognize.
—Sassan, "Emptiness's Decaffeinated Sense"

CONTENTS

PREFACE

I worked at a job-placement desk in a small nonprofit agency in California, as the United States responded to a massive refugee crisis in the aftermath of the Vietnam War. The US Refugee Act of 1980, riding an immense wave of popular support, provided for job-placement services, several years of cash assistance, mental health services, and small-business assistance. Aihwa Ong's brilliant study of Cambodian refugees described my goal: "daily figuring out ways to produce subjects who can be induced, nudged, and empowered to become self-sufficient and goal-oriented citizens."[1]

On the wall facing my desk hung a sign in English that read, "A positive attitude at work can make your daily routine more rewarding and enjoyable. Whatever your job, success depends on your attitude. How do you develop positive attitudes on the job? Courtesy, Consideration, Knowledge, Enthusiasm, Dependability, Respect, Pride."[2]

Of all immigrant types, refugees are the most captive of audiences for what I call acculturation "camp," tethered to the state and its service agents through cultural orientation, English as a second language (ESL), and job development. Like the other staff, I assumed that refugees should be grateful for American rescue (from a crisis we engineered). Wasn't unconditional gratitude one of the "unspoken conditions" of their acceptance in the United States?[3] We produced job placements in order to maintain state funding, as well as our own morale. Part of the job was preparing refugees for work in the low-end service sector—janitors, maids, burger flippers. Why was I surprised to learn that refugees might not want those jobs for long? How inconceivable that a Cambodian teen would only stay at Burger King for two weeks!

I mention my work with Vietnamese and Hmong refugees because there are striking parallels between the displacement caused by the Vietnam War (or the American War, depending on which side you fought) and the Iraq War (2003–2011).[4] Both wars led to the establishment of new and significant refugee communities in the US. In both instances, the US justified its support for resettlement programs out of a sense of responsibility for the plight of military and/or civilian allies who were forced out of their countries. Both groups' pathway toward belonging in the US was shaped by severe economic recession, racial stratification, and geopolitics: "They [Vietnamese, Cambodians, and Laotians] arrived *en masse* (fully 450,000 during 1979–82 alone), and at the worst possible time: the peak of their arrival (1980) coincided with the highest domestic inflation rates in memory, followed (during 1981–1983) by the most severe economic recession in nearly half a century, and by an accompanying socio-political climate of intensifying nativism, racism, xenophobia, and 'compassion fatigue.'"[5]

The Iraqi refugee narrative bears many similarities to that of the Vietnamese and Hmong in the trauma of violence and flight, struggles to build livelihoods during economic recession, cultural adaptations of children and adults, and stigmatizing otherness. There are parallels as well in how both groups began their American lives in unique cultural geographies: Vietnamese and Hmong found themselves in impoverished urban neighborhoods in cities like Oakland, and Iraqis found themselves in working-class Latinx neighborhoods.

Despite the abrupt defunding of the job-development program for resettled refugees, my experience there left me feeling a natural resonance with that kind of work. This led first to Washington, DC, and then to Khartoum, Sudan. My interest in Arabic and the people of the Middle East and North Africa grew from previous travels to Turkey, Jordan, and Syria. That experience had affected me in a profound way, and I believe it had to do with the fact that I was a vulnerable stranger in a strange land, with very little money, which forced me to avail myself of the traditional hospitality of the Arab and Turkish people.

When I arrived in Sudan in September 1986, the country was recovering from "famine," a euphemism for war- and climate-induced economic collapse and food insecurity, which left huge numbers of people displaced and vulnerable to malnutrition. The neighboring countries of Ethiopia and Somalia had been the arena of proxy wars for the disputed Ogaden region, and the Eritrean struggle for self-determination had left tens of thousands of refugees living a tenuous existence in the eastern part of Sudan. The capital city of Khartoum was home to large populations of ethnically distinct southern Sudanese who had fled civil war and lived in simple shelters on the outskirts of the city. In Khartoum, I worked for an international agency, helping to manage a program that supported thirty government Mother-Child Health clinics that served people displaced by war and famine.

During this time, I also worked with displaced Hawaweer nomads in Sudan's Northern Province who had been forced by the "famine" to leave their ancestral lands to work as day laborers on the date farms along the Nile. The plight of the Hawaweer illustrated the intersectionality of climate change, superpower intervention, political oppression, and unjust economic policy, leading to the erosion of livelihood.[6]

I spent the year immersing myself in the Sudanese dialect of Arabic and was subjected to the relentless Sudanese hospitality in the homes of my coworkers. Like Iraqis, the Sudanese are a welcoming and social people, and the joy I found in their homes helps explain how easy it was later to claim ethnography as my most natural expression as a researcher. Sudan also left me with a desire to continue a connection with the Arab world. It explains why, of all the refugee populations in Southern California, Iraqis were the ones I gravitated toward in 2010.

Sudan was followed by five years of work managing mostly rural community-development projects in Kenya. Inspired by Wangaari Maathai's Green Belt Movement, much of our effort went in support of women's microfinance, health education, and training in organic farming. Always there was the specter of migration in the background. Rural villages, based on subsistence farming, were disproportionately made up of the old and very young. Women were the mainstay of what was left of the subsistence farming economy, working the *shambas* (kitchen gardens), "stretching the week" with *sukumuweeki* (kale). Men had migrated to the cities, once again a way to diversify the household economy, much like some ranchos in Mexico that are characterized by outmigration of men, and increasingly women, of working age. As in Sudan, the most rewarding part of life among the Kenyans was sitting with people and listening to them talk about what was happening in their lives, their families, and their communities.

Six years in East Africa were followed by doctoral work in the rural midwestern US, where I joined a group researching the Mexican settlement within the larger economic and demographic shifts that were transforming agriculture and rural communities. Supported by the Julian Samora Research Institute at Michigan State University,[7] I explored the role of Latinx religious congregations in helping individuals, particularly the US-born children, find a place of belonging within a sometimes hostile host community.[8]

After returning to California in 2008 to teach at La Sierra University, I began reading press reports about the hardship of the newly arrived Iraqi refugee families. Several things struck me as unusual and unique. Iraqis were being resettled in majority-Latinx communities like Fontana and Moreno Valley instead of Middle Eastern enclaves like El Cajon. This spatial reality raised even more questions; not only has very little research been done on the new Iraqi refugee groups in California, but even less is known about the Arab American experience in majority-Latinx communities.

The decision to pursue a study of the emerging Iraqi refugee community in my corner of California finally coalesced in 2010 in Washington, DC. I went there to interview people involved with refugee advocacy and resettlement in the US, including the International Catholic Migration Commission (ICMC). It was there that I met Abel, an Iraqi man in his early forties who had been in the District for two months and had just landed a restaurant job. Over curried chicken in his small apartment that he shared with his parents, Abel told me his story. He had majored in engineering at the University of Baghdad and studied English at schools in Egypt, Syria, and Jordan. His father had left Iraq because some government officials had taken his writing as critical of Saddam Hussein. He was exiled for a time in Egypt, where he met an Egyptian woman, and they married. Abel's English skills were what landed him the job of translating for the British in Basra, later for the Americans in Baghdad. As Iraqis who worked for the coalition were systematically hunted down by militias, he went into hiding for four years.

I had been introduced to Abel by John, a young staff member for the List Project to Resettle Iraqi Allies. What brought these two men together was that Abel's asylum application had been successful because of the work done by John's organization. State Department officials claimed that Iraqis were not fleeing in large numbers until 2006, when sectarian violence broke out in response to the bombing of the Al-Askari Mosque in Samarra, one of the holiest sites for Shi'a Islam. The List Project, however, documented that well before that, many Iraqis who worked for the US and its coalition partners had been targeted for assassination by insurgents. (The organization's name derived from the lists it had created of those who had been hunted down or forced to leave the country.) The doors to asylum in the US remained essentially closed from 2003 to 2007 for Iraqis like Abel who were staff and translators associated with the US military or the Coalition Provisional Authority.

I was moved by Abel's story and outraged by American indifference toward the suffering of the country's former allies. A jarring reminder of this occurred on the flight back from Washington, DC. My loquacious row-mate asked what had taken me to DC, and when I recounted my meeting with John and Abel, her response was (I paraphrase), "Why should I care about them? I know so many Americans who have plenty of problems. And besides, we kicked Saddam's butt. They should be grateful." Was it the gin talking, or were the American people truly in deliberate denial about the ongoing consequences of the Iraq War? Appalled by the apathy toward the very real violence that Iraqis fled from, the economic struggles they faced in the US, and the willful ignorance toward the interplay of empire and forced migration, it was at that moment that my future research came into sharper focus.

This anecdote reveals to a fuller extent the political bias I brought into this research. I plead guilty to Marc Manganaro's accusation that "the question ought not to be if an anthropological text is political, but rather, what kind of sociopolitical affiliations are tied to particular anthropological texts."[9] While my initial approach to the study of the Iraqi resettlement in the US was to examine the traditional questions of refugee resettlement—the struggles of fleeing violence and building new lives—my research had a political motive. I wanted their story, the brute fact of their presence in the US, to be seen as a testimony to the enduring affects of *our* war, rather than to the generosity of *our* humanitarian ideals.

A few weeks after meeting with John and Abel, I contacted Catholic Charities, the agency responsible for resettlement of refugees in Riverside and San Bernardino Counties. After having scrutinized me thoroughly, the directors provided me with introductions to four Iraqi families. I unexpectedly encountered another group of Iraqi refugees at La Sierra University, where a small number of Christian Iraqis (Chaldeans, Armenians, and Seventh-Day Adventists) showed up as students in my classroom. This provided further introductions to parents and extended families. After interviewing them, they approached me to serve as faculty sponsor for an advocacy group formed to support religious minorities in the Middle East. This gave me an opportunity to engage them in a (sometimes uneasy) dialogue about the sectarian violence set in motion by the Iraq War that threatened all religious groups in Iraqi society, not only the already vulnerable Christian minorities but Muslims as well.

These two sites of contact—resettlement agency and university—became the locus for a convenience sample, which eventually snowballed into fifty individuals.[10] Over time, I developed a close relationship with a group of six families. Time spent with these families involved mostly conversation in living rooms over tea and meals, helping with homework, rides to appointments and ESL classes, filling out forms, and many celebrations at mosques, churches, birthday parties, and picnics. This pattern of fieldwork lasted from the winter of 2011 until the end of 2018. Maintaining relationships over seven years allowed me to observe changes that were happening in their lives—finding and leaving jobs, graduations, starting college, and in some cases, moving away to other cities. As youths graduated from high school and began college or full-time jobs, I was able to meet them individually, outside the gaze of their parents, at coffee houses or hookah lounges.[11]

Through seven years of sustained listening, I continually and deeply felt the truth of these people's experiences as they narrated them to me. This truth was not static; their stories lived and breathed in open-endedness. Details were added later that in the first telling had been left out (purposefully?). For some precious moments, I was invited into a "place where we feel the truth of how things are."[12] Much of this "truth" was found in the intimate and ordinary realms of life—work, school, family life, and picnics.

Introduction

Achieving a sense of belonging in the United States is complicated for all new immigrants. But imagine that your home country is blamed for a terror attack it did not cause, and then the president of the United States decides that you are part of an unholy trinity he calls the "axis of evil."[1] When that is your starting point, only the most optimistic of souls would predict a good outcome. This was the challenge facing the 124,159 Iraqi refugees who were resettled in the US between 2008 and 2015. This book is a witness to their uphill climb as they have sought membership and belonging during the displacement of the Iraq War and the seemingly endless global War on Terror.

"National belonging" is commonly understood as legal citizenship. Hannah Arendt writes in her seminal work *The Origins of Totalitarianism* that citizenship confers the indispensable "right to have rights."[2] But even after the oath is uttered—"I absolutely and entirely renounce and abjure all allegiance and fidelity to any foreign prince"—the *felt sense of belonging* can be elusive. In the pre–World War II Europe analyzed by Arendt, refugees challenged the nation-state's homogeneity and imagined rootedness in ancestral soil: the *xenos* that threatened the national *ethnos*. Meaningful societal participation was denied for those who were "born into the wrong kind of race or the wrong kind of class."[3] In the post-9/11 United States, legal citizenship has not protected Arabs and Muslims from Islamophobia or from the hard edge of the Patriot Act.

It is vital for subordinated groups, writes Renato Rosaldo, to be "conscious and articulate about their needs, to be visible, to be heard, and *to belong*."[4] The felt experience of social belonging hinges on the immediate and daily experience of inclusion, captured in the concept of "cultural citizenship."[5] Iraqi refugee lives demonstrate that belonging is not only something granted but something people claim, even under appalling circumstances, alongside the daily rounds of life.

President George W. Bush's decision to invade Iraq in 2003 left an irrevocable imprint on Iraqi lives, triggering the largest forced migration in the Middle East since 1948. Bush's first attorney general, John Ashcroft, allowed surveillance aimed disproportionately at Arab and Muslim Americans. Just when it would be hard to imagine a more unfriendly environment for Iraqi refugees, a bellicose Donald Trump ran for president and named refugees from Iraq as threats to national security. Once elected, he greatly restricted refugee admissions. For Iraqi refugees in this time and place, what shall be their cartography of belonging, their pathways and possibilities? That is this book's central purpose, to see if the felt experience of belonging is possible even for people who face active hostility.

The pathway toward belonging is inevitably preceded by the loss of belonging. Refugees are commonly portrayed as suddenly and cruelly uprooted from an idealized normality. Liisa Malkki reminds us that more often refugees have found that their country ceased to be a place of belonging before they left, the welcome mat already removed.[6] They saw the writing on the wall, which said, "You do not belong." They left with no home to return to, only certain arrest by security police or someone else occupying their house in an ethnically cleansed neighborhood.

The invasion of Iraq by US and coalition forces in 2003 caused a loss of belonging for Iraqis on a scale previously unseen in their turbulent history. In chapter 1, we meet four individuals and their families who serve as our windows onto the wider experiences and pathways that Iraqi refugees took toward finding safety and livelihood. They initially intended to wait out the war in neighboring countries, but their hopes that the security situation in Iraqi would improve were not realized. This book focuses on a group of those who after years of waiting in exile were eventually accepted for resettlement in the US.

The door to resettlement of Iraqi refugees in the US did not open easily. It took an intense and successful lobbying effort to convince Americans that Iraqis, as collaborators with the coalition in the Iraq War, earned their eligibility to be resettled in the US. They were labeled "good" Arabs, that is, allies of US geopolitical interests in the Middle East. It was as if being accepted as a refugee in the US required a worthiness quotient.

Of the 124,159 Iraqi refugees who arrived in the US, approximately 500 were placed in California's Inland Empire, located sixty miles east of Los Angeles. I cannot say why this region is burdened by the label of "empire." There is probably a historical reason, but I prefer Lewis DeSoto's lyrical explanation: "It was an empire of things. Oranges, tract homes, steel, freeways, earthquakes and floods, desert and deep water. Crackling fire in the hills . . . It was the empire of mountains, deserts, and weird inland seas. It was marvelous and abject. It was filled with opposites: blue mountains and white snow presiding over crispy weeds and sunbaked lots, balmy palms."[7] The vastness and extremes of the Inland Empire, its diverse social and physical geography, are what garnered the appellation of "empire," four and a half million people concentrated in the metro areas of Ontario, Riverside, and San Bernardino, as well as in smaller blue-collar towns along iconic Route 66—Rialto, Fontana, Colton, bordering the metropolis of Los Angeles to the west, Orange County to the south, and the Mojave Desert to the east. Only a small community of people of Middle Eastern descent lived in the Inland Empire prior to 2008. Earlier settlement patterns taken by Iraqis after the Gulf War were to the well-established Arab American enclaves of El Cajon and Anaheim's Little Arabia. After 2008, the unusually large number of Iraqis settling in the US pushed the newer arrivals into new frontiers of the majority-Latinx neighborhoods of the Inland Empire.

Historically, the immigrant pathway to belonging has been shaped by finding specialized neighborhood gateways into ethnic business, political, and religious institutions. But what is the pathway to belonging for Arab immigrants within the sprawling urban majority-Latinx communities of the Inland Empire? Understanding refugees in this region of California that is not densely populated by people of Arab descent will tell us something about how Arab immigrants have survived outside their ethnic communities.[8]

As it happens, Iraqis arrived in the US in the throes of the Great Recession and in a place suffering from foreclosures and bankruptcies. For immigrants in the US, the meaning of belonging and good citizenship has been historically tied to their economic value as laborers and entrepreneurs. The refugee success story in the US offers membership and belonging to those who make a valuable economic or social contribution to society: the high school valedictorian, the successful entrepreneur, those who combine a high level of acculturation with economic success. Successful cultural adaptations and economic success implicitly grant permission to say, "Now we belong." In chapter 2, we find out how Iraqis navigate through their economic discouragement and financial strain. I explore the relationship between societal belonging and the ability to find meaningful work. Iraqi youths had much to say about the meaning of economic success in the "money country," fearing that preoccupation with money could tear families apart. By the time Iraqi families arrived in the Inland Empire, they were already fragmented—some children and siblings still in precarious exile in the Middle East, others building new lives in Germany, Denmark, Australia, and Canada.

How Iraqi parents and their children were clearly troubled by the freedoms of the United States and the potential impact of those freedoms on the family are the concern of chapter 3. Youths feared that the authoritarian parenting styles that worked in Iraq would backfire in the American culture of expressive freedom. Youths had lived enough of their lives in Iraq to recognize and appreciate those parts of Iraqi culture that are grounded in communal ties of faith and family, and they had witnessed how mosques and churches provided a vehicle for celebrating and passing on values. This was of particular urgency for ethnic and religious minorities like Chaldeans, whose cultural survival relied increasingly on its diaspora outside the Middle East.

Iraqi refugee women in the Inland Empire named security as something they valued highly in the United States. Yet for women whose religious dress makes them more visible targets for hate crimes, Muslim women find themselves in the epicenter of the ongoing process by which Arabs and Muslims have been made into racial Others. Chapter 4 situates Iraqi women within the context of the gendered experience of the War on Terror, the atmosphere punctuated by anti-Muslim rhetoric coming from the highest levels of the US polity, such that the act of claiming belonging in public spaces, whether bus stops, graduations, or garage sales, can never be far from the specter of violence. The Iraqi women narrative broaches the question of multiple forms of citizenship, one for them (as Others) and one for "white" Christian America.

Refugees find and create belonging in real, physical places, each shaped by a particular regional history. The process of becoming American for Iraqi refugees was happening within the cultural-political borderland of Latinx California, among people who had also survived a century and a half of their own marginalization. What did "becoming American" mean in this particular cultural geography, with its own layers of racial history? Immigrant strategies to achieve national belonging have historically involved differentiating from subordinate racial groups. Chapter 5 shows how, as Iraqis embarked on the path toward belonging and membership within the majority-Latinx communities of the Inland Empire, they both navigated difference and found a nascent solidarity with Latinx neighbors, despite frustration, confusion, and ambivalence.

As long as the War on Terror continues to fuel fear of Arabs, Arab Americans, and Muslims, the work to prove worthiness to fully belong will never be over.[9] Arab Americans know that a terrorist attack that involves a Muslim (or anyone who looks Middle Eastern for that matter) has the potential to set the worthiness scale back to zero, as it did in the fall of 2015. The year 2015 saw historic levels of refugee movements out of Syria, Iraq, and North Africa coinciding with major terrorist attacks in Paris, France, and San Bernardino, California, which is one of the most populous cities in the Inland Empire. While the Republican presidential candidates that year singled out refugees from Syria and Iraq as existential threats, a larger "Islamophobia Industry" foregrounded an anti-Muslim discourse in the presidential primary, naming Arab refugees as a potential *fifth column*.[10] So successful was the political opportunism employed to conflate terrorism and Arab refugees that it led to the passage of the American Security Against Foreign Enemies (SAFE) Act by the House of Representatives in 2015, profiling Iraqi and Syrian refugees as threats to national security.

So it was that seven years after being deemed worthy of asylum, Iraqis were singled out (alongside Syrians) as undesirable refugees and threats to our way of life.[11] While the SAFE Act did not become law, the discussion itself made me wonder how people—many who had put their lives on the line for the US coalition—would feel about the United States' radically changing stance toward Arab refugees from the Middle East. As refugee policy became driven by the ideological constructs of "stealth jihad" and "sharia creep," what strategies would they adopt on their path to belonging in the United States?

I was particularly concerned about what these changes meant for Iraqi youths and how they saw their future in the US polity. In my interviews with Iraqi youths up until 2015, they had imagined the United States as a space to express individual and collective identities without fear of judgment, a place to find belonging without having to compromise their cultural and religious values. After the seismic political shifts of 2015, what would belonging in the United States look like to them? Chapter 6 draws on their fears and hopes, captured in a focus group I conducted with them in 2016, just two months after the San Bernardino terrorist shooting on December 2, 2015, which left fourteen dead and twenty-two wounded. I wondered if they would continue to embrace this American identity even as the mosque in Indio was attacked and anti-Arab/Muslim rancor lifted its ugly head in national politics. Chapter 6 explores the experience of belonging among Iraqi refugee youths as they confronted the disturbing ways in which they—Arabs and Muslims—were being so brazenly profiled in the public arena.

This book is more about the reclaiming of belonging than its loss. I have tried to bear witness to how cultural citizenship was worked out in the everyday experience of belonging. João Biehl and Peter Locke have written about what belonging looks like for people who are potentially unwanted, how "powers and potentials of desire" can "break open alternative pathways."[12] In a similar fashion, Iraqi lives in this book bear witness to a people's ability to claim belonging even in the face of such appalling circumstances as being named the "enemy" and to the way they have made their way in a country as perpetual players within the theater of the War on Terror.

Violence was the essential commonality for the fifty individuals who participated in this study. Whether they were Chaldean, Assyrian, Armenian, Kurd, Arab Sunni, or Arab Shi'a, they were all Iraqi citizens who felt the heat of violence—on their bodies, their friends and families, their faith communities. All of them experienced the removal of belonging even before they crossed the border to Syria, Jordan, or Turkey. This is not to gloss over profound communal and religious differences, group power differentials, and vastly different histories of vulnerability. This is a testament, first and foremost, to the pervasive and widespread nature of the violence inflicted on Iraqi civilians in the postinvasion period. No demographic was shielded from the terror that burned through Iraqi society after 2003. Their story begins, in chapter 1, with the terror that removed the possibility of belonging.

1

Belonging and Displacement

If only memory, or hope, or regret
Could one day block our country from its path.
If only we feared madness.
If only our lives could be disturbed by travel
Or shock,
Or the sadness of an impossible love.
If only we could die like other people.
—Nazik Al-Malaika, "New Year"

The removal of belonging for Iraqis happened suddenly after the US invasion in 2003. This unfolded in different ways. Letters were delivered with religious symbols crossed out, hinting that people of a certain religion would be killed if they stayed in the neighborhood; family members were murdered or kidnapped and held for ransom; armed thugs came to places of work; churches and mosques, sacred symbols of religious communities, were bombed. For some Iraqis, the message was less violent but still effective. Messengers came to tell wives and daughters that they must dress differently; employment was contingent on membership in a certain tribe or political party. Whatever the means used to get the message of nonbelonging across, the chaotic and violent aftermath of the 2003 invasion was a crisis point for a huge swath of the Iraqi population.

In the years following the invasion, violence toward civilians escalated to the point that no group was left untargeted. Millions of Iraqis were faced with decision points—to stay or flee, where to go, how to get there, for how long, how do we survive, and what comes after that? The words "crisis" and "decision" are etymologically connected. "Crisis" originates from the classical Greek verb κυίν-ειν—"to decide"—and in English, it has come to mean, among other things, "a turning point."[1] The violent denial of belonging precipitated a crisis—a search for its recovery.

What follows is a series of individual and family migration histories that represent common experiences of the violent removal of belonging, followed by exile and survival in surrounding countries, and finally the momentous decision points about asylum seeking and resettlement in countries outside the Middle East.[2] While each of these individuals' stories is unique, they illustrate common features of the Iraqi refugee experience.[3] These portraits are by no means an exhaustive portrayal of the entire range of Iraqi experience but rather heuristic devices to explore individual lives as windows onto the loss and search for belonging. Their experience of resettlement in the Inland Empire of California, which is the focus of this book, was not an endpoint but rather a station along a continuum of belonging.

Belonging and Loss

Yousef, Suha, and Ibrahim recalled living in neighborhoods with varying degrees of ethnoreligious diversity. None spoke of growing up in completely homogeneous Muslim or Christian, Sunni or Shi'a, neighborhoods. There may have been communal tensions brewing under the surface, but the different groups had achieved a more or less peaceful coexistence. Overwhelmingly, Muslims and Christians spoke of each other as "good people." This relatively peaceful coexistence, however, changed after 2003.

The US invasion, achieving its goal of defeating and disbanding the Iraqi army and laying waste to the country's infrastructure, created a political vacuum in what had been a Sunni-minority-ruled regime under Saddam Hussein. Along with civilian casualties, there was an increase in organized crime and an emerging Sunni insurgency. Clear targets were those who were associated in some way with the coalition forces and the Coalition Provisional Authority of the occupation. After the first elections, which brought a Shi'a-dominated Iraqi government led by Prime Minister Nouri al-Maliki into power, professionals such as doctors were seen as indirectly supporting the government and were targeted by insurgents.

After graduating from medical school, Ibrahim survived the economic sanctions (1990–2003) by scavenging the smoldering junkyards for car seats and other spare parts, with which he fashioned dental chairs

and clinic equipment. The economic sanctions imposed on Iraq following the Gulf War had resulted in a shortage of medical equipment, and
he did brisk business.[4] He would have preferred to practice medicine at
one of the government hospitals, but that would have left him vulnerable
to conscription into the military. Ibrahim had seen this happen to other
doctors who had died in one of Iraq's wars since 1981. After the 2003 invasion, he felt it was safe to take a position at Al Kadhmiya Hospital for
Children, and he also opened a private clinic with a dentist partner. One
day, after buying some drugs at the pharmacy, he returned to the clinic
to find that a group of thugs had just gunned down his friend. Ibrahim
gave his brother the keys to the clinic and never returned. Police later
claimed to have arrested the assassins and told Ibrahim that he had been
on the same hit list as his dentist partner. Ibrahim believed that while
the assassins were simply doing it for money, the people behind them
had political motives, to destabilize the country and take power.

Even indirect associations with the coalition could be deadly. Yousef,
an engineer who worked in wastewater treatment in the oil fields, owned
a shop in Baghdad that sold women's accessories, cosmetics, makeup,
and jewelry. It was a mixed neighborhood of Sunnis, Shi'a, Kurds, and
Christians. After the invasion, Yousef's shop began to have a large clientele of US soldiers who bought items for family members back home:

> So the American army used to come to the shop to see why the shop is
> crowded. And also they used to buy from me some gifts, or they would
> ask me, "How much is this? What is this? What is that?" So, as a shop in
> general, drew their attention. So the terrorists that were in Al-A'amiriya
> [a neighborhood of Baghdad], they imagined that I—how to say it—that I
> was helping the Americans. Meaning, they considered me that I'm letting
> the Americans inside, I'm helping them; therefore, and according to this,
> I received a threat to kill, so I left.

After the death threats, Yousef and his wife, Nuha, along with their three
sons, moved in with his brother for several months while deciding what
to do next.

Interethnic and religious divides substantively widened with the increase of attacks on symbols of collective identity, such as the bomb-
ings at the Al Kadhmiya mosque. Both mosque and hospital are located

in an elite Shi'a section of Baghdad, near the sacred Shrine of Imam Musa al-Kadhmiya, the seventh of the twelve imams in Shi'a sacred history. Ibrahim was on duty that horrible day in 2004 when the hospital was overwhelmed with casualties from deadly bomb attacks on people gathered for the sacred event of Ashura at the Al Kadhmiya mosque: fifty-eight people died, according to official counts, but Ibrahim believed that the number was much higher, in the hundreds. He remembered the scene: "A big hell, body parts everywhere in the street, by the mosque." The hospital was overwhelmed, there were no beds, and surgery was being done on the floors.[5]

Attacks on religious symbols were accompanied by the escalation of communal tensions at the neighborhood level. As the conflict in Iraq came to be drawn along communal boundaries, there was a deliberate strategy by warring parties to physically displace each other at the neighborhood level—Sunnis from Shi'a-majority areas, Shi'a from Sunni-majority areas, or religious and ethnic minorities from Sunni or Shi'a areas.[6] Outside of Baghdad in Northern Iraq, the Turkoman (a Turkish-speaking minority), already oppressed by Saddam's efforts to replace ethnic minorities with Arab populations, were squeezed between Kurds and Arabs for control of Kirkuk. The violence that displaced people was not random but intentional, argues Jan Gruiters of Amnesty International: "There lies more behind people being forced to flee than simply a consequence of violence: the violence is often deliberately intended to purge cities, neighborhoods and villages of people who belong to another political faction, a different religion or ethnic group, or those who are voices of dissent."[7] Yousef believes not only that was he targeted because of his hospitality to US forces in his shop but also that he was in danger because he was a Shi'i in a majority-Sunni neighborhood.

The same was also the case with Suha, who grew up on her father's farm in the small village of Alanish in Kurdish Northern Iraq, a region where Assyrian Christians have lived for two thousand years.[8] In 1975, Suha and her family moved to the Baghdad suburb of Al Jadeeda for work. It was a mixed community, Sunni, Shi'a, and Christian; according to her father, "They [Muslims] were very kind to us." Suha managed to complete only third grade before the bombing raids during the Iraq-Iran War, which began in 1980 and prevented her from continuing at school. Suha eventually got married in Baghdad, but her husband died from illness several years later. To support herself, she went to work in a textile factory, where she stayed for seven years.

In 2006, the family's church, St. Elias Chaldean Parish, was attacked. With the attack on the church and intensification of violence, Christian friends and relatives began to leave the area. In the post-2003 turmoil, already-vulnerable religious and ethnic minorities became even more susceptible to threats, kidnappings, and attacks. Before the major sectarian conflicts broke out, there had already been mass expulsions of Christians from Basra, despite the city being controlled by coalition forces. Suha and her family did not leave. Finally they were the only Christians left in the neighborhood. For many Christians, attacks on churches meant that they were being targeted as a whole group and that the government was unable to protect them. Many felt it was no longer safe for Christians anywhere in Iraq, even in their stronghold of Mosul.[9]

In 2006, a young man came to the grocery store of Suha's brother Daoud and delivered a threat, that his sisters should wear hijab and stop attending their church or face the consequences. Daoud threw a can of tomato paste at the young man and told him to get out. The family feared that the young man would return with an armed group. At that point, they knew it was now too dangerous to stay in Iraq. In April, Suha and her father, mother, and older sister drove north through Iraqi Kurdistan and crossed the border into Syria. There they met up with other Iraqi-Assyrian and Chaldean refugees living in northeastern Syria, not far from the Iraqi border. Suha's father, Aodish, stressed that they did not run away in the middle of the night: "It was six in the morning. We took our time. It was normal." Daoud and two younger sisters followed soon after.

The diversity of people I interviewed spanned most religious and ethnic groups in Iraq. All left because they were threatened with violence. As one Muslim woman told me, "It didn't matter which group, Christian or Muslim: they were trying to kill all of us." The Dutch journalist Geert van Kesteren was told something nearly identical by a woman he interviewed: "There is no end to the list of civilians who are victims and targets of the violence in Iraq; it affects everyone: Muslims—both Sunni and Shia—Mandeans, Yezidis, Kurds, Turkmen, Assyrians, Chaldean Catholics and others."[10] By 2006, the drift into chaos and civil war had left no ethnoreligious or political group untargeted.

The terror unleashed on the Iraqi people reached its zenith in the year of the murder attempt on Suha's brother in 2006. That year witnessed thirty-four thousand documented killings of Iraqi civilians.[11] For each "documented" killing, there were myriad other undocumented events, kidnappings, threats, and killings, particularly of women and children, that went unrecorded.[12] Lindsay Gifford found that "all neighborhoods were equally exposed to violence," rather than official portrayals of places like Sadr City being the locus of violence, an assessment with which my respondents would agree.[13]

The common perception of the civil war in Iraq is that existing sectarian tensions had been held in check by the repressive regime of Saddam Hussein, simply to rise to the surface after the "liberation" of the country, according to some natural law of nation-building. In fact, the effect of Hussein's security regime did much to erode civil society and national identity, using factions within the Baath Party apparatus to control dissent. A weak government and the fractured nature of Iraqi society forced people to lean more heavily on localized political actors (tribal leadership and religious authorities) for support, security, and protection.[14] In short, consensus has built around the following factors as primary drivers of the communal conflict that ensued after the invasion: the collapse of governance structures, the mismanagement by the occupation and its failure to establish security, massive unemployment after the firing of the armed forces, fears among Sunnis of the new Shi'a-governed Iraq and fear of reprisals against former Baath Party members, and the presence of the US military as a magnet to foreign fighters who poured into the country to join the growing insurgency.[15]

The reasons behind the postinvasion meltdown will no doubt be debated for years. What is not up for debate is the consequence of the postinvasion violence: a massive displacement of an estimated 1.5 to 2 million people within Iraq and an estimated outmigration of 750,000 and 2 million, respectively, to the neighboring countries of Jordan and Syria.[16] Lebanon gave protection to 50,000, Iran to another 48,000, and Turkey to an estimated 18,000.[17]

Exile and Contingent Belonging

The individuals whom we have followed up to this point—Yousef, Suha, and Ibrahim—survived in these countries by following family and ethnoreligious networks built and expanded by exiles fleeing political unrest and two decades of oppression under Saddam Hussein.[18] Constituting a diverse class of people, ranging from butchers and electricians to engineers and doctors, they blended into the informal economies of neighboring countries, like Al-Seida Zeinab district of Damascus, where up to half a million Iraqi refugees lived by 2007.[19] Assisted by principles of Arab solidarity, they were commonly referred to not as refugees (a label reserved solely for Palestinians) but as guests—*dhuyuf*.[20]

Iraqi social networks throughout the Middle East should not be underestimated as a means of survival during this time. The human capacity to move across borders is largely enabled by social networks, with an internal momentum by which migration becomes progressively easier for successive migrants.[21] Social capital, building on the "embeddedness" of social relations within networks—solidarity, reciprocity, and enforceable trust—facilitates mobilization of economic and informational resources.[22] Social networks can be translocal, meaning that they are not bounded by borders and allow resources to be mobilized both locally and through transnational relationships.[23] The social capital mobilized through Iraqis' social networks is how they survived outside the confinement of camps. This is not to say that they were shielded from real and consequential hardship: gaps in education for their children,[24] working underpaid jobs in the underground economies of surrounding countries,[25] and the vulnerability to "survival sex" for war widows and forced marriages for girls.[26] In addition, they carried trauma with them from the war and the terrible violence they had witnessed.[27]

In 2007, the year Yousef and his family left Iraq, no visa was required to cross the Syrian border.[28] Yousef and Nuha found protection in Syria but were terribly exploited in the informal economy and faced constant threats of deportation by security police.[29] Yousef's friend in Aleppo helped him find work in a textile factory that made children's clothes. Yousef, trained as an engineer, now described himself as a "laborer" who worked fourteen hours days for minimal pay. His wife, Nuha, did jewelry piecework from home.

Yousef and Nuha had rented a house in Aleppo for six months, thinking that they would be able to return to Iraq in a few months. Two years later, they were still in Aleppo, where Nuha delivered their youngest child. They had not expected to be in Syria this long. But the news from Iraq still wasn't good: "We realized that Iraq was moving towards the worst. The situations there were deteriorating. So, with this deterioration, the decision [to seek resettlement] becomes stronger." Eventually the situation in Aleppo became dangerous, and Yousef and his family had to leave for Damascus, where he managed to find similar work with the help of a cousin while they waited for the United Nations High Commission for Refugees (UNHCR) to act on their application.

Suha and her father, Aodish, who were also in Syria at this time, found jobs in textile warehouses. Over time, this Chaldean family came to the conclusion that there was no future for Christians in Iraq. All of Aodish's siblings had by this time left Iraq for Australia, France, Germany, Finland, and the US (San Diego). In 2011, Suha, along with her parents, brother, and sister, traveled to the UN offices in Damascus, where they were interviewed by US Department of Homeland Security (DHS) officials as part of the arduous security screening process required for resettlement applicants.

Like Yousef and Suha, Ibrahim and his wife, Zaynab, first headed to Syria. Ibrahim had friends in Al-Zabadani, a small city in southwestern Syria, where he had gone once to purchase a car.[30] He looked into working at one of the Syrian hospitals but would have only been able to make $200 a month, not enough to live on. They ended up in Amman, Jordan, where a friend from medical school offered Ibrahim work in his private clinic.[31] Ibrahim worked there for three months, then was given a final three-month extension.

In Jordan, Iraqis did not have the fear of an impending war but rather a government growing impatient with half a million Iraqi refugees in a country with a total population of only about ten million. Many Shi'a Iraqis felt that the Jordanian government, predominantly Sunni, did not want them in the country. Iraqis in Jordan whose visas had expired were being deported. Ibrahim applied to the UNHCR to receive refugee protection and permission to stay in Jordan without fear of deportation. Two months later, he was told by UNHCR that he could apply for resettlement to the US, where he had relatives.

Ibrahim and Zaynab were ambivalent about applying for resettlement in the US. Ibrahim liked his work and would have preferred to stay in Amman had his "legal residency" been more secure. Even with UNHCR giving Iraqis temporary refugee status, Jordanian refugee policy toward Iraqis was in constant flux. Another difficulty was the education of the couple's three school-age children—Raiya, Malik, and Masim—whose attendance at a private school was assisted, for the time being, by UNICEF. But how long could that continue?

Having given up hope of returning to Iraq, and with the long-term prospects in Jordan unclear, Ibrahim and Zaynab decided that resettlement was the best option. "USA is not bad. Maybe good. Maybe I suffer also, but its okay, let me try," Ibrahim reflected. They thought about the long-term prospects for their children's education. Another strategic thought occurred to them as well, that with US passports they would be "free" to "live anywhere," and they could finally fulfill their dream of making the pilgrimage to Mecca, a dubious possibility with an Iraqi passport.

Even as the violence in Iraq subsided somewhat after 2007, the conditions that would have allowed Iraqi refugees to rebuild their lives were missing. Ibrahim returned briefly to Baghdad to discover that conditions had not really improved. "The killer," he said, "was in the street everywhere." Ibrahim, Yousef, and Suha realized that the Iraq they had known would never return, and probably neither would they. With their old neighborhoods ethnically cleansed and property confiscated, they knew their futures lay outside the Middle East.

As Syria began to slip into its own war, and compassion fatigue was besetting Jordan, Iraqi refugees waited in vain for the situation in Iraq to improve, and many became increasingly desperate. Rana, a mother of three children, and her husband had hired a smuggler to take them from Mosul to Europe but found themselves stranded in Istanbul. Rana supported herself and her children with her modest earnings as a hairdresser in Tarlabaşi, one of Istanbul's poorer neighborhoods. Her husband worked as a day laborer. Their situation was made more precarious by having been denied refugee status in Turkey. Things got worse when Rana's husband eventually abandoned the family. She and her children moved in with an elderly couple, paying daily for room and board. She and her children found themselves homeless when they were locked out of their apartment after she fell three months behind in her rent. Eventually Rana and her children returned to Iraq. The charity that had helped Rana in Istanbul eventually lost all contact with them, their fate unknown.

Like Rana, many Iraqis were desperate enough to attempt reaching Europe via Turkey. Suha's brother Daoud, after fleeing to Syria, tried several times to join family in France and Finland. The border crossing from Turkey to Greece at the Evros River, used by smugglers, however, was heavily guarded. Daoud was caught both times trying to cross into Greece, each time being sent back to Turkey. He finally returned to Syria to rejoin Suha and Aodish.

The reason Iraqis risked taking the smuggling routes to Europe was because Germany, Sweden, and Denmark had by this time well-established diasporas of Iraqis. Previously liberal refugee policies in the European Union (over 50 percent asylum recognition rates for Iraqis) had allowed significant numbers of asylum seekers temporary and permanent protection during the Iran-Iraq and Gulf Wars. Ibrahim's sister and her family, fearing that Saddam Hussein was on a collision course toward another war, left Iraq in 1997 for Yemen, where they applied for asylum at the German consulate and arrived in Germany in 2000. Germany had by that time granted asylum to over fifty thousand Iraqis who had fled during and after the Gulf War.[32] Sweden already had close to one hundred thousand Iraqi immigrants and gave asylum to over thirty thousand more from 2003 to 2007, the proportional equivalent of the US accepting five hundred thousand refugees.[33]

Asylum had been applied liberally by European countries to Iraqis fleeing Hussein's brutal dictatorship. Hence, after the overthrow of Hussein by the coalition forces, asylum acceptance rates for Iraqis in some of the major destination countries in Europe dropped, and even some Iraqis who had made it to Europe were later deported when their asylum claims were rejected.[34] Unfortunately, the EU at this time, unlike the US, did not have formal refugee relocation programs for those fleeing countries like Iraq. Instead EU countries processed asylum seekers as they arrived as irregular migrants.[35] Reaching Europe, therefore, meant that Iraqis had to hire a smuggler to take them through Turkey into Greece. As we saw in the case of Suha's brother, however, Europe had tightened the land border between Greece and Turkey. With the land border with Greece more militarized, Iraqis began attempts to cross the Aegean Sea from Turkey. With their options running out, and resettlement doors still closed, trying to make it to Europe, with all of its risks, was better than doing nothing. If they managed to make it to Greece, then it was northward through the Balkans to Germany, Denmark, and Sweden.

Like the strategic land bridge that Turkey has been for centuries between East and West, it was a key transit country for Iraqis fleeing toward Europe after the Gulf War.[36] In Turkey, Iraqis could apply for refugee status with the UNHCR office in Ankara, which gave them legal permission to stay on a temporary basis. Those with refugee status were assigned by Turkish authorities to live temporarily in about fifty "satellite cities" throughout the country to prevent them from congregating in cities that were already crowded with refugees. The downside to this arrangement was that many experienced isolation while they were living within a non-Arabic-language community. To assist them, the US State Department sponsored Turkish-language classes and counselling for people who either suffered during their adjustment to Turkey or who were dealing with trauma associated with their flight from Iraq.

It is not surprising that Iraqis in Turkey found ways to circumvent the satellite-city restriction in order to live at least part of the time in Istanbul, "a place where people find help from those culturally like them," according to one NGO source.[37] The social geography of Istanbul held characteristics vital for Arabic-speaking Iraqis in a Turkish-speaking country—religious communities and family networks provided them a form of contingent belonging and a means of survival while they either waited for resettlement or prepared for the boat crossing into Greece, onward to Europe.

A longer and even riskier route to asylum emerged through Southeast Asia to the shores of Australian territory. In contrast to the US, Australia responded to the postinvasion refugee crisis by formally resettling one to two thousand Iraqis per year beginning in 2004.[38] Iraqi refugees coming through Malaysia to Indonesia were trying to rejoin family members in Australia.[39] Once they were smuggled into Indonesia, they attempted to hire a small fishing vessel, often captained by a teenage boy, to take them on an uncertain voyage to Australia.[40] In a tragic incident on December 15, 2010, twenty-eight people drowned when a boat carrying eighty Iraqi and Iranian asylum seekers wrecked on Christmas Island, a territory off the Australian coast close to Indonesia.[41]

Iraqi "boat people" who did manage to land safely on Australian territory, such as on the rocky shore of Christmas Island, would have found themselves immediately transferred to a very crowded prison-like complex, where over two thousand men, women, children, and unaccompanied minors lived in a facility run by SERCO (an Australian corporation that operates prisons), meant to accommodate four hundred.[42] Like other destinations for asylum seekers from Iraq at that time, as well as from Iran and Afghanistan, Australia had begun taking a harder line to deter boat people, eventually putting a freeze on granting security clearances, a prerequisite for granting asylum. Eventually they would be declared ineligible for refugee status in Australia. Policies would eventually emerge that denied the possibility for asylum for boat people who arrived on Australia's shores.[43]

Despite the harder line emerging toward boat arrivals, Australia was at least doing its part in accepting refugees from the Middle East through its official humanitarian refugee-resettlement program. From 2003 to 2006 Australia accepted 5,170 Iraqis who had applied for resettlement, including one of Ibrahim's sisters. The US during that same period accepted only 770.[44]

The Social Construction of the Worthy Refugee

At the peak of the violence in Iraq, the door to the largest resettlement country still remained closed. This lays bare the brute fact that who gains entry into the US as a refugee is an intrinsically political, rather than humanitarian, decision. To gain entry to the US, it must be demonstrated that refugees serve a government's political interests.[45] During the Cold War, refugees fleeing oppressive Communist states were an essential motif in the West's narrative as the "beacon of freedom," evidence of the superiority of its political system. Another interest served in refugee policy has been to protect those who have been the allies of the US in its imperial projects. "In general, the U.S. does not welcome refugees," wrote Reginald Baker and David North to explain why one hundred thousand Vietnamese were allowed into the US in 1975 with little public debate on the matter. "We do, however, have a specialized interest in those who are our defeated allies in our world-wide struggle against Communism."[46] As the "world-wide struggle against Communism" has given way to the worldwide War on Terror, Iraqis became a litmus test for whether the same logic would hold about "defeated allies" in far-flung conflict zones being deserving of protection.

The US opened its doors to Iraqi Shi'a and Kurdish refugees immediately following the Gulf War (1990–1991), once again as acknowledgment of some culpability for the two million people who were displaced during the uprisings that followed. Prior to the US-led offensive that liberated Kuwait and routed the Iraqi army, George W. Bush had called on the Iraqi people to rise up and overthrow Saddam Hussein. In the aftermath of the defeat of Hussein's army by the US and its coalition partners, there were in fact large-scale Shi'a and Kurdish rebellions. These were brutally suppressed with nerve gas and helicopter gunship attacks on civilians. The Shi'a refugees fled to Saudi Arabia and Iran, the Kurds to the Turkish and Iranian borders.[47] In response to that crisis, the US accepted 29,080 Iraqi refugees for resettlement between 1991 and 1999.[48]

Iraqis who faced mass displacement after 2003 did not receive the same sympathy as those following the Gulf War. Total refugee admissions for the years immediately after the terror attacks of 9/11 had been reduced to 26,839 and 28,306 in 2002 and 2003, respectively.[49] The US Refugee Admissions Program (USRAP) was essentially shut to Iraqis from 2003 to 2007. Deborah Amos, whose seminal work *Eclipse of the Sunnis* provides one of the best accounts of Iraqis exiled in the wake of the 2003 invasion, detailed the many barriers facing Iraqis applying for asylum to the US during this time. The Patriot Act disqualified anyone suspected of "material support for terrorism," and the Department of Homeland Security, responsible for security checks on asylum applicants, extended this liberally to families who had paid ransom to release a family member, to Shi'a who had risen up against Hussein after the Gulf War, and to former members of the Baath Party, to which the vast majority of Iraqis belonged for practical rather than partisan reasons during the Hussein era.[50]

Instead of the US government ramping up its resettlement operation to accept refugees from Iraq, it channeled humanitarian assistance to those countries shouldering the burden of hosting the displaced, either through direct support to the Jordanian government or to the UN and NGOs in Syria, Lebanon, or Turkey. This strategy allowed scenes of suffering to be effectively decoupled from the violent morass arising from the invasion. Jordan, a country of ten million hosting half a million Iraqi refugees, challenged the US to step up its resettlement operation: "The U.S. has demonstrated time and again its ability to be a leader in durable solutions for refugees," observed HRH Prince Ibrahim bin Talal of Jordan in reference to the successful resettlement of refugees from Vietnam, Cuba, Russia, and Bosnia.[51] Jordan had opposed the US invasion in 2003, and Prince Ibrahim's message to the US signaled that doing something more to address the Iraqi refugee problem was in the US strategic interests; it would help alleviate the burden on one of its few friends in the Arab world. Thus, the concern for maintaining a strong relationship with a US ally, known as the "politics of neighbors," became a political factor in moving the needle of US refugee policy toward Iraq.[52]

Refugee policy in the US has always lived in a tension between humanitarian concern and fear that refugees could be an existential threat to the US cultural and political order. In the massive resettlement operation in the wake of the US withdrawal from Vietnam, a nation's gratitude toward non-Communist allies was enough to override fear of the "Yellow Peril." A similar sentiment emerged within the US among those who had formed ties with Iraqis during the invasion and occupation. During this time of widespread asylum denial, Iraqis who had collaborated with the coalition forces and occupation were being systematically targeted for assassination by insurgents. The List Project to Resettle Iraqi Allies, an organization founded by Kirk W. Johnson, a former USAID administrator in Fallujah, began calling attention to the plight of Iraqi allies—engineers, translators, and advisers—who worked alongside US troops and contractors: "As our military rolled into villages, this linguistic and cultural gap between occupier and occupied was bridged by a unique group of Iraqis who stepped forward to help as interpreters. They became, in effect, our eyes, our ears, and our voice as we tried to make the best of an increasingly harrowing situation. Without question, their work has saved American lives."[53] Being the eyes, ears, and voice of the "occupier" subsequently made Iraqi staff vulnerable. Johnson argued that the US was on track to repeat previous abandonments of its allies to death or imprisonment (e.g., the Hmong of Laos): "The terrorist group that has already abducted, tortured, and assassinated hundreds of our employees just announced plans to redouble their efforts as America leaves Iraq."[54] The List Project's website listed the names of Iraqi collaborators who had been murdered, injured, or forced to flee Iraq. As a matter of saving these individuals' lives, the organization advocated for asylum and the permanent resettlement of Iraqi allies and their families to the US.

The lobbying by the List Project and other refugee advocates led to an amendment to the Department of Defense authorization bill of December 2007, the Refugee Crisis in Iraq Act, sponsored by the late Senator Edward Kennedy.[55] The act prioritized admissions for Iraqis and their families who had collaborated with the coalition. This included those who had worked on the reconstruction of Iraqi infrastructure by the US government and its contractors. The act opened the door to other vulnerable Iraqis, not just those who worked with the US government and its agents, and mandated that humanitarian concerns be taken into account for religious and ethnic minorities and "other persecuted groups," as identified by the secretary of state. Asylum advocates in Washington, DC, were especially worried about war widows and young women and girls working the nightclubs of Damascus.[56]

The Refugee Crisis in Iraq Act provided criteria by which Ibrahim, Yousef, Suha, and their families deserved to be considered for resettlement in the US. Suha was doubly at risk, as part of a religious minority and a widow. Yousef and Ibrahim had loose ties with the Americans or the reconstruction efforts under the occupation, enough to put them on hit lists, as well as exposure to violence in ethnic cleansing at the neighborhood level. This transmutation of an asylum seeker, a temporary and merely tolerated migrant, into a "refugee," as set forth in 101(a)(42) of the Immigration and Nationality Act, is dependent on these calculations, which tilted the worthiness scale in favor of these Iraqis and others like them who passed the various types of scrutiny.[57]

Thus, becoming a refugee in the US bears the imprint of governmental determinations of citizenship worthiness. For Yousef, Ibrahim, and Suha, the worthiness process began with the asylum interview at the UNHCR office. That interview began their evolution from migrant, exile, guest, or asylum seeker into "refugee." Because they had been judged to have a "well-founded fear of persecution" and because they had relatives in the US, their case files were recommended to one of the processing centers managed by the US Department of State's Bureau of Population, Refugees, and Migration (PRM).[58] The Refugee Crisis in Iraq Act authorized the establishment of PRM processing centers where significant numbers of Iraqi refugees had already fled: Amman, Damascus, and Istanbul.

From the point when a refugee status determination is made by the UNHCR to the moment when a refugee arrives in the US, a minimum of two years will have elapsed (as in Ibrahim's case) or as many as eight (as in Yousef's). During this time, their lives will have been touched by several UN agencies, several NGOs that have provided some humanitarian support, and at least five agencies of the US federal government, as well as the International Organization for Migration, which coordinates travel arrangements. The US Citizenship and Immigration Services (USCIS) will have coordinated a series of security-clearance interviews by the Department of Homeland Security (DHS), Central Intelligence Agency (CIA), and Federal Bureau of Investigation (FBI). Medical exams will have followed, then coordination with Office of Refugee Resettlement (ORR) and its NGO partners at the federal, state, and municipal levels. Each government player had a role in the construction of that person's status as a refugee and in setting his or her final destination. This Foucauldian knowledge-power of the state exerted on asylum seekers, observes Ong, is intended to mold future citizen-subjects who will contribute to "the security and strength of the state."[59]

The Refugee Crisis in Iraq Act named and justified to the American people a specific nationality group of people to be authorized for resettlement in the US. To be so named in an act of Congress requires that support to Iraqi refugees had to be justified. The act implicitly considered them good future citizens on the basis of their support of the US war effort and the reconstruction of Iraq. Like the Vietnamese decades earlier, the US had a "moral debt" to Iraqis who had supported the US military. Resettlement of "up to 25,000" (for fiscal year 2008) was in alignment with the US foreign-policy objectives in the Middle East, by helping to mitigate the destabilizing effect of three million refugees spread through the region and by removing a "fertile recruiting ground for terrorists."[60] The reference to countries like Afghanistan and Iraq as breeding grounds of potential terrorists has been the constant background noise of the War on Terror since 9/11. Iraqis, like the Arab Americans they would soon join in the US, exist for Americans primarily within this narrow frame of reference. As such, Iraqi refugees came to the US as both potential good citizens and potential terrorists.

The refugee narrative as a whole tilts toward vulnerability. Humanitarian crisis is what opens the wallets of the American people, while the "moral debt" argument, along with foreign-policy interests, especially those claiming to mitigate the terrorist threat, justifies congressional appropriations. The Iraqi experience follows a well-worn pattern, that refugees are admitted for resettlement on a large scale when there is a convergence of foreign-policy interests, moral obligation, and humanitarian appeal.

The year 2008 saw Ibrahim and Zaynab and their three children get on a flight from Amman to Los Angeles; they were part of the 13,822 Iraqi refugees admitted to the US that year, enabled by the passage of the Refugee Crisis in Iraq Act. Yousef and Suha and their families came five years later. Yousef and his family had endured eight years in exile. Between 2008 and 2015, a total of 124,159 Iraqi refugees were resettled in the US.[61] Iraq was the number-one refugee-sending country to the US for four of those seven years.

The lives of Yousef, Ibrahim, and Suha are windows onto a world of both the loss and the creation of belonging. Having lost it in the violence of postinvasion Iraq, they re-created contingent forms of it within communities in exile. Once they made the decision to apply for resettlement, they became engaged in a process in which they were vetted and prepared for the path to citizenship in the US. Toward that end, they arrived with immediate permission to work, a green card soon followed, and legal citizenship was expected in five years. Once they arrived, however, they discovered that the meaning of national belonging and good citizenship was intertwined with cultural notions of work and self-reliance. Refugee programs were implicitly justified to US taxpayers by the presence of model refugees—successful entrepreneurs and professionals who realized the American dream and were not a drain on the US welfare system. And yet there was a problem, because in the year 2008, when Ibrahim arrived with the first major wave of Iraqi refugees, the United States was facing a financial meltdown.

2

Work, Autonomy, Belonging

Work does not integrate one into the public household but
estranges one from it. It becomes hard to do good work and
be a good citizen at the same time.
—Robert Bellah et al., *Habits of the Heart*

Immigrants have traditionally been judged on the worthiness scale in
the US polity in terms of the their potential economic harm (taking jobs
from native workers and competing for government assistance) or their
benefit (as labor, professional expertise, or entrepreneurial job creation).
During the Senate debate over legislation that would provide amnesty
for undocumented agricultural workers in exchange for tougher controls on unauthorized immigrant labor, passed as the Immigration
Reform and Control Act in 1982, testimony on the Senate floor included
language such as "When God's bounty is ready to harvest, they have
got to get the horses ready to harvest." The horses metaphor, observes
David Sandell, refers to (undocumented) immigrant labor as a "beast-
like agency to be harnessed and controlled, ensuring the economic and
social wellbeing for those in power."[1]
    Refugees are not granted entry on the basis of employment eligibility
or labor-recruitment criteria and hence do not have the right of national
belonging justified, at least initially, by their potential economic benefit.
Yet some refugee groups have historically been vilified for becoming
part of an underclass of welfare-dependent poor, as happened to the
Hmong of Cambodia and Laos.[2] Due to their marginalized and rural
origins, the Hmong did not meet the standard by which many Asian immigrant groups (particularly those from urban centers of India, China,
South Korea, Vietnam) have been perceived as model minorities, as
having demonstrated worthiness through industry, hard work, and economic success. The primary measure of success for refugee-resettlement
programs according to annual reports to Congress by the Office of Refu-

gee Resettlement (ORR)—getting refugees to become financially self-reliant—had not changed in the decades since the arrival of refugees from Southeast Asia. In this chapter, I explore how the need to prove economic (market) worthiness became an element of cultural citizenship for Iraqi refugees as they sought belonging and membership in the throes of the Great Recession.

Work and Belonging in the Great Recession

In one corner of the Inland Empire is where I met Majid, Miriam, and their two children, Fairuz and Musa. They lived in a small, well-kept apartment at the foot of Box Springs—dry hills from which the strip malls, subdivisions, and megawarehouses of Moreno Valley sprawl eastward. "MoValley" is a former agricultural zone that grew up around the US Air Force base at March Field. We sat together, watching their TV alternate between Al Arabia, the Dubai-based cable news channel, and Nickelodeon. A photo of the Virgin Mary was taped to the wall. Majid was in his early thirties. He had a somewhat angular face with Elvis sideburns, about five feet eight, a solid build. He had done some trade school in Baghdad and learned how to do electrical work. Miriam was about five foot one and usually wore jeans and a T-shirt, sometimes hijab. She had some experience as a beautician in Iraq and hoped that someday she could pursue her trade here. They had a three-year-old daughter, Fairuz, and seven-year-old son, Musa, going into second grade.

After tea, they showed me a bill for $157, the first installment to pay back the $6,000 it cost to get them to the US. Over time, I came to know that money problems were often on their minds. Rent for the apartment was $850, but they only get $720 from Temporary Assistance for Needy Families (TANF) in support of the children. Majid earned some money working for a Lebanese American contractor, doing electrical work on a construction site, but it was only several days a week at most and only as needed. They sold some of Miriam's gold jewelry to pay for a new couch. They complained about the caseworkers who were constantly asking them for evidence that they were looking for work or taking ESL or college classes. Miriam could not understand how she could leave her three-year-old with a babysitter while she looked for a job or went to classes.

During the next two years, I visited the family about every other week. Over time, Majid revealed his version of events, which led to their fleeing Iraq. After the invasion, he worked for six years on the security and logistics team for a US contractor in Ramadi, including fitting Chevy SUVs with bulletproof glass and installing surveillance cameras in buildings. His work sometimes required him to travel to Ramadi, which meant passing through Fallujah in the "Sunni triangle," where the insurgency was most entrenched. Getting to Ramadi meant passing through checkpoints controlled by various militia, and he had a bad feeling about the way some looked at him. (It was during 2004 that four US contractors were killed by Sunni insurgents in Fallujah.)

Miriam said she was constantly worried about Majid whenever he left for Ramadi. Although there were no specific threats made against him, it was becoming apparent that Iraqis who worked for US contractors were prime targets for assassination by insurgents. Since he had worked for a US contractor, he was eligible for asylum under the Special Immigrant Visa (SIV) provision. A "cousin" in Moreno Valley sponsored them. In contrast to Ibrahim, Suha, and Yousef, who spent years in exile waiting, Majid and Miriam were flown directly from Iraq to the US, with only a one-day layover in Amman.

Majid told me that he was "maybe interested" in learning heating and air-conditioning maintenance (HVAC). In December, I drove him to Riverside Community College (RCC) to register on campus, instead of struggling with the online application. It had taken Majid three weeks just to register to take an ESL placement test. We found a person behind a counter, and with the person's help, he registered for the test. I felt that it was a milestone worth celebrating and took him to my favorite downtown cafe, Back to the Grind, where we bought coffee and croissants. It was also his birthday, so I wanted to do something special for him. We sat for over an hour, slowly sipping coffee, chatting about stuff. He looked genuinely happy. He remarked how close it was to the RCC campus: "This is want I want to do after classes, come here and just sit, relax, drink coffee with some friends." I asked if he missed that kind of thing. Yes, he missed going out visiting every night to be with friends and family, at their houses or in coffee shops.

Majid began taking ESL classes in February 2012 but by April had dropped out. "The ESL classes," he said, "are a headache for Arabic speaker[s]." In the class, he had met some Egyptian students who told him that they attend for a while and then drop out and claim financial-aid money: "same shit, it's business" (one of his favorite phrases when something disillusioned him). The classrooms were crowded, he hated having to take the bus at six a.m., and he claimed that he could smell marijuana smoke at the downtown Riverside bus depot. But by the following fall, he had reenrolled, this time taking general education and required courses toward a degree in HVAC: Business Math, Electronics, English for Business, Computer Science. He said his homework online was tough; but the tests in class weren't too bad, and he gets tutoring help in class.

Majid and Miriam kept getting bills from Catholic Migration Services to begin payments on the $6,000 bill for transportation from Iraq. Their money problems and the inability to find work were compounded by health issues. Miriam experienced chronic stomach problems and some side effects from medications. She often seemed weary. Majid's ability to look for work was hampered by reoccurring symptoms from a knee injury when he was hit by a flying piece of concrete from a bomb explosion. Eventually he was able to work it out with insurance and his doctor to have surgery. This involved six months of rehabilitation, incredibly expensive unless insurance covered it. I visited Majid right after his surgery. He was resting on the couch while Musa was playing a video game on Majid's laptop. I asked him if he was fasting for Ramadan, and he said he was not expected to because he was recovering from his leg operation and on medication. Fairuz sat down next to me on the couch. They told me her birthday would be next week. I asked her if she wanted a toy truck or a doll. Musa looked up from the laptop and yelled, "Trucks are for boys!" Majid said they were going to all go to Chuck E. Cheese pizza. Fairuz got up and brought back a Dora book for me to read to her. I started to read, then asked her to read parts and noticed that her vocabulary was growing fast.

Early in October 2013, Majid called and said that Musa had been in the hospital. I was shocked and told him I would come right over. When I got there, Musa lifted up his T-shirt to show me his stomach with three bandages where they had removed his appendix. Majid told me the whole story: Musa had a stomachache that didn't seem to get better, so they went to the emergency room. Majid told me some surprising news:

that they might be moving to Anaheim. I called a few days later, and he told me that they would be moving at the end of the month. Although rent is higher there, an Iraqi friend who arrived in 2008 cosigned with him on a lease for an apartment and offered him a part-time job installing car windshields. He wanted the job to be part-time until his knee felt stronger. The HVAC-degree courses were never completed.

The day before the family moved to Anaheim, I went to see them. Majid gave me a big hug at the door and called me "brother." Miriam was visiting the Palestinian neighbor. Two months later, I visited them at their new apartment in Anaheim. Their neighborhood had a Coptic church, with a greater number of Arabic-speaking people, mostly Egyptians, living there. The Coptic parish offered ESL classes and child care, so now Miriam could attend the classes to improve her English. Musa liked his teacher. The job seemed to be working out for Majid, and overall it looked like life was better in Anaheim.

The lives of Majid and Miriam reveal ways in which becoming American for refugees requires so much more than becoming legal citizens. Becoming American grows out of a process of interactions with an array of societal institutions that "suggest, define, and direct adherence to democratic, racial, and *market norms of belonging.*"[3] Reflecting on my relationship with Majid and Miriam, it struck me that in my zeal to "rescue" these "poor struggling refugees," I reverted to a practitioner role by which I participated with other "service agents" who "teach clients to be subjective beings who develop new ways of thinking about the self, acting upon the self, and making choices that help them to strive for personal fulfillment in this life."[4]

My role toward Majid and Miriam had been informed by my earlier work with Vietnamese and Hmong refugees in California, teaching them the models of American labor decorum, timeliness, deferred gratification, flexibility, and willingness to settle for any job, basically making refugees into citizen-subjects and furthering the ORR's goal of keeping them off the dole. Market norms of belonging and good citizenship are defined by moving out of welfare dependency into the labor market, pursuing education because it contributes to moving toward economic self-reliance, and utilizing outsourced child care.

The regulatory programs of the human service and international humanitarian type (social welfare, resettlement, aid, and development), with their façade of benevolence, are exertions of knowledge-power that clients must navigate in ways that match their values and life goals and needs. That knowledge-power is thus similarly subverted because "subjects interpret and act in ways that undo systems of classification . . . and thwart rules of surveillance and punishment."[5] I saw this pattern repeated over and over during the six years I implemented microenterprise and sustainable-agriculture programs for displaced and vulnerable populations in Sudan and Kenya. I likewise saw it in the way Majid and Miriam resisted classifications imposed on them in order to move toward life goals that they saw as appropriate. As it turned out, pursuing an HVAC certification was more my idea of a good career move than Majid's.

It is with some reluctance that I tell Majid and Miriam's story, for there will no doubt be those who draw the conclusion that they are one more example of deviant refugee-subjects trying to circumvent the rules of good citizenship by cheating the welfare system. But I feel that an important lesson is to be gained from witnessing Majid and Miriam's struggles with the resettlement bureaucracy during the economic collapse of the Great Recession. Their actions reveal how "subjectivity does not merely speak as resistance, nor is it simply spoken (or silenced) by power."[6] Biehl and Locke's description of Catarina, a woman in Vita (an institution where people went who had been abandoned by families or discarded by state systems dealing with the mentally ill), reminded me (absent the mental illness) of Majid and Miriam: "Catarina's puzzling trajectories and desires required a different analytical approach. . . . Her knowledge revealed complicated realities and the noninstitutionalized spaces in which life chances crystallized."[7] The language of "puzzling trajectories and desires" seemed to aptly describe the way Majid and Miriam moved toward their particular life goals, constantly bumping up against a system that wanted them to be rational participants in the labor market, even as the labor market itself had become utterly irrational, beset by what C. Wright Mills called a "crisis in institutional arrangements,"[8] the perverse collapse of a financial assemblage causing massive unemployment in the Inland Empire. Majid and Miriam had "complicated realities"—lingering health issues from the war, an uninsured car, an absentee sponsor, social workers sending them out to look for jobs that did not exist and asking Miriam to leave her kids with people she didn't know, and other "unreasonable demands."

What I observed, in my ill-conceived role as unofficial "service agent," was not simply a new "reterritorialization" of their lives by yet another regime, the ostensibly benevolent country that rescued them. Nor was it waiting for state power to decide on a subject's fate and rights as a holder of "bare life."[9] What I saw in Majid's and Miriam's lives looked more like the "primacy of desire over power."[10] Alessandro Monsutti, in his study of the migration strategies of Afghan Hazara refugees in Pakistan, argues that refugees can indeed become "agents of their own life in spite of all the hardship they are facing."[11] What we learn from Majid and Miriam is that even within the highly bureaucratic and programmatic structures of refugee resettlement, with their array of "humanitarian" knowledge-power, there still exists the expression of personal agency, even if it is poorly understood.

More Misery in the United States

Beginning in 2009, the news media began highlighting the economic distress that recent Iraqi arrivals were experiencing. Articles with headlines such as "War-Scarred Iraqi Refugees Find More Misery in America" called attention to the economic and health challenges that newly arrived Iraqis were facing: unemployment, eviction, physical and mental health problems due to war-related trauma.[12] I found these stories both mystifying and troubling—in six years, Iraqis had gone from "good refugee" allies to the United States' newest working poor. How did this happen?

There was one particularly revealing story in the local newspaper, the *Press Enterprise*, by the reporter David Olson, which profiled an Iraqi Chaldean family who arrived with the first wave of refugees in 2008.[13] In Olson's story, Shimon, the wife, suffered from cancer, and her husband, Dawod, a carpenter, was unable to find work in a region where the housing industry had collapsed. They were kept alive by cash payments from TANF (two of their minor children were under the age of eighteen) and from the income of two older children who had found jobs in a shoe warehouse. Dawod and Shimon are described as "struggling" yet "optimistic." The wife in the sponsoring family was conscientiously helping the family get adjusted—translating documents, driving them to appointments, helping them get their house furnished.

Three years after the article appeared, I managed to find Shimon and Dawod through Deacon Zaker at the Chaldean parish. By this time, I had met Zaker several times at the Chaldean mass and at a gas station where he occasionally cashiered. Zaker had agreed to introduce me to Shimon and Dawod and translate from Aramaic and Arabic for the interview. We were also to meet a newly arrived Iraqi family who were staying temporarily at Shimon and Dawod's house. We arrived at Shimon and Dawod's house in the evening; some of the men and teenage boys were fixing an appliance in the garage, and the women were inside the house cooking. We settled onto a large and well-worn leather couch in the partially finished garage for the interview.

In my interview with Dawod, I learned that he had still not found any steady carpentry work and was driving cars for a dealership. About his wife, he only said that she was "doing okay." During the interview with Dawod, his two sons came in, and the oldest one, Simon, plopped down on the couch. Sizan, the younger, stayed standing against the garage wall. I asked Simon, who wore a cast on his finger, how he had broken it, to which he replied, "I was hitting a wall at RCC. I was pissed off." I didn't have time to follow up with Simon about what he was angry about because at that moment Suha, Aodish, and Daoud came into the garage.

That was the night I first met Suha (the same woman from the introduction and chapter 1). Suha's family had arrived in Riverside from Syria earlier that year (2012), in late summer. They were sponsored by Aodish's wife's cousin, Dawod, whose house they were living in temporarily. Aodish was a short and wiry man in his late fifties who sported a significant graying mustache on his dark-brown, sun-weathered face. The questions about his family took some time; there were eight children—one in Finland, one in France, three in the US, a daughter still in Northern Iraq, two sons still in Syria. Due to various complicating factors, the two sons had not managed to leave Syria with the rest of the family. One son had been in the delicate phase of marriage arrangements and decided to apply separately with his wife. Aodish was also told that these two sons did not qualify for resettlement, since they had left Iraq from the Kurdish Autonomous Region, part of which had been established as a no-fly safe zone in 1991; in contrast to Baghdad, this region was considered secure enough not to warrant granting protection status to those who chose to leave Iraq.

Whatever the reasons, the fact remained that when Aodish and his wife, their daughters Suha and Janeen, and their son Daoud left Syria for California, the two remaining sons were not with them. By now, the war in Syria was raging, and the family was extremely worried about what might happen to them. Aodish seemed to think that I might have some kind of official capacity or connection to the government and kept urging me to help him get his sons out of Syria. He would renew his request to me at every subsequent interview.

As I was finishing my interview with Aodish, his son Daoud, who had been working with the other young men in the garage, sat down with us. Daoud, in his early thirties and a butcher by profession, said he was interested in doing the same kind of work in the US. In Syria, Daoud had worked four jobs, including carpentry and in the lingerie factory/warehouse. One of the jobs was for an Iraqi businessman exiled in Syria; that was "not a good situation," he said.

Over the next two years, I visited the family several times a month. Because none of them spoke enough English to translate, I always took along Eva, who is fluent in both Neo-Aramaic and Arabic and served as my translator for the entirety of my fieldwork. Eva was also somewhat of a natural-foods enthusiast and often brought herb teas for the family. Daoud's favorite was ginger, which he felt helped his stomach problems. On our visits, Daoud would show us the pigeons he kept in the backyard coop, a hobby he carried on from Iraq.

Like the other Iraq families I interviewed during this time, Aodish's family struggled to find work. Their difficulties were compounded by the fact that none of them spoke English well enough to get along without a translator. The war with Iran had interrupted their education in Iraq so severely that none of the children had even finished elementary school. I offered to take them to the ESL class at a nearby church. Daoud agreed, and when we showed up at the church, there were eight people in a "beginner level" class. The teacher, a native Spanish speaker from Costa Rica, realized that there was a problem when Daoud did not even know the English alphabet. The rest of the students were native Spanish speakers, so she could talk to them a bit in Spanish; but with Daoud, it was different. She scrambled to do one-on-one instruction with Daoud while giving the other eight students exercises. Daoud never returned to that class.[14]

The Catholic Charities resettlement coordinator, sensing that this family would have difficulty even in beginning ESL classes, asked me to organize some student volunteers to teach ESL in the home. With the help of an Arabic-speaking ESL instructor from La Sierra University, we worked up a curriculum. With Eva and a student volunteer, we started making weekly "ESL home visits." During these language sessions, we continued to talk about the family's lives in Iraq and how they felt about life in Riverside. Aodish would often derail the class by rambling on about various topics instead of focusing on the lessons.

Not having anyone employed put tremendous strain on the family. At every visit, Aodish and his wife, Rebekah, would talk about their money problems and their sons in Syria. All the children were adults, so they did not qualify for cash support under TANF. It was a year and a half after their arrival that Daoud found a job working several days a week installing windshields, but the windshield business closed six months later. Eventually Suha became the sole provider for the family. She found a job at the local *tienda* (small neighborhood grocery store catering to Mexican customers) where she shopped, which was within walking distance of the house. The shop was owned by a Palestinian. Suha worked three hours a day, stocking shelves and cleaning.

From 2010 to 2014, despair and frustration about finding work was the dominant theme emerging from my ethnography. What surprised me was not just how frequently but how candidly and bitterly those emotions were articulated. A man who had been looking for work "every day for the last six months" told me that he was thinking of giving up and just dealing drugs. It was meant as a joke, but I sensed the desperation in his voice. A former schoolteacher in his early fifties complained that the resettlement program had not prepared him in any way to find work in the US.

It was not only in the Inland Empire, one of the regions in California with historically high concentrations of poverty, where Iraqis were struggling. The International Rescue Committee (IRC), one of the major resettlement agencies, submitted a special report on Iraqi refugees in the US. *In Dire Straights* described many of the problems that recently resettled Iraqis were experiencing in achieving economic self-reliance. The report cited a Reuters story that unemployment of Iraqis throughout the US was three times higher than the national average.[15] These revelations were accompanied by a number of reports that sharply criticized both government and resettlement agencies for their inability to move people toward self-sufficiency.[16]

Most of the research on the emerging Iraqi refugee communities throughout the US after 2008 identified the salient presence of financial problems exacerbated by the Great Recession.[17] Even where resettlement agencies offered job-readiness and placement services, as in Charlottesville, North Carolina, half of the Iraqis reported at least one instance of being unable to provide enough for their family. Most had not expected to remain unemployed for so long after their arrival. Even employed Iraqis felt that their income was insufficient for their needs, suggesting that the jobs they were able to obtain did not pay a living wage.[18] The authors suggested that the premigratory higher socioeconomic status of urban Iraqis led to higher expectations and hence higher levels of dissatisfaction, presumably based on unmet expectations, financial stress, and downward mobility. Refugees from Bhutan and Burma, on the other hand, who had lived in refugee camps before being resettled to Charlotte, expressed greater levels of satisfaction with their economic circumstances than did the Iraqi cohort. The Iraqis had lived for less time in the US than the Bhutanese and Burmese had, which could also have been a factor, since unemployment rates for refugees tend to decline over time.

When refugees from Vietnam, Cambodia, and Laos arrived in the early 1980s, they also faced a serious recession. The nation's unemployment rate during the 1981–1983 recession was around 8.5 percent.[19] This second wave (the first wave included higher-socioeconomic-status Vietnamese who left in 1975) not only suffered from higher unemployment than the earlier wave had but were much more ethnically diverse, many coming from rural Cambodia and Laos, unfamiliar with urban life, and with lower levels of education and literacy than the 1975 wave had. Even those who found jobs experienced the vulnerability of "temporary, dead-end jobs offering few fringe benefits or avenues of advancement."[20]

Iraqis like Majid, Miriam, Aodish, Suha, and Daoud, having arrived in the Inland Empire as skilled workers and technicians, represent a significant subgroup of the Iraqis who were particularly vulnerable to the high unemployment in construction and related occupations. Like the later waves of refugees from Vietnam, they came with less English proficiency than those with college degrees. During the depths of the Great Recession, things were not that much better for the more highly educated Iraqis, like Ibrahim and Zaynab, who, like the refugees in the early 1980s, also found themselves in mostly dead-end jobs.

The initial months after arriving in Fontana could only be described as bewildering for Ibrahim and Zaynab. In contrast to Dawod and Shimon, their sponsor family did nothing to help them figure out daily life in the US. Their sponsors were an Iraqi couple; the wife was an acquaintance of Ibrahim's sister in Germany who had lived in Austria before coming to the US in the late 1990s. Her husband, an Iraqi man who had lived in nearby Rancho Cucamonga, had purchased another house in Fontana. It seems they signed up to be sponsors primarily to find tenants for their rental house. The husband at the time was not even in the US, and the wife showed up for the signing of the lease and then disappeared from the picture altogether: "They [sponsors] didn't do anything," said Ibrahim. "Nobody told me anything about the USA. I cannot go to the bus. I cannot go to the anywhere. I was go the store to bring the stuff, and the grocery and the shopping by hand, and for mile, one mile or more. . . . I didn't have a car. I didn't know where is the DMV? Where is the library? Where is anything? I ask them [sponsors]. They don't know." Not having a car, Ibrahim would take his wife and four children on the city bus to go shopping. To get anywhere in the Inland Empire by bus involves long, often hot, waits at terminals and bus stops.

The resettlement coordinator showed up several days later and quickly realized that the sponsors were not doing their job. For the next several months, she helped Ibrahim and Zaynab figure out how things worked in the Inland Empire. But this was not the end of their troubles. There was a constant tug-of-war with social services staff to access their refugee cash assistance. Things finally improved when they were befriended by a parent at their children's elementary school who happened to be a social worker. She became their advocate and guide through the bewildering maze of social services eligibility. With the cost to be certified in the US to practice medicine impossibly expensive, Ibrahim began working on a degree at Chaffee Community College to become a physician's assistant.

Iraqi professionals like Ibrahim and Zaynab came to the US with university diplomas and credentials in engineering, medicine, and teaching and with greater fluency in English. They struggled with a situation that typically affects immigrant professionals, that their credentials are not recognized or are subject to a long and expensive process of recertification; meanwhile, they experience a sharp decline in status as they are forced to take lower-paying jobs, having to settle for menial work for which they are vastly overqualified, and basically occupying a lower socioeconomic status than they enjoyed in Iraq. Research on Iraqi refugees in Detroit and St. Louis found that Iraqis saw this situation as both demoralizing and unjust.[21]

None of the professionals I interviewed in the years 2010–2012 were working at anything approximating their previous training. Highly trained engineers were now cooks and grocery-store clerks, and those were the lucky ones; those with less education were unemployed. Naturally they expressed disappointment in their leveling of career prospects: "[Here] everything is wrong for me," lamented a math teacher after applying for work at Walmart.

Catholic Charities relies primarily on the anchor-family system to help refugees adapt to life in the Inland Empire, meaning that every person or family has to be sponsored by a person, who orients them into their new surroundings and helps them deal with bigger issues of getting jobs, maneuvering through government bureaucracy, and avoiding scams. Programs in other parts of the country with larger caseloads will sometimes have the funding to hire staff to provide services such as job development, cultural orientation, translation, and the like, but even those programs will not have the levels of funding that existed for the Southeast Asian refugees in 1975–1980. In the Inland Empire, the anchor-family system mostly worked out, especially when new arrivals were connected to Iraqi families who had stable, well-paying jobs, often themselves embedded within wider support networks like church and mosque congregations, who took a hands-on approach in the early months and years after a new family's arrival. The prospects for success were not nearly as good when anchor families were barely managing themselves or when anchor families were hardly ever in the picture. In cases where anchor families failed, Iraqis never spoke of Catholic Charities as having been uncaring or indifferent toward them. Research from other parts of the country suggests that agency-provided services can be perceived as inferior to sponsor-family-provided services.[22]

For the ORR, helping refugees become "economically self-sufficient" is a top priority, and to facilitate this, refugees arrive in the US with immediate permission to work and eligibility for a green card within one year.[23] In order to fulfill the ORR targets of refugee self-reliance, refugees are encouraged to find any kind of employment quickly, especially with the clock ticking on their eight months of federal cash support. Yet challenges to reaching this goal have emerged frequently, particularly in recessions. After 2008, in that historical moment in US economic history when the middle-class was facing record-breaking foreclosures, was it realistic to think that even good sponsor families alone could effectively facilitate achievement of self-sufficiency for refugee newcomers? When the first wave of Iraqis arrived in 2008, resources for programs to address unemployment for all vulnerable populations in the Inland Empire, nonrefugee and refugee alike, was already stretched to the breaking point.

From 2009 to 2014, the Iraqi refugees coming to the Inland Empire followed a pattern similar to that of Southeast Asian refugees from 1975 into the 1980s, in which over time the socioeconomic status and human capital of refugees decreased with each successive wave.[24] As described in the previous chapter, the Refugee Crisis in Iraqi Act prioritized the most vulnerable members of such refugee populations, not just those who served the cause of the US military or the Provisional Authority (e.g., Majid and Miriam) but also ethnic or religious minorities (Suha, Janeen, and Daoud) and "other priority groups" and their families, which often included disabled or older dependents. This makes refugees, potentially, the least employable category of immigrant. In fact, resettlement programs have eschewed attempts to use employability as a criterion.[25] If employability is one of the criteria for refugee admissions, warn Baker and North, then "the nation should admit refugees with the most human capital and subsequently provide only short-term cash assistance to them."[26] And herein lies a fundamental contradiction in the public perception and acceptance of refugees in the US. Their vulnerability and weakness is what makes them our object of humanitarian outpouring, yet if this vulnerability and weakness leads to unemployment and dependency on government support, then refugees fail to obtain a critical component of good citizenship—the achievement of economic self-reliance.

"America Is a Money Country"

My conversations with Iraqi refugees in the Inland Empire about their experiences with work or the lack of it, its relationship with personal choice and the meaning of success, eventually turned to the role that it played in their sense of belonging in the US. Success is of course culturally defined, and Khalid, a young man who had just become a citizen, summed up the cultural problematic succinctly: "America is a money country." This aphorism punctuated his observations about how becoming American was affecting his relationship with his parents, informed by competing notions of success within American and Iraqi culture and further complicated by looming career decision points, all of which seemed to threaten his own idealized notions of family loyalty. Of all the young Iraqis I came to know well, Khalid was the most candid with me about the struggle he was having with his parents over career decisions. His parents were struggling to reengineer their careers, were unemployed, and had not attained fluency in English. They depended on Khalid and his older brother, Saddiq, for financial support. Khalid was what you would call a "creative": bright, thoughtful, artistic, and outgoing. He arrived in Fontana in the middle of his junior year in high school and by the next year was directing the senior-class video and going to prom. After his graduation, his parents wanted him to continue his education toward a degree in nursing, something reliable that paid well. He knew in his heart that he wanted to work in film and television. Over a four-year period, I observed an ongoing tug-of-war with his parents and within himself. He had extremely strong notions of family obligation and equally strong aspirations toward what he knew he wanted to do with his life.

Khalid's father was an artist who studied at the Art Institute of Baghdad, but his career as an artist was continually frustrated by war and economic necessity. He taught art in primary school but had to sell pastries as a street vendor to make ends meet. When he took the family to Syria in 2006, he did silk-screen work and ran a grocery store in Damascus. Khalid and his brother worked in the store, delivering groceries on bicycle. Despite his father's frustration as an artist, Khalid felt that he could still look up to his father. In Iraq, according to Khalid, the act of working to support your family defined you more than what kind of work you did: "There, it didn't matter what kind of work [you did]. But here, people start to think about how much you make, your position. It's a money country." The first time Khalid used the "money country" phrase was when his cousin Bilal, after finishing a two-year technical degree, decided to move to San Francisco to take a job at the airport.

When Khalid and his family became citizens, I asked him if he felt any differently about being in the US. "Do you feel more American now?" His answer took me by surprise: "Actually what makes me feel American was what I was already doing, like working at Jack in the Box." When I asked him why, he said, "I'm contributing, doing something good for the country. Most people just see it like a job, just for money. Not me. If somebody foreign sees me, I'm like them, working and doing something good even if it's serving an order of fries. They can say, 'He's like me. I can do that too.' That's what makes me feel like I belong here: I'm doing something good—same with my internship at KVCR [public television]." For Khalid, a sense of belonging grew out of participating as a worker, even in the low-end service sector of the US economy. Sunaina Maira observed in her study of South Asian Muslim youth that their involvement in work is their primary exposure to public culture in the US; in the US neoliberal capitalism system, "cultural citizenship is embedded in and mediated by work practices, because these young workers [South Asian youth] provide the flexible labor that the globalized United States economy relies on for maximum profit."[27] Khalid saw his Jack in the Box job as more significant for him than formal citizenship when it came to the daily experience of belonging. The role that work has played in inclusion and exclusion for immigrants in the US has a long and complicated history involving recruitment, exploitation, niche markets, entrepreneurship, xenophobia, and economic scapegoating, but it has been one way immigrants have proven their worthiness to belong as Americans. For refugees like Khalid, the basis for their admission is asylum rather than potential economic benefit to the nation, although refugees who achieve high levels of economic success become poster children for keeping open the golden door. This harks back to the cultural meaning of work itself, which Khalid alluded to when he referred to his father's work in Iraq. The work itself, as a contribution to the family—whether it added up to "economic success" was irrelevant—had intrinsic worth.

Because refugees are usually tied to resettlement programs, they are subjected to more citizenship preparation than other immigrants are. This preparation is tinged with expectations of economic self-reliance. The formal cultural orientation courses that I observed focused on instilling what could be called "market norms of belonging," that is, securing a driver's license, following immigration laws, setting up bank accounts.[28] The essence of US culture could be boiled down to the importance of showing up on time for a job interview, which is not surprising given that programmatic success is defined in terms of refugee employment. Ong describes the sociocultural process for achieving citizenship for Cambodian refugees as the "cumulative effect of a multiplicity of bureaucratic figures who are concerned with the practicalities of democracy."[29] The practicality at hand, of course, is ensuring that refugees, whose resettlement costs taxpayers $1 billion each year, do not become a drain on the system: get Majid and Miriam off food stamps and TANF; get Dr. Ibrahim a minimum-wage job as fast as possible.

Given the powerful ideological pull toward individualism of US culture, I wondered how long it would be before Khalid would begin to define his work in the context of the autonomous self, the freedoms enabled by money to move outside restrictive cultural boxes. "Becoming American," conclude Robert Bellah et al., "means learning how to think about economic progress. In American culture, personal choice and finding the good life depend on economic success."[30] Khalid and his family, like many who left Iraq as professionals, found themselves grasping for ways to think meaningfully of their experience of downward mobility. Maira found that South Asian working-class refugee youth were "more ambiguously positioned" in relation to what Ong calls "the neoliberal ideology of productivity and consumption" with its allure of "freedom, progress, and individualism."[31] Khalid transformed his experience by reinterpreting the meaning of work and individual choice. The relationship between those two centrifugal forces was mediated by his connection with his family and his own vision of "economic success." In turn, he "rejected, modified, or transformed" the dominant ideologies of work.[32] In his vision of individual choice and work, he could make compromises that opened some doors of opportunity, but he resisted the allure of money-enabled autonomy. As Khalid and his brother witnessed their cousin succumbing to its temptations, they argued that they would never "abandon" their families by moving away, and if they did ever move away, they would send their paychecks to their parents so they could buy a house.

This ideology of success within our quintessential capitalist society, however, "is not very helpful in relating economic success to our ultimate success as persons and our ultimate success as a society."[33] Circling back to Majid and Miriam, their failure to enter the formal labor market or complete a college degree will be interpreted by some people as a failure to assimilate to US norms of rational economic behavior. I see it another way, as oblique resistance to the "technologies of governing"—as relayed through social programs and experts seeking to shape people's subjectivity. In reality, Majid and Miriam were working out their own ethos of economic success, one attached to another system of cultural meaning. For Khalid, this larger system of cultural meaning was expressed in his second-favorite aphorism: "Family is everything."

3

"Just Trust Us"

I worked hard to get where I am today, and I am proud of
what I accomplished. However, I did not work alone.
—Raiya, graduation speech

The effect of war on families is devastating. Between flight from
violence and the arrival in a resettlement country, refugee families
commonly experience separation, death and injury of family members, and uncertainty of the whereabouts of loved ones.[1] Iraqis in the
Inland Empire were intensely distressed by the potential violence that
their loved ones continued to face, especially those stranded in Syria.
The Iraqis in the Inland Empire had lived in Syria, Lebanon, Jordan,
or Turkey for as many as eight years. Most had managed to keep some
part of the family unit (broadly construed) together, but their migration survival strategies, together with state-bureaucratic decisions about
resettlement and asylum, meant that Iraqi refugees arrived in the US
as global families, sisters and brothers and children spread around the
Middle East and the resettlement countries of Germany, Sweden, Australia, and Canada.

Migration can create new configurations in the primary groups to
which most individuals are attached, especially in family relationships
and structure. Parents and children usually adapt to new cultural worlds
in different ways that can lead to generational rifts, and family separation can strain and redefine parent-child relationships: "Situated within
two cultural worlds, [children] must define themselves in relation to
multiple reference groups (sometimes in two countries and in two languages) and to the classifications into which they are placed by their
foreign-born parents, native peers, schools, the ethnic community and
the larger society."[2] Attempting to negotiate both worlds (of parents and
host-society peer groups), children fail to find a sense of full belonging
in either world that would reduce anxiety about one's identity.

Nadine Naber's research and own personal history delve into the two worlds of Arab and American imaginaries: the Arab world, perceived by the US through the lens of Orientalism (submissive and sequestered women and sexually aggressive males), and the US imaginary, as seen through the eyes of Arab parents (decadent, lawless, and sexually permissive). For Naber, finding belonging in the US, while tasked with the project of integrating these two incompatible worlds, seemed "overwhelming and irresolvable."[3] This chapter is driven by the question of how Iraqi refugee families would resolve the tension between the cultural worlds of parents' and youths' emerging imaginaries of Americanness and how this becomes a strategy of finding belonging for a displaced people within the Latinx-dominant US of the Inland Empire. (The youths would eventually have to resolve their own tensions with the US imaginary within the context of the War on Terror and a rising Islamophobia in national politics, which is the subject of chapter 6.)

As I posed questions along these lines to both adults and youths, I was interested in learning what aspects of Iraqi culture were absolutely critical to keep. Which had been irreparably lost by leaving Iraq? What did they see as forces pulling families apart? "What values," I asked parents, "do you hope to pass on to your children?" "What parts of Iraqi culture," I asked youths, "do you feel are valuable as you contemplate your future as an American citizen?"

The majority of the youths in this study were born in Iraq. With the exception of a few who were born while exiled in Syria and Jordan or shortly after their parents arrived in the US, they had spent a formative, adolescent phase of their lives in Iraq. During the years spent living in countries of first asylum (Syria, Jordan, Turkey, Lebanon), they found jobs alongside parents or sometimes continued with some form of school. They arrived in the US in their high school or early college years. Immigrant youths of this vintage are termed by social scientists as the "1.5 generation."[4] Members of the 1.5 generation are uniquely positioned within the family as generational bridges—they share a frame of reference common with their parents of the home country yet are young enough for US culture to be a vital element in the crucible of adolescent identity formation.[5] This dual frame of reference makes them distinct from the second generation, those US-born children of Arab immigrant parents who are so incisively portrayed by Moustafa Bayoumi or Nadine Naber.[6]

Belonging in human society first emerges out of individuals' relationship to the primary social groups to which they are attached, and the need to remain part of these groups places constraints on our behavior. In this chapter, I pay a great deal of attention to the way language, cultural values, and religious belief converged or diverged between the parents and their children and how these tensions played out as they found their social spaces of belonging within the family and in religious institutions that intersected with the family. Dera, a Seventh-Day Adventist Christian who along with her parents fled Iraq shortly after the 2003 invasion, articulated well how the 1.5 generation approached these tensions: "I try as much as possible to keep my culture, to keep the things up, you know—because, honestly, I don't see anything wrong with it, and I am proud of it—just to keep everything, you know, basically good, to keep the same . . . not exactly the same style, but, you know, I'm still, like, kind of going and acting . . . not acting, but going with the flow basically: keeping certain stuff here, keeping stuff there."

"Keeping Certain Stuff"

As previously mentioned, Iraqi refugee families in the Inland Empire lived in a Latinx-dominant cultural geography rather than in communities where Iraqi and Arab populations were concentrated. In the absence of supports for the maintenance of language found in ethnic enclaves, they faced the pressure to adapt to both Spanish- and English-speaking communities. (I will address interactions with the Spanish-speaking community in chapters 4 and 5.) One concern that emerged for parents was the importance of staying fluent in the mother tongues, which included not just Arabic but, depending on ethnicity, Aramaic, Kurdish, or Armenian.

Iraqi parents with small children of elementary school age (not the 1.5 generation) observed with concern that in a very short span of time their younger children were losing fluency in the mother tongue. At home, they would try to prevent this by insisting on speaking Arabic or Aramaic in response to their children speaking to them in English. Over the course of the study, I witnessed dramatic changes in attitudes toward language at home. Parental concerns about poor school performance in writing and spelling English shifted over time, sometimes in one or two years, to fears that children were no longer speaking good Arabic. Additionally, choices in TV channels soon changed for children, away from Arabic-language channels to English-language programs on Netflix or Nickelodeon.

In a curious role reversal, youths worried about their parents not learning English fast enough and feared their parents would become isolated from the wider community, not mingling with English speakers at work or school with the facility of the younger generation. (This was particularly critical for some women who, because of age, health, or caregiving, tended to be more linguistically isolated, which I will say more about in chapter 4.) Some youths anticipated a troubling scenario, articulated by Musa, who was attending community college: "The way they [parents] learn is not like us. . . . For us, within a year, we'll master the language; maybe after six months, we'll be able to read and write, because now we are only speaking, and we can manage conversing. . . . They [our parents] are struggling." Mustafa anticipated a common problem faced by immigrant families: differential rates of language acquisition. Parents' lack of language skills results in an inversion of roles as parents depend on their children in dealings with public entities such as teachers or social workers, which shifts power differentials within the family. The inability of parents to learn the host-country language can undermine parental authority. Within this "dissonant" mode of acculturation, the second generation (US born) is less connected and guided by parents, with parents and children embracing conflicting sets of cultural values, experiencing a rupture of family ties that often correlates with youths' involvement in risky behavior, teen pregnancy, and gangs.[7]

In an alternative scenario, children and parents adapt at roughly the same rate, which often happens with strong support and encouragement from immigrant institutions—religion, schools, and clubs. In this scenario, the language acquisition of parents helps prevent role reversal. This more "selective" path of acculturation involves a preservation of parental authority, mutually embraced cultural values, and higher rates of bilingualism and biculturalism and is usually associated with more upward mobility. Some aspects of selective acculturation, such as bilingualism, are highly correlated with better school performance and psychosocial well-being.[8]

Fluency in the mother tongue situated the 1.5 generation and their parents within a common cultural frame of reference. The Iraqi 1.5 generation, having lived a significant period of time in Iraq, maintained a high level of understanding for their parents' cultural world. Even when they did not agree with some of the cultural norms that their parents continued to embrace, those norms were not utterly incomprehensible, and they still held a certain degree of respect for them. Shared language and cultural frames of reference, even when there was difference of opinion on the value of those shared understandings for life in the Inland Empire, helped families avoid the dissonant path of acculturation with its associated generational rift.

Parents were clearly troubled, however, by what they saw as an overly permissive US youth culture. Parents saw their children being exposed to new ways of relating to parents, which in Iraq would be considered "disrespectful."[9] Ali, who had been a primary school teacher in Iraq, observed that the US system of education is so different from that in Iraq; he felt there was too much distraction with both sexes in the same classroom. He saw too much physical contact between boys and girls here: "Why do they do that? It is better in Iraq, where they are separate. Here it is too relaxed. In Iraq, it was—what's the word?—'strict.' And what about drugs?" Ali's concerns were common among Arab parents in general, as Naber observed of her own parents: "They seemed to share a tacit knowledge that Amerika (America) was the trash culture, degenerate, morally bankrupt, and sexually depraved. In contrast, *al Arab* (Arabs) were morally respectable—we valued marriage, family, and close relationships".[10] Iraqi youths seemed aware of their parents' disapproval of popular music and fashion. One youth recalled the time he shared with his father a drug-themed music video that had gone viral, to which his father reacted, "Don't be like them." When the father dropped him off at school, he pointed to some of the other boys and then told his son, "Put your pants up." Some parents opted for private religious schools in order to remove youths from what they saw as the negative social environments of public school.

Given these fears, it was not surprising that youths complained of their parents' tendency to be overprotective, as in this public-park adventure recalled by Ibrahim's son Malik, a high school sophomore: "We were at the park before we came here, and my dad called at least five times to make sure that we were still in the park and we are not dead." One is reminded here of Bayoumi's story of Lina, who, after a protracted battle with parents to get permission to attend the homecoming dance, was asked by her friend, "Isn't that your mom over there?"[11]

Malik, who had met a wide swath of the local Iraqi community at the mosque and private Islamic school, gave some accounts of Iraqi youths engaging in some of the behaviors that Iraqi parents feared most: "I think it's mainly [concerns about] drugs and women. That's what I see in other families: usually, mostly drugs." Iraqi youths told me how their friends and classmates freely shared stories of drug use and sexual adventures. Some youths seemed surprised at the openness surrounding sexuality in the US. Mohammad, who had become an expert YouTuber, found the condom-dispensing machine in the college student center of great interest in his vlog, (the episode also reported on eating sushi for the first time): "Wait you, they are selling condoms out in the open! Basically just telling people to enjoy!" To be fair, Iraqi parents were not one-sided in their messages to youths about the dangers and excesses of US culture. They urged their children to be open-minded toward the "good things" in the US, that both Iraqi and US cultures "have bad parts and good parts." The good of the US was mostly couched in terms of economic opportunity, religious freedom, and security, never in behaviors that contradicted Arab cultural sensibilities.

When youths were asked what might cause conflict between parents and children in the US, they named as potentially problematic the following issues: relationships with the opposite sex, freedom to make their own career choices, and the strictness of religious teaching. To avoid conflict would depend not only on their compliance with parental standards but equally on whether parents approached disagreements in the traditionally authoritarian manner. This is what Malik meant when he said, "So, they [parents] don't know how to deal with it. So, they fail, as parents." That is a strong indictment of parental performance, and a depressing conclusion to come to, unless we dig deeper.

Culture is not static but always in constant flux. Dera, in her stated project to "keep certain stuff," implicitly admitted to being complicit in a process of cultural change. Her own cultural universe already had layers of complexity: her great-grandmother was Indian, her mother Baptist. She admitted to appreciating the values of her culture (i.e., what she had received from parents and community and her own lived experience in Iraq until she was ten years old), while embarking on a pathway of an evolving sensibility about the Iraqi family in a new context of belonging. She and others of the 1.5 generation were formulating an alternative to what is assumed to be a reified and unchanging authoritarian-traditionalist culture, which in Malik's view is doomed to certain "failure." This evolving formulation was most clearly articulated when they discussed the highly volatile matter of relationships with the opposite sex.

Relationships

Dera said that she respects family norms that conflict with "American culture," especially those that govern the social propriety of opposite-sex relationships. There was a lack of confidence, however, about whether these norms can be maintained over time. For example, Dera's parents were adamant that the US modality of courtship is unacceptable:

> KEN CRANE (*to parents*): If a guy called her [Dera] up and said, "Let's go out to the movies," what would you say?
> DERA: No.
> BROTHER: It would be a war at home.
> MOTHER: No, no, no, she'd go with the cousin.

Here is a clear delineation between the Iraqi norms regarding relations between unmarried young people held by Dera's parents and those of the typical practice of "dating" in the US. Dera's mother made it clear that this is out of bounds. Likewise for Ibrahim, a Shi'a Muslim, there was a stark contrast between "dating" and what was acceptable for him and his wife in Iraq:

> KEN CRANE: Would you let a young man take Raiya out on a date?
> IBRAHIM: What is that: "date"?
> KC: When young people go off together somewhere; he calls her [Raiya], then comes here in his car and picks her up, and they go off to a movie or to In-N-Out Burger.
> IBRAHIM: If he wants to marry her, yes, it's okay.

> KC: Then they have to be engaged?
>
> IBRAHIM: I only did that [go unchaperoned together in public] when my wife and I were engaged in Iraq; we were engaged for six months, we met every weekend, we go to a restaurant and talk.

In Ibrahim's view, the romantic interaction of "dating" belongs to a phase of engagement and is inappropriate as a form of "courtship" preceding the engagement. In his understanding of the US practice of dating, this is desired by youths because they are sexually curious; hence, unchaperoned dating is unwise. Likewise, for Dera's parents, they would only allow her to "date" with "cousins." (On further inquiry, I learned that "cousins" included close friends of the family.) Dera explained that this practice was not a problem for her or a source of any serious conflict with her parents, at least not yet: "So pretty much, I respect it. My parents have certain cultures that they like to go by here, and I understand it. Like, I mean, dating for example. I mean, it's not . . . that important to me. I mean, sure, it is kind of—to get to know people and stuff like that. But some have, you know, when they date, they forget about their schooling, their education, and all that, which basically, right here, is important to have an education so you can work as a certain profession." Dera submitted to the dating practice acceptable to her parents, that of "going out" with cousins (broadly construed), not just to appease her parents but for reasons that made sense to her, as she elaborated: "Here I've seen a lot of them make a lot of mistakes, and I just don't want to make any mistakes at all . . . focus on school, focus on work, and that's it. I mean, that stuff can come later." For this reason, Dera respected her parents' approach to dating, that it should avoid couples being alone together and be restricted to young men of good reputation who are known to the family. Being in a large public high school, she had heard of cases where dating led to more serious relationships that led to girls dropping out of school, interfering with their getting into a good university and having career success, which is an extremely high priority for her and her family (and most Iraqi families I interviewed).

Parents, for their part, demonstrated increasing flexibility, particularly if youths did not overstep serious moral boundaries. About a year after the interview with Dera, her brother Iewan started dating a Caucasian, non-Iraqi Christian woman at the university where he majored in biology. Iewan began his relationship with her as a freshman, and they continued in a relationship over their four years of college. Right after graduation, they were married with the parents' full blessing.

I found Ibrahim also to be moving toward a more flexible stance on the matter of his daughter's future choices regarding marriage. He admitted that Raiya could not be sequestered from contact with young men. After all, she was applying to several universities at the time we spoke: "I know I can't do everything like it was for me and my wife in Iraq, but I want her to talk to me about the guys that she thinks about marrying. If she wants something, I want her to talk with me. We'll talk, then she might marry someone she wants." Ibrahim recognized that in the new US context, there needed to be some flexibility, but serious relationships that may lead to marriage would require intense parental involvement.

Thiqa: "Just Trust Us"

I was told by my translator that in Iraq there is a saying: "Cultivate honesty and seriousness and you will harvest confidence and security." The Arabic word for "confidence," *thiqa*, can also be translated "trust." Trust was at the center of the youths' narrative about their relationships with parents. Trust was a key factor for Dera in approaching the matter of dating with her parents; she eventually admitted to trusting her parents' judgment on relationship matters: "But I mean, if my parents know the person . . . and they're comfortable with them . . . and they know that person's parents, then it's fine with them. They just got to trust. And they trust me, and I don't want to ruin that trust, basically." Moreover, she recognized that there were grounds for trusting her parents: "they have more experience." This sentiment about parental wisdom was shared by Ibrahim's daughter Raiya, who felt that her parents were influential in her life precisely for these reasons: "They have lived longer than me, they know better, they've experienced much more." Both the refugee experience and the "culture shock" experienced after arriving in the US had helped Raiya draw her and her parents closer into a kind of trust relationship: "I mean, living in Iraq, and then in Jordan . . . it's very different from living here. . . . And, like, when we first came, as I said, we didn't speak English, so the person to turn to was obviously your parents, because no matter how much you learned at school at first, they knew better; different now, but they did. So I guess that brings me closer." Family solidarity is one of those notions of authentic Arab culture whose articulations within the Arab middle class "meet desires for connection, attachment, comfort, and security that come from displacement, immigrant marginality, and the pressures of assimilation."[12] Raiya described how family solidarity was strengthened by the refugee experience, the recognition of parental sacrifice during exile, and the collective struggle of rebuilding lives and finding belonging in a new country, contributing to a certain amount of deference to parental "wisdom" and enabling Raiya's willingness to trust her parents in major life decisions.

Dera admitted that without the wisdom of your family, you will end up "working at McDonalds," that family solidarity protects you from making bad choices. Her choices should demonstrate that she deserves her parents' trust and that this trust is not unconditional—it can be "ruined." But it is not just that she trusted her parents' judgment but that her parents also needed to trust her. What is unique in this emerging perspective is the growing expectation that there needs to be a reciprocity of trust.

Raiya's brother Malik admitted that his parents were influential in career choices even more than in matters of religion: "Well, I mean, with career choices, well, they are pretty much the ones getting me to my career, so I take their advice." (It was not that Malik was in some kind of rebellion against the religion of his parents—in fact, of all the Muslim youths in the study, Malik and his sister Raiya were the most engaged and devout—but he was adamant that religion must be a choice and cannot be forced on an individual.) In a pragmatic sense, he admitted that parents hold some strings when it comes to certain choices because of the level of support, but it also has to do with what parents can do through persuasion within an ongoing dialogue, rather than through an authoritarian approach. Having spent many hours with Raiya and Malik at their home, I was witness to numerous discussions during which both she and her brother openly disagreed with their father and mother. During those debates, their devout Shi'a parents always responded to their opinions with respect, as though they would respond to reason, rather than needing to be forced into submission. Raiya made it clear that her parents do not actually force her to do anything: "They can't really [force me], but . . . I mean . . . I would take their advice, and in the end, they know a lot more. And sometimes we argue back of course—you are not going to like anything your parents say. But most of the time they are pretty influential." The primary importance of trust identified by the youths flows, in part, out of recognition that parents' cultural and religious values are still relevant for their lives in the US. These youth had lived enough of their lives in Iraq to recognize, and perhaps even appreciate, some of what their parents valued. When Dera said, "I don't see anything wrong with it, and I am proud of it," this was based on her own knowledge and experience gained from growing up with Iraqi culture. It was from this vantage point that she engaged with the ongoing process of sorting out what was vital for her present and future, as she put it, "keeping certain stuff here, keeping stuff there." The parental voice was not left out of the equation but was integrated, as much as possible, into the decision of what to keep and what to change. Finding a way to accommodate her parents was consciously identified as a critical factor either in heading off conflict or in causing it to arise. She could do this because she held, as did most other youths, a sense of trust and confidence that her family could steer her in a positive direction: "If your family is good and they are helping you to build good morals, . . . then . . . you are just grabbing whatever is good in the culture."

A common dilemma for immigrant parents is that parenting styles that work well back home are ineffective with children in the US context. Youths are quickly aware of these cultural differences because of the contact they have with people outside Iraqi culture, particularly in public school. As previously mentioned, the 1.5 generation actually anticipated this problem, realizing that life in the US operates in a much less authoritarian manner. They predicted that it would be very problematic for families if parents were to fall back on traditional ways, as expressed by twenty-one-year-old Mustafa: "He [an Iraqi child] is seeing something else, and then at home his parents are insisting on him, as they have brought with them their *customs and traditions of the old time in Baghdad*, following the way his father brought him up and trying to teach it to your child. And there are others, no, they leave their son to be free, as *they trust him*, as long as there is a *line of communication* between him and his son and knows *when to be strict and when to be liberal*" (emphasis added). The "something else" that Iraqi youths "see" in the US is not the traditional Iraqi family of the "old times in Baghdad," of authoritarian father and submissive children, but a freer, more open type of family. Iraqi youths argued that parents needed to adapt to ways of discipline and socialization that were better suited to a new cultural reality. They expected parents to adapt to this reality and be more democratic, with "lines of communication," dialogue that would gauge when to be "strict" or "liberal." If parents were simply authoritarian, they would run the risk of youths rejecting them totally, the result being that the youths would "take the wrong road." The traditional practice of parents forcing children to submit and obey was neither desirable nor effective. Parents needed to allow their children freedom and "trust" them. This sentiment was also argued by Bilal, a high school senior, that the best parent-youth relationship is based on trust and dialogue: "They trust me. And . . . they just say that in my religion we have system, they say, . . . 'Don't break the system. . . . Don't drink alcohol' or something like that, you know. Because it's bad . . . for my life. . . . But, . . . I can do *anything*" (emphasis added). Mustafa, Bilal, and to some extent Dera engaged in the project of "keeping certain stuff" by arguing that instead of parents being overprotective or increasing scrutiny over their teens, they should adopt a different strategy—parents and youths should just trust each other and be in dialogue about what is happening in their lives.

In sum, youths identified three different family scenarios. In the first, parents do not adapt to new realities but rely on child compliance based on traditional modes of parental authority. This inevitably drives a wedge between parents and their children, who have adopted more "American" attitudes toward parent-child relationships that request more personal freedom and expect more trust and flexibility. In the second scenario, youths reject wholesale the cultural and religious values of their parents and uncritically embrace the morally dubious freedoms of *Amerika*, with their associated risk behaviors, for example, drug use and sexual promiscuity. In that scenario, family obligations go out with the bathwater, at the expense of youths' well-being. These first two scenarios are described in the literature on immigrant second-generation youth as dissonant patterns of acculturation.[13] These scenarios were not apparent in the families I studied in the Inland Empire but were frequently reported by youths to describe certain other youths whom they knew about: "the guys smoking weed in the Starbucks parking lot across from the mosque." They tended to be highly critical of these individuals. In the third and more desirable scenario, parent-child relationships rely less on traditional lines of authority but more on trust and dialogue, which my young interlocutors believed would pose the lowest risk of family division and risky behaviors among children. One important factor in this outcome, at least for some, was the role played by their faith communities.

Faith, Family, and Communal Belonging

Geographical dispersion of immigrants decreases the possibility of deep involvements with religious, social, and political associations. Rapid and dissonant forms of assimilation, where divergent trajectories of cultural adaption bring children into conflict with parental values, are more prevalent where immigrant families are not integrated into strong ethnic communities.[14] Findings that emerged from studies conducted in the Program for the Analysis of Religion among Latinos and the Julian Samora Research Institute show religious institutions playing a key role in youths resisting rapid and disruptive patterns of acculturation; Latinx religious institutions helped to foster youths along a path of selective acculturation, characterized by high levels of bilingualism and a positive regard (albeit at times reluctant) of the cultural values that are important to parents.[15] For youths who attended Latinx religious congregations with their parents and extended families, the congregation functioned as an extension of the family, and it was through the narrative of family that these youths experienced their religious socialization. Religious values in turn reinforced family solidarity and respect for parental guidance.[16]

More relevant to questions of belonging for geographically isolated Iraqis in the Inland Empire, Latinx religious congregations were one of the key places of face-to-face interaction for geographically dispersed newcomer Latinx populations in rural communities of the Midwest. It was not unusual for families to drive over an hour to attend churches of their particular faith, whether Catholic, Protestant, or Pentecostal. Churches were the largest regular, public meetings for Latinx in those regions. Latinx churches were a fundamental way in which a geographically dispersed community came together on a regular basis, and in the process of enacting religious meaning, a social space was carved out to honor the community's language and tradition.[17]

For geographically isolated groups, religious congregations may be the only place (outside the family) where a person meets face-to-face with people of similar cultural background and where cultural symbols are publicly affirmed: "Religion is often at the center of immigrants' sense of identity and religious institutions serve as focal points for ethnic gatherings, celebrations and *re-creations of ethnic language and customs.*"[18] The faith community, for immigrants and refugees, can provide the social space for the felt experience of social belonging. Using the language of cultural citizenship as articulated by Renato Rosaldo, it is where people emerge from the social subaltern to be "visible" and "heard" and to "*belong.*"[19]

Youths and parents may value the religious community for different reasons. For immigrant parents, the religious community can be a crucial mechanism for coping with the trauma and anomie of displacement and uprootedness, of preserving cultural values and identity.[20] "The future is connected to the past by the slender thread of memory," observes Raymond B. Williams.[21] For immigrant youths in general, finding the place of belonging in the present and future is of greater salience than preserving a connection to the past. (This is not true for some Iraqis, like the Chaldeans, whose identity depends on a connection to the glories of ancient Mesopotamia.) Remaining primarily a "community of memory," however, is the reason that many US-born youths eventually leave the immigrant congregation entirely.

The goal of retaining US-born youth has forced immigrant congregations to become more than places that allow an uprooted community to reconstitute itself. They have become a vehicle for the "vital expression of groups within an increasingly diverse society."[22]

The widespread creation of immigrant religious congregations, rather than simply being attached to an existing native congregation, reveals many facets of US religious culture, of racial and class hierarchies, of inclusion and exclusion. As I did fieldwork at Iraqi religious congregations in the Inland Empire, both Christian and Muslim, what I observed was the human agency of claiming and creating the social spaces of belonging.

In January 2014, I was given a special invitation by Ibrahim to attend a service at his mosque to honor his return from completing the hajj, the pilgrimage to Mecca. When I arrived, I was met by Ibrahim's son, Malik. I was taken to chairs outside an open side window, where I could see what was happening inside the mosque. Ibrahim went to the front to read a short prayer, stood in the mihrab to face Mecca, and prayed, giving thanks for completing the hajj in October. Women in the back were ululating and clapping during the songs. During Ibrahim's testimony, one of his physician friends whispered to me, "I appreciate Ibrahim, devout but open-minded."[23] Outside was a beehive of activity: people were milling about, getting food from the buffet tables; kids were doing typical kid things, swinging, running, and chasing each other around. Ibrahim's two daughters walked by on their way to the classroom for the Qur'an lesson, both in long dresses, sleeves, and hijabs. Ibrahim later joined us, and we sat with Ibrahim's friends and family and discussed many things, including the merits of a particular used car, my research, how the kids were doing in school. It was clear to me that what was happening was consistent with how immigrant religious institutions in the US are social spaces that provide more than spiritual needs, where a great many other needs are met, from finding a marriage partner of the same religion and ethnicity to teaching children Arabic and networking about jobs.

On further reflection, I saw how this mosque was similar to the Latinx churches in Michigan and Indiana, in that the Iraqi Shi'a Muslims were driving sixty miles from Orange County or Los Angeles through terrible traffic to attend. By doing so, they were, again paraphrasing Rosaldo, emerging to be "visible" and "seen" and "to belong." It saw this vividly during the reenactments of the martyrdom of Hussein and as the congregation reenacted the worldwide Shi'a pilgrimage from Najaf to Imam Hussein's burial site in Karbala, Iraq, the "Arbaeen Walk." It is estimated that twenty-seven million Shi'a around the world celebrate this pilgrimage wherever they are in the world. In doing so, they "reaffirm their commitment to the principles" for which Hussein lived and was ultimately martyred.[24] Youths are at the forefront of organizing and participating in these events, as providers of food and water, traffic control, and security. Speeches are given about the need for peace. In Dearborn, with the large Iraqi community, the march was hailed as a "march for justice," and participants held large banners with statements such as "no extremism in Islam," "the Islamic community condemns ISIS crimes around the world," and "Imam Hussein is a sword over oppressors."[25]

By gathering at this mosque, an interstate freeway on one side, a Starbucks and McDonalds on the other, the Iraqis of the Inland Empire were able to tap into broader social networks beyond their kinship groups, vital to obtaining critical social and economic resources, or social capital.[26] One of the most significant ways in which Islamic centers of the Inland Empire directed their social capital was in their response to the terrorist attack in 2015, in which they mobilized money and goodwill to head off Islamophobic attacks. Immediately after the San Bernardino shooting, the Muslim community shifted into high gear, organizing numerous events at local mosques, where they publicly honored police and other first responders. They invited Christian and Jewish clergy to these events to join in denouncing terrorism, and they participated in similar events at churches and temples, taking every opportunity to affirm Islam as a religion of peace.[27]

I observed the human agency of belonging of a different type in the Chaldean church, where I came to know Deacon Zaker well. The congregation was formed around small groups of very close-knit families. Several families at this parish had sponsored refugees like Suha and were helping them get on their feet in the Inland Empire (see chapter 2). The Chaldeans shared the church building with a Latinx congregation. As I arrived at the four p.m. mass, there would be Latinx families leaving from the previous mass, and families would be eating together at picnic tables or barbecuing meat and making food items to sell for various fund-raising projects.

The priest who presided over the church and conducted the mass was based at a much larger parish in Orange County. He explained to me the different parts of the prayerbook in Neo-Aramaic, Arabic, and English, emphasizing that it is the Aramaic language, along with doctrine, that defines their community. (Chaldeans and Assyrians still speak a form of Aramaic, known as Neo-Aramaic/Neo-Syriac.) Neo-Aramaic is the liturgical language used in the Chaldean mass, and many of the ancient texts of the Eastern Church are written in Syriac. During the mass, a group of three women, all with heads covered in black, would face the priest and lead the congregational prayers. The Bible was held up frequently by the priest, who then touched his forehead with it. Deacon Zaker waved the incense as he walked down the aisles of the church.

Chaldeans are Christians with ecclesial origins in the Nestorian Church of the fifth century. Deacon Zaker claimed that geographically speaking, their base was the Nineveh plains in Northern Iraq, the center of the ancient Assyrian empire. The name Chaldean was given by Pope Eugene IV to Eastern Rite Christians who entered into communion with Rome in 1445 CE. Later, the Anglican Church began using the label "Assyrian" to refer to people of essentially the same ethnicity and language as Chaldean but to designate those who were not Catholic.[28] The identification as Assyrian also became associated with a movement for a separate nation on the Nineveh plains of Northern Iraq.

Among the Chaldeans in the Inland Empire, the identifications of Chaldean and Assyrian seemed to be used interchangeably. Suha's father, Aodish, in reference to his sponsors in the Chaldean parish, exclaimed, "These Assyrians, thank God, along with their children are doing their duty towards us."[29] I saw how the various ethnoreligious identifications of Chaldean and Assyrian played out among the student group Persecution Relief Organization, which, according to its mission statement submitted to the university, formed to "focus attention and bring relief to religious and ethnic minorities around the world who face persecution," although their concerns were clearly in solidarity with Christians in the Middle East. The student organizers were members of the Chaldean parish in Riverside; a few were members of the Seventh-Day Adventist Church.[30] The students held a series of fund-raising events that generated a considerable sum, which they decided to send to the Assyrian Aid Society in Iraq. The prime movers in the student group were Yakoub and Gina, a brother and sister who fled Iraq in 2005 after their father, a government engineer, narrowly escaped an attempted kidnapping. Their great-grandparents were Chaldeans who fled the eastern Turkish city of Mardin during the genocide against the Armenians (which included Assyrians and Chaldeans) starting in 1915.[31] They migrated first to Syria and Lebanon and finally to Iraq. At some point after fleeing the Turkish and Kurdish forces who attacked Mardin and their arrival in Iraq, they joined the Seventh-Day Adventist Church, which by this time had begun missionary activity in Iran, Lebanon, and Iraq.[32] Given this family history, it is no surprise that Yakoub and Gina poured themselves so vigorously into this cause, despite the pressure on them to maintain the grades needed for acceptance to professional school.

Yakoub identified himself as Assyrian, rather than Chaldean, clarifying his Protestant rather than Catholic affiliation, and explained that

"Assyrian" referred to his ethnicity and that, as far as race was concerned, he was "white." His identification as Assyrian further disassociated him from being Arab or Catholic. The Iraqi Adventists who had no Chaldean ancestry referred to themselves simply as "Christian Arabs." Yasmeen Hanoosh points out that the term "Assyrian" has been used as "an ethnic and nationalist identity that firmly subsumes the Chaldean branch and all other splinter Eastern Syriac branches that exist today."[33] She cautions the reader, however, to avoid using these two georeligious "appellations" to refer to any kind of actual racial, ethnic, or linguistic distinction; rather, they represent a "cultural divergence" stemming from schisms between the Western and Eastern branches of Christianity and later sharpened during the missionary projects of the colonial period.

Today most Chaldeans live outside Iraq in a global diaspora. Previous to 2003, there had been a small but steady outmigration of Christians from Iraq, but the outmigration of Chaldo-Assyrians accelerated after 2003 and again in 2014, when the Nineveh plains were overrun by ISIL.[34] The minister of human rights for Iraq, appointed after the fall of Saddam Hussein, predicted that "in 20 years there will be no more Christians in Iraq."[35] A nonpartisan commission estimates that in 2003, eight hundred thousand to 1.4 million Christians called Iraq their home, spread across a spectrum of ethnoreligious confessions, including Chaldeans, Assyrian Orthodox, Syriac Catholics, Syrian Orthodox, Armenian Catholics and Orthodox, and various Protestants denominations (Baptists, Seventh-Day Adventists).[36] It is now very likely that over 50 percent of the Christian population has fled since 2003, with the present Christian population estimated at two hundred thousand to five hundred thousand and dropping.[37]

For the shrinking religious and ethnic minorities of the Middle East, like the Chaldo-Assyrians, the majority of whose people live outside Iraq, religion as a "community of memory" holds a certain significance within the diasporic community. In the US, Chaldeans have significant communities in and around Chicago and Detroit; and in California, large Chaldean communities thrive in El Cajon (San Diego) and in Orange County (Yorba Linda). Efforts have been made by leaders of Chaldean and Assyrian communities in the US to combine both populations with the title "Chaldean-Assyrian" for purposes of being counted as a single group in the US Census.[38]

Hanoosh argues that to understand the Chaldean community in the US, we must understand how people see their religious identity through a transnational lens, one that connects the local with the global, the present with the past.[39] "Our people were discriminated against because we are the minority Christian population in an Islam-ruled part of the world. . . . Constant war and conflict forced us out of our homeland and into foreign cultures," said Jasmen, a college student attending the Chaldean Catholic parish. She spoke further of what it meant to her, as part of the Chaldean diaspora in the US, to celebrate the mass in Aramaic: "[Aramaic] language is something that connects people in my community, and unfortunately my family has been scattered across the globe. . . . Now we are faced with the challenges of trying to keep our dying language and culture a part of our [future] children's lives. How would they [her children] communicate with their cousins who are being raised in Germany and France?" For Jasmen, the Chaldean church, with its cultural repository of Aramaic in the mass, symbolizes the survival of a people whose presence in the Middle East is diminishing, whose cultural survival relies increasingly on its diaspora. The Chaldean parish in Riverside was one hub within a larger transnational community of memory in which rituals in Aramaic are enacted simultaneously throughout the world. For Jasmen, by seeing her congregation as part of a transnational community, language and religious identity are the link by which solidarity is maintained in the ethnoscape among a global diaspora; even if people never meet face-to-face, they are powerfully tangible as an imagined community.[40]

In sum, both Christians and Muslims pointed out that the US, a highly secularized society, is different from Iraq, where families are embedded within cultures that reinforce religious observance. Youths, in spite of the freedom and opportunity of the US, admitted that they missed their very close-knit communities in Iraq, with their associated social life and friendship, that they did not expect to see that kind of life being reproduced here. Christian parents lamented the loss of an enmeshed religious community, with its strong institutional supports of observance. Parents of all faiths confessed to being worried about how challenging it was to "keep that link between themselves and their children" in the US, as one Iraqi Christian put it.

Within immigrant families, members of the 1.5 generation tend to have a closer connection to their faith communities than members of the US-born generation do. Religion, however, never ceases to be a potential arena for conflict between the generations. Not every youth I interviewed, or adult for that matter, was an avid attender of mosque or church. Much of the level of conflict surrounding religion can depend on how hard parents push their children to adopt the traditional religious practices and beliefs. Circling back to the trust paradigm proposed by youths like Malik, the choices about religious belief must grow out of a dialogue with, rather than out of obedience to, parents: "With religion, I mean, they can teach me, but they can't really force me because . . . in our religion, you are not allowed to force your kids to choose your religion. . . . You are not allowed to force anyone. So they just try to teach. . . . My dad is a good debater, so I usually have to agree." This statement is all the more interesting because Malik (along with his sister Raiya) was one of the most devout Muslim youths in the study, strictly adhered to the daily ritual and dietary practices of Islam, was an active attender of the mosque, and was an organizer of the Arbaeen March; he joined a group of American Muslim students that took a summer study tour to the Islamic seminary in Najaf. We spent many hours discussing theological and ethical questions that he brought up. Malik's father, Ibrahim, was very devout and participated in a global conversation (via Skype) on Shi'a doctrine. Even so, Malik maintained that the teaching of religious belief and observance to children should be based on persuasion rather than submission to parental authority. Malik's cousin Bilal argued that forcing religion could drive a wedge between parents and children: "You see parents insist a lot on their children, especially that we are Muslim. . . . They insist on prayer, fasting, and such things. Especially here, you know, so they keep insisting, and there are young people who get fed up with this behavior. So maybe that person will go far away, might take a wrong road and leave . . . because of the parents' insisting." Bilal's statement suggests that even when something as vital to parents as having their children follow their footsteps in religious practice religious practice, it is still best to make choices out of freedom, not coercion. Overwhelmingly, youths felt that it was not a good idea for parents to be rigid in requiring religious observance from their children.

"Family Is Everything"

Despite parents' fears that their influence was waning in the power-ful and secular cultural currents of the US, youth like Raiya affirmed the enduring influence of parents in making important decisions, such as choosing a career. Raiya admitted that she allows her parents to be influential:

> I mean, of course, they want me to go to be a doctor or to be like an en-gineer. Of course, everybody's parents want them to do that, but then, as I thought about it, you know, they know me, and at the end of the day, I thought about it myself, and I thought what they were advising me to do was what I actually wanted to do. And if I chose something else, I don't think they would have forced me to not do it or to stop me. I mean, if I liked it, at the end, I think they would have still been supportive. They never told me, "You have to do this," but they were like, "I think you should. . . . I think it suits you."

Raiya was observant enough to know that Iraqi parents tend to push their kids into certain professions—medicine and engineering. She felt that in her own experience, there was no serious conflict with her par-ents over her choice of pharmacology. In fact, it seemed a reasonable compromise—it was a well-paying and respectable profession, she did well in science, and she was interested in psychology. In her junior year, however, she decided to drop pharmacology for psychology. She was cor-rect in her prediction: her parents remained supportive. Raiya's brother, Malik, also switched from premed biochemistry to neuroscience, as he was not getting good-enough grades to stay in the biochemistry program. He said he was only "80 percent sure" that he wanted to be premed. When his father, Ibrahim, challenged him, "Unless you are 100 percent sure, [then] it's not a real option or plan," Malik disagreed, argu-ing that it was better to "stay open." Malik seemed more comfortable with an open-ended future than did his father.

Not all youths were as sanguine about reconciling personal and pa-rental aspirations. Iewan had joined the ROTC at his high school and hoped to apply to the Air Force Academy in Colorado Springs after graduation. His long-term ambition was eventually to become an Air

Force surgeon. He realized, however, that his parents would never approve of him leaving home until he is married. Iewan weighed the pros and cons of his aspirations with those of his parents' preferences. He expressed some dismay that these dreams could not be realized, and he admitted that he got into arguments with his parents on such matters. On the other hand, he understood the logic behind his parents' wishes, especially as he observed his friends in the ROTC program moving out of the house at age eighteen to join the army:

> They're all moving out at this age. They go fight in a war, and they're eighteen. I think that's a little too much. I mean, there are things that I want to do, and if something goes wrong, I might end up in jail for it when I'm eighteen. But they [parents], they'll keep me out of trouble. I'll stay here, and when I want something, I talk to them about it. They say "yeah" or "no," and then we start arguing about it, then we fight about it, but its usually ending up going to their way. It'll definitely keep me out of trouble.

Like his sister, Dera, Iewan saw the risks of going against his parents' wishes as potentially damaging in the long term. He linked his parents' concern for his academic performance with their Arab cultural expectations, which limited some aspirations (leaving home) but kept him "out of trouble." In fact, this circumspection preserved his long-term prospects as his life played out over the next six years: he lived at home, attended a small religious university, got married, and started medical school in the same city where his parents lived.

Open rebellion with parents over career aspirations was rare. What youths most often expressed was distress about wanting to please parents and clearly not being happy about it. As we saw in chapter 2, Khalid felt pressured by his parents to pursue a career in the health professions. Both his parents were unemployed, and he felt that he and his brother were expected to assume financial responsibility for the family. He despaired that family obligations would outweigh his personal career goals, which lay in film and television.

Bilal was in a similar situation. He enjoyed tinkering with computers, but his father, who had just paid a thousand-dollar dental bill for Bilal's brother, urged him to consider the income potential of a medical career. (Bilal's younger brother headed for dentistry, a decision he made as a junior in high school.) Bilal claimed, however, that his father was not taking a hard line on this and had told him that he could study whatever he wanted; Bilal admitted that he was looking into a degree in nursing. But he ended up pursuing a degree in aircraft maintenance at a local community college, very different from nursing but with good employment potential.

The main source of distress when it came to the choice of a career was how it could break families apart. Maintaining strong "family connections" was vitally important, even if it meant relinquishing some personal ambitions or having to stay at home rather than move out on one's own. Dera tended to play down the cultural factor, claiming that it is natural: "It's not just a cultural thing that happens. I mean, just the fact that they care about you living with them and keeping the family close." She went on to say, "That's the idea of a lot of Arabs. It's not because they don't want you to go and see, or they don't want you to get interacted with other people."

Given this fear of pressures from the US economic culture, particularly the tendency to go to where the jobs are, which could break families apart, I wondered what would happen over time to Iraqi families if local employment opportunities did not materialize for youths. Would they resist the temptation to go to other cities and states? Pressures to find employment were indeed affecting Dera's family precisely in the way that she feared. When Bilal finished a two-year degree in aircraft maintenance, he was unable to find a job in the Inland Empire and decided to move four hundred miles away to take a job with the airline KLM at the San Francisco International Airport. When I mentioned to both Khalid and his brother, Saddiq, their cousin leaving to take the job in San Francisco, I received very similar responses. Khalid opined critically, "See, we are in a 'money country' now." Would he, Khalid, ever do that? I posed that question knowing that he was at a similar decision point. He was now finishing his two-year degree in communications and had applied to several four-year universities, all in Southern California, but some would require him to move away from home. He admitted that his parents did not like the idea of him studying film and TV production in the first place, so his choosing a major in communications was a compromise but still left the door open to specialize in film or TV production at a four-year university. He stressed that if he moved away for two years, it would only be until he finished his degree, then he would come back. Like his brother, he wanted to be able to "help them out someday": "I owe it to them. They sacrificed, and I need to pay them back. Family is everything to us." Khalid had made his own decision about his career in spite of his family's disapproval, but he drew the line at moving away from them.

I asked a similar question of Saddiq, who like his cousin Bilal still had not found a job in aircraft maintenance: "Wouldn't you do the same thing, if a job offer came your way and it meant you had to move far away, even to some other state?" Like his brother's, Saddiq's response was immediate and clear: "I could not do it. My parents sacrificed a lot. [I] remember my dad pushing a cart on the street, selling pastries. My parents, I owe them. [They made] too much sacrifice for us." For now, he was working as a security guard at the Amazon warehouse in San Bernardino. "It's boring," he said, and so he would listen to books and English-language lessons to pass the time. He admitted, "Most American kids would just go [to take a job somewhere far away]. I want to buy my parents a house so [we could] all live there together."

Both Khalid and Saddiq found the actions of their cousin disturbing; in fact, it seemed to have caused a bit of a scandal. They were upset that Bilal had moved away and left without even telling them. It had saddened Bilal's family that he would move so far away. When I spoke to Yousef, Bilal's father, about his oldest son moving away to take the job, he seemed sad: "We do this in America, may God keep him." Yousef seemed somewhat embittered by the fact that his son had deviated from the Arab cultural ideal of family; he hoped that his son would work for a while, get some experience, and then return and find a job closer to home.

If there was one aspect of Iraqi culture that everyone felt at risk of losing, it was family cohesion. The importance of family togetherness was one thing that the parents and children agreed on strongly. Parents expressed concern that the weakening of close family ties could lead to their children's involvement in "bad behavior, drugs, sex." Parents felt that too much freedom within families had been driven by a preoccupation with money, so Khalid's aphorism, "This is a money country," rings true. Youths feared that rigid parental authoritarianism combined with the US ethos of success would lead to family disorganization.

The preoccupation with money is often perceived as the main cause of family breakdown, yet parents nudge children into high-paying careers and want them to adopt solid American middle-class values.[41] Even to speak of middle-class values, however, assumes a kind of homogeneous normative American family—a "normal American family" that only exists in the American imaginary as two parents and children, flexible and tolerant of expressive individualism, committed to helping children move along the path of personal autonomy and their own construction of the self.[42] This is where reified notions of culture, such as "family is everything," are actually in a state of flux. Culture is a moving target, always evolving into something new despite attempts to preserve it in some permanent form. As youths engage a US culture that elevates the autonomous self, new "articulations" of both Iraqi and US imaginaries are inevitable and expected.[43] People are in motion; they evolve as cultural worlds collide and the ensuing fusion forms new cultural elements.

The "money country" and "family is everything" aphorisms are one way youths have begun to critique the US middle-class values and engage critically with the ideology of the American autonomous self, even as they have to some extent embraced it, as seen in these lines from Raiya's graduation speech: "But here's the thing: saying good-bye is less about something ending and more about new beginnings and exciting possibilities that the years to come hold." Variations of the trope of "new beginnings and exciting possibilities" were heard at a thousand commencement ceremonies throughout the country. This is an essential American cultural script about the self—with origins in Ralph Waldo Emerson's "insist on yourself," morphing during the 1970s and 1980s into the therapeutic construction of the self.[44] The autonomous self is further constructed in "techniques of the self," "which permit individuals to effect by their own means or with the help of others a certain number of operations on their own bodies and souls, thoughts, conduct and way of being, so as to transform themselves in order to attain a certain state of happiness, purity, wisdom, perfection, or immortality."[45] The project of enlargement of self-expression, and the type of freedom that the self requires for its fulfillment, is more than ever the driving principle of US culture. The graduation script flows out from middle-class values as we have come to know them, undergirded by the ideology of achievement and its unlimited possibilities for those who model hard work and believe strongly and fully in themselves.[46]

US society has historically maintained a healthy balance between civic responsibility and individual freedom. But Robert Bellah and his colleagues identified in the 1980s a tilt toward "expressive individualism," an ethos in which the United States' quintessential values are revealed in the spaces of economic possibility and freedom of expression. The "self-expressive attitude" has been identified more commonly in US-born than first-generation Arab Americans.[47] Among the 1.5 generation in this study, we heard it in Malik's reflection on identity, "I try to keep my identity, so that it's not part of anything else but me." This seems very much a project of individual self-expression. What makes his stance all the more striking is that it seems delinked from membership in any ethnoreligious, kinship, or political solidarity group. And yet it comes from someone who was solidly connected to family and religion. Malik was not the only one who could speak about realizing their identity within family solidarity while at the same time embracing the American imaginary as a space of expression. In this emergent family, mutual trust prevails, and reasoned rather than coercive dialogue exists between parents and children, working to cumulatively dampen the extreme "money country" ambition that breaks families apart.

Clues to reconciling these seemingly contradictory notions of the self come from a close reading of the narrative of friendship in Iraqi and US cultures. Friends in Iraq, Mustafa said, were there for him very much like family:

> Like, not just friends, and that's it, but . . . now I have friends [from Iraq] that text me. . . . They ask about how . . . I'm doing in . . . in school, . . . how is my language now. And they ask me every day that—they call me. Yeah, I like . . . I like that. Not like here, in US: . . . they have the daughter and sons, but . . . they don't care about them, not like Arabs, or like Iraqi. We always together. . . . Like, if my mom wasn't there, my aunt will give me her advice. . . . Yeah, I like that.

The 1.5 generation feels deeply that in Iraq, "when you make friends, they are more than just friends." They are people you can actually depend on. It is more than just going out to have fun; you can actually depend on them to do stuff for you. "Here," said Raiya, "people just want to do what's good for them." This lack of tighter friendship solidarity was one of only a few deficiencies Iraqi youths identified in US culture yet one of its most troubling. Raiya lamented that friendships in the US are indeed different, and it is because relationships are prioritized according to a different calculus, one bending toward the autonomous self, or as she put it, "Every man for himself kind of thing." What preoccupies the individual is the thought that "I need to get along with my life, you know. . . . I help as I can, but my life comes first." Most of the youths were resigned to the fact that solidarities that were natural to Iraqi culture could never be fully reconstituted in the US, but Raiya persisted in believing that people should still try: "One person can make a change, I think. You can call the gathering. I'm sure like some people will say no, but some will come. That's . . . something, you know." I love how she put it: "You can call *the gathering.*"

According to the grand narrative of the Iraqi personality formulated by the sociologist Ali Wardi, friendships are taken very seriously, even among urbanites who had shed some of the deep traditions of hospitality and fierce loyalty of Bedouin society: "In the past, the predominant motto prevailing among city dwellers was 'your neighbor, our neighbor, then your neighbor.' That is, a neighbor should receive attention and assistance even before one's own family. The emphasis on this neighborly relation is not without conditions, the important part of which is that every member of a neighborhood must be 'noble' and 'clean,' with no immoral trait(s). Otherwise, 'neighbors' will be evicted."[48] Wardi feared that neighborly solidarity was starting to weaken as cities grew rapidly, as people migrated to suburbs, and as attitudes of "individualism" emerged among urbanites. Wardi believed that one thing still remained constant: despite people caring less about their neighbors, they still cared very much if their "neighborhood ha[d] an immoral reputation."[49] The neighborly locus of solidarity in Iraq was also the space where attitudes that constrained and judged could prevail, even as the bonds of solidarity weakened.

Youths described their appreciation for friendships that involved tangible forms of mutual obligation. And yet, if Iraq was a place of strong and loyal solidarities, it could also be a place where the individual was hindered by judgment emanating from those same solidarities. This seemed to be Raiya's concern: "Even if it's not necessarily bad over there [in Iraq], it's about, are they going to judge me? Even if it's a good thing, even if you are helping that someone, or that group there doesn't like that someone, so I shouldn't help them, they'll judge me. It's like that; it's a very judgmental society within." Raiya was clear that she preferred the freedom available in the US: "Here it's better. It's more you are free to be who you are and do what you want to do." Malik agreed: "Here people don't really care about what other people think. . . . To a certain extent, that's a good thing." In their cartography of freedom and rights, the US is the quintessential space for expression of individual or collective identity—without fear of judgment (or worse). In their US imaginary, the essence of US values is in its stated commitment to protect individual freedom and human rights.

What I saw in the Iraqi 1.5 generation was that the path to finding belonging in the US was like walking a tightrope. Just as in Wardi's portrayal of the Iraqi personality, the good and the bad about the US inhabit the same locus—the individual construction of the self, with its excesses and erosive effect on group solidarity, is enabled by a country in which "you are free to be who you are and do what you want to do." By embracing the US imaginary and its freedom, these youths risked falling into the belly of the beast. But humans are active creators of culture, not passive recipients. The Iraqi youths were starting to make their own pathway through a hyperindividualistic society, celebrating the freedom to express cultural and religious identities without fear, but deviated from the full exaltation of the independent self. They chose to remain grounded in Iraqi family values that they helped to create—where mutual trust prevails, rather than rigid adherence to a static and idealized notion of family values.

Dera was figuring out how to "keep certain stuff" and realizing that what gets kept is "not exactly the same." Some people would say that you cannot hold in the same hand values that are irreconcilable, recalling Nadine Naber's observation about the difficulty of reconciling what seem to be two irreconcilable worlds. Indeed, it did not work out to everyone's satisfaction. Traditional Iraqi family values were challenged as Bilal moved to San Francisco, Khalid majored in film instead of nursing, and Malik expressed an ambivalent "80 percent" surety about pursuing medicine. Dera's "keeping certain stuff" is an apt metaphor for the cultural project that the Iraqi 1.5 generation has embarked on: to create Iraqi institutions that do not hide in the reified past but rather accommodate new realities and change in ways that adopt what is good in US culture yet still manage to preserve essential Iraqi values. There was much at stake in this project: if it failed, so goes the family.

Notions of what is good for a community, what it values most dearly, tend to delineate the boundaries of that community in contrast to other communities.[50] The project of "keeping certain stuff," "money country," "family is everything" is very revealing in how youths are engaged in discourses of what Naber calls the "politics of authenticity," in which true Arab culture is a static, unchanging feature preserved by the immigrant generation in the face of erosion from the US dominant culture. As youths interact and negotiate their pathway of belonging, the "keeping certain stuff" involves a kind of "selective assimilation . . . as it provides middle-class Arab diasporas with a meaning system for conceptualizing a *sense of belonging*, empowerment, and cultural grounding in the context of displacement and diaspora."[51] Still, the US imaginary also contains freedom of expression, to take action without being judged and to negotiate choices, but within a context of trust.

A Conversation with Women about Families

The beauty of San Diego tortures me.
The silver clouds slaughter me.
How can I live comfortably in a country?
Where swords are sharpened for our people?
—Lamea Abbas Amara, "San Diego (On a Rainy Day)"

Three Iraqi women sat together around a table. Hiba, in her early fifties, arrived in 2014 with her husband and two sons. She had been a school secretary in Iraq. Maryana, in her late fifties, had been an agronomist for the Iraqi government. She had arrived with her husband and four adult children in 2013. Eva, an Iraqi woman in her midthirties was the translator. Lisa, the research assistant and interviewer, began by asking them a poignant question, "Could you please tell me a fond memory you have of either your mother or your grandmother?"

MARYANA: There are lots of memories, . . . lots of memories of my
    mother. We had . . . Please go ahead. . . .
HIBA: No, no, go ahead. . . .
MARYANA: No, please, you go first.
HIBA: No, you started, so go ahead, dear.
MARYANA: Sorry . . . sorry.

The conversation took some time to pick up steam, and what had been
intended as a "discussion" unfolded into an intimate conversation
between two women, Maryana, a Chaldean Christian, and Hiba, a Shi'i
Muslim. I describe their exchange as an honest telling of experience
through the lens of memories of their mothers. Maryana remembered
fondly how she and her mother made a sweet and salty pastry called
klecha during the Christmas holiday, then added, "Mother was very
important to me . . . especially to me. Because my mom and I, we were
always together. I used to tell her my secrets. She always sewed clothes
for me and my children. I have four children, and she used to sew
clothes. Until now, I have kept some of the clothes my mom sewed. So
my mom to me was 'top,' you know."

Hiba's memory moved the conversation into a somber direction as
she recalled the pain and separation inflicted on families by both wars
with the US. They were difficult times, especially how it played out in
her relationship with both her biological mother and her mother-in-law:

> Honestly, I didn't get enough of my mother. We were in Syria as refugees
> for seven years. We used to buy phone credits and make phone calls, and
> she was ill. I even had that malignant disease in my breast. . . . [Maryana
> and Eva: "May God protect you."] Yes, and her responsibilities were a lot,
> because of my brothers and sister. My brother was a martyr at the war
> in 1990; . . . and the other war, the last war in which Baghdad was fallen,
> in that war I lost my other brother, the eldest one. And then my father
> passed away because of his grief. And we didn't see my mother because
> we left Iraq for seven years, and we couldn't see them.

Hiba remembered what it was like in her neighborhood of Al Amiryiah,
which forced her husband to leave in 2006. She followed him to Syria
a year later: "The killing was something unbelievable. Even people who

came to collect the bodies were shot." Her mother-in-law, however, was stubborn in the face of the pressure to leave: "My mother-in-law, God rest her soul, [she] told my husband, 'I'm not going to go to a Sunni area nor to a Shi'a area. We are secular people; we have no discrimination between a Kurd or a Sunni or a Shi'i or . . .'. As my mother, God rest her soul, used to say, 'The Jews lived among us, and they used to call me to their house to turn on . . . [the stove during Shabbat]." Her memory of her mother and mother-in-law was integral to the family's story of displacement. Her husband's leaving Iraq was very difficult for his mother, since he was the only child. After leaving for Syria, she tried to stay in touch with her mother: "but she was always crying after us." Eventually her mother-in-law followed them to Syria, only to become terminally ill. She requested to be taken back to Iraq: "I want to die in my house. I want to see my female friends." She died before they left for the US. "Abu [her husband], poor thing, didn't have enough of his mother. . . . The story of my husband is also painful, honestly." Only three months after arriving in Fontana, she got the "sad news" of her own mother's death.

"But it [life in the Inland Empire] is safe," Maryana said. Refuge from violence was named by the women in this chapter as one of the very good things about life in the US. But the uncomfortable memory of loss remains, recalling the words of the poet: "How can I live comfortably in a country where swords are sharpened for our people?" Hiba's sister-in-law Nuha recalled the loss of brothers in the wars with the US.

The memories of loss evoked in this conversation are examples of the deep elements needed to develop a sense of belonging. A similar truth was articulated by a Bosnian refugee in Germany, who fled the Serbian siege of Sarajevo. She believed that critical to "belonging" was the ability to effectively communicate at an emotional, empathetic level: "Because only those who can express their needs and opinions, those who can explain their misunderstandings and their sadness, can say in this society: 'I have arrived' because only those who feel understood and those who understand the others are part of the society."[52]

Both Hiba and Maryana faced severe health challenges, either personally or among their families. Hiba was a cancer survivor, had been given chemotherapy in Syria, and had been in treatment since arriving in Fontana. Maryana's husband had recently had prostate surgery and was frail: "He is tired from the time he came until now." Neither was she feeling healthy: "I sweat a lot. And if I start something for a short while, I sit down to rest. I get tired, and then I get nervous easily."

The women's conversation moved into what they faced in the US. "Thank God, now we have come to the US. All we want is to be safe, to settle down. . . . Despite the distance and alienation and the expensive life here—honestly, the rent! . . . But it is safe." Hiba's mention of rent reveals how financial need weighed on her, and the inability to find work was frustrating. Both Hiba and Maryana had hoped to work in the Inland Empire, but neither they nor their husbands could find work. They needed to speak both Spanish and English in order to get a job here. Maryana was frustrated by seeing people unable to find work in the professions they had been educated and trained for: "If someone completed their education there in Iraq and has come here, all that education is gone. . . . They can't make their degree equivalent. . . . We are very hurt because of that." What Hiba found very troubling was that the inability of adults to find jobs had turned family roles upside down: "I wished for them [her two sons] to study, only study. I wished to work and their father to work. . . . So my eldest son was obliged to work to pay the rent." She recalled that in Iraq it would not be that way; parents would work, and children could pursue their university or technical degrees. "But here, you get puzzled about what to do." Hiba then quoted the proverb "Whoever leaves his home, his value lessens."

Security is a good thing about the Inland Empire, the women admitted, but it did not mean immunity from financial need or social upheaval. Family relationships had been turned upside down for economic necessity. Four years after the interview, Maryana and her family moved from their small apartment into a modest house, immensely spacious compared to the apartment, with a backyard and in a middle-class neighborhood. But she was discouraged. Her family was embroiled in a divorce case involving one of her sons. Maryana felt that this would not have happened in Iraq: "It is our custom and traditions, and of course, they are different."

Hiba, the mother of Khalid and Saddiq, spoke about freedom, a good thing but also sometimes not so good when it came to her children: "This freedom, honestly, makes us worry about our sons and daughters, honestly." Freedom, embraced by youths as a quintessential element in the US imaginary, frightened parents. And yet, as we saw earlier in this chapter, youth also worried about what cultural and religious values might be lost and what was worth "keeping." Hiba and Maryam, as well as their children, were grappling with the meaning of freedom in their families as they sought belonging in the unique cultural spaces of the Inland Empire.

Hiba and Maryana spoke about the challenges faced by Iraqi women to thrive socially. Both had first lived in apartment complexes that were occupied by predominantly Latinx families. Language barriers frustrated their interaction with neighbors. "We don't have neighbors who can speak with us. They are all Mexicans as well," Maryana lamented. Hiba concurred: "Yes, and . . . even if you want to say 'Hello,' they wouldn't understand, unless you say it 'Allo.' It is like in Mexico." As Lisa and I studied the situation that women like Hiba and Maryana found themselves in, we wondered whether it would ever be possible to overcome the cultural and linguistic barriers between Iraqi refugee women like Hiba and Maryana and their Latinx neighbors. Friendships across cultural barriers are crucial to a felt sense of inclusion. Lisa, who by this time had befriended both Hiba and Maryam and had visited their homes, was optimistic. She believed that Iraqis and Latinxs could find common ground, which could facilitate "community and friendships so that struggles in daily life can be a little more tolerable."

Lisa proceeded to guide the conversation toward an exploration of that possibility. In response to the question about what the women felt they could have in common with their Latinx neighbors, Hiba proceeded to describe the Mexican women she had met at adult school. These friendships, she said, helped her stay motivated with her English classes and gave her more positive feelings about the "Mexican" people surrounding her, especially the women: "I got to know female friends, honestly, the first time I started adult school in San Bernardino, friends who are Mexicans. I mean, beautiful, nice and pretty . . . And if I don't attend a class, they call me to see why I didn't attend, even though they don't [speak] English and I don't know English. . . . It is a good school, and they are patient with the older people." Other Iraqi women spoke of similar experiences with making friends in English classes. Nuha invited classmates from her early-childhood education program, mostly Latinas, to her house.

In fact, Maryana and Hiba found many good things about "Mexican" people. Maryana appreciated that they "bring their own relatives [to the

US], they love each other." Hiba agreed, observing that "their natures, characters, and traditions [are] just like ours, almost, . . . their food, their gatherings." Hiba also pointed to their similar migration experiences, that both Mexicans and Iraqis had been forced to cross borders to survive: "And they also flee to here. They also have bad situations as we do, poor people, . . . just as Iraq and Syria, we cross the borders."

Older Iraqi women not only faced language barriers but, due to poor health or caregiver responsibilities, tended to be more isolated than Iraqi men. Ibrahim's sister Maya arrived in Fontana several months after Ibrahim. During my interviews with Ibrahim and his wife, Layla, and their older children, Maya was always present with us, interested and attentive, sometimes asking me questions. She spoke only a few words of English, and so I exchanged greetings and simple phrases with her in Arabic. She was in poor health and was either using a walker or wheelchair. She would accompany the family on trips to the mosque or to the park. Her life was very much contained within the family circle. I finally had a chance to interview her:

> My life? . . . Born in 1959, in the eighth month. . . . I was an employee in archaeology. . . . Now, all the years of my work, the service, were gone. . . .
>
> Here [Fontana], the situation is normal. People mind their own business. There is no restriction on a person. A person is given his freedom, There is nothing difficult. All is good. I'm comfortable. I don't have anything that is difficult. No, praise God. Whatever was not available there is available here. What is available here compensates for there.
>
> Is there anything about Iraq that I miss? Only visiting the Islamic holy places [visiting Ziyarat]. When you are feeling uncomfortable or bored, you go there to find rest. May God keep you safe.

Women like Maya, who were not pursuing a career or education, lived lives that were contained with the family, somewhat isolated, nevertheless surrounded by family members, nieces, nephews, and cousins. Hiba, who had family nearby that shared her culture, religion, and traditions, found that they were busy just trying to survive: "[My brother] is the only one living close to us. My sister-in-law is also living close to me. Honestly, I don't see them. They are busy, and they are studying, and she [sister-in-law] has taken so many subjects. She didn't even come to visit us, even though she would love to." Hiba's relationships with students in English classes at adult school were an example of how important these social spaces were in connecting the Iraqis to people outside their own solidarity group and in experiencing some form of acceptance within the wider US community.

Listening to Hiba and Maryana talk about their lives, their challenges faced as mothers and ESL students, and their inability to move into employment, Lisa and I wondered about the need for women to be able to move beyond small, close networks that were established through the sponsor-family resettlement system. Lisa felt that what she heard in Hiba's accounts of the family being busy and the joy of friendship in the ESL classes was that she cannot count solely on her extended family to fulfill her social needs or help her to adequately adjust to life in California. Even though she had two families of relatives living within a three-mile radius, friendships outside those families were clearly important to her life.

As we reflected on the conversation with Hiba and Maryana, including what we had observed with other Iraqi women, we wondered about the sense of isolation that some women felt. And yet through the simple attendance at adult school, they had enlarged their networks to include people outside their cultural group. Lisa believed that this was a simple but effective means of breaking the isolation they found themselves in:

> Not to say that they are not close, but each individual is forming a new identity outside the home and what they were previously familiar with. . . . Hiba had the chance to build a friendship with women in her class despite the language barrier. . . . Not only were people friendly to her but also made her feel accepted despite the other students being predominantly Spanish speaking. Since she is an older woman, the classes were her only way to really interact with people in the community who are of a different nationality and religion than her.

Making friends in adult school moved people toward a sense of inclusion, even if that inclusion was with newcomers who were also seeking belonging in the US.

Another question that Lisa and I pondered was whether the women's expanding the social network outside their family and ethnoreligious group could change their sense of dependency for all their social needs, as in Hiba's case, on a group of Iraqi families. One dramatic example of this was what happened to Suha (whose story was introduced in chapter 2). Suha was a widow when she left Iraq, with less than an elementary level of education. She and her family's sponsor in the Chaldean parish were still struggling to get on their feet, and she felt isolated even within her own small Iraqi Chaldean community. Her educational level contributed further to isolation; her English-language ability was too low to qualify for the ESL classes that were within walking distance. The consequences of these intersectional vulnerabilities were starkly revealed in a terrifying incident that occurred several months after she arrived in Riverside. According to Suha's sister, after an argument with her father, Suha had walked to the local *tienda*, a neighborhood store several blocks away that served the mostly Mexican clientele of the area. Unable to read the street signs and afraid to ask for directions from people on the street, she got lost. Her father and sister drove around the city with Deacon Zaker and his wife, searching all day. Finally she was found in the late afternoon, several miles from home, in front of a *tienda*, shaken but safe.

"Articulations of Arabness," writes Naber about her interviewees (both immigrant and second-generation Arab Americans in the Bay Area), contained a division between the "inner Arab domain"—constructed along lines of appropriate behavior for Arab women, heterosexual marriage, and family cohesion—and the "outer American domain," exposed by its loose morals (again, pertaining to women) and disregard for family obligation and parental authority.[53] This split, she says, "provided a sense of empowerment and *belonging* and also *constrained the lives of many of my interlocutors*."[54] Among the Iraqi refugee families in the Inland Empire, the idealized notions of family contained in the aphorism "family is everything" were juxtaposed with "the money country" of the US imaginary. The inner world of the idealized Iraqi family was seen in contrast to the outer US world of hyperindividualized consumerism that threatened to erode and break families apart. In this chapter, we have seen how women confronted this dialectic of the inner and outer worlds and what it meant to them as it produced notions of ethnic familiarity with and distinction from other groups in the Inland Empire and challenged assumptions of the family as all sufficient, as "everything."

4

Two Kinds of Citizens

The week that Nuha, Yousef, and their four children passed their citizenship exams I brought them two pies to celebrate. When I got there, they were watching a live feed on their large TV screen of people in hajj pilgrimage around the Kaaba in Mecca. Nuha was very excited because her sister and brother-in-law, who live in Baghdad, were in the Al-Haram mosque that very moment. She showed me a photo of them, both garbed in white for the hajj. We watched while eating baked fish (Sam's Club salmon), rice, and a yoghurt, cucumber, and mint salad. We caught up on what everyone was doing. Bilal had finished his degree in aircraft maintenance and was looking for a job. His parents hoped he would find one close by. I asked him if he would move away if a job was offered. He answered, "I can't do that. I have to stay here." His youngest brother joked, "He doesn't want to leave me." Their Syrian-born daughter and youngest child was starting fourth grade. On the wall was a photo of her taken during her third-grade year, with the inscription, "Mi nieta, mas bonita de estrella de las universas" (My granddaughter, prettiest star of the universe). She studies Arabic at the Mosque every Friday, and they showed me a photo of Koranic verse she wrote that was on her bedroom ceiling. Nuha was finishing up classes for a degree in early-childhood education at the community college. We drank tea, ate apple and razzleberry pie, with generous scoops of ice cream, and watched the hajj live feed. Suddenly Nuha jumped up and took a photo of the TV screen, trying to capture her sister on one of the mosque balconies.

After a while, I asked them if they felt any different now that they were anticipating the upcoming swearing-in ceremony in Los Angeles. The question did not get much traction, so I asked it another way: "Do you feel more comfortable, more accepted, now that you are almost citizens?" Bilal said, "Sure, no problem." Nuha reacted immediately: "But it's different for me." When I asked what she meant, she told me what had happened to her on the day of the terrorist attack on December 2, 2015, in San Bernardino: "On that day, Yousef called and said he can't take me to appointment, so I take the bus. Later, coming home, I was at the bus stop. [There were] three women talking really loud, looking at me, scared me the way they looking at me. They talked loud, looked at me funny. One walked toward me shouting, then stopped, then kicked the sign. When I got home, I told Yousef what happened. He was watching TV news. It showed the woman with hijab like me, then I knew why those people were angry at me." The woman in the hijab was Tashfeen Malik.

Tashfeen was born in Pakistan, where she studied to be a pharmacist. She later obtained additional education in Saudi Arabia, where she met Syed Rizwan Farook through an online dating site. Farook was born in Chicago in 1987 to parents of Pakistani origin and raised in Southern California. He earned a bachelor's degree in environmental studies and worked as a health inspector for the county.[1] What Nuha's husband was watching on TV was the unfolding story of how Tashfeen and Farook had just killed fourteen people and wounded twenty-two at the County Regional Center. Both died later that day in a shootout with the SWAT team. On the day of the attack, Tashfeen reportedly claimed allegiance to the ISIL leader Abu Bakr Al-Baghdadi on a Facebook post.[2] The mass shooting was, at that time, called the "worst terrorist attack in America since 9/11."[3] Media depictions of Tashfeen Malik showed several photos of her wearing hijab.

In an NPR interview immediately after the San Bernardino attack, Professor Shazia Rahman described her and her family's fears of public anger: "My husband on a daily basis sends me stories of women in hijab who have been attacked. . . . He is very much scared for me and my safety."[4] Attacks on Muslim women have been linked to the anti-Muslim rhetoric of the 2016 presidential election, as documented in a report published by the Bridge Initiative at Georgetown University.[5]

Bilal's comment that for him "it's no problem" illustrates the difference in the way Iraqi men and women are seen in public spaces of the Inland Empire. Iraqi men are assumed to be Latinx, as Bilal's cousin Khalid put it: "Actually they think I'm Hispanic, except for my nose. It's an Arab nose." Khalid's brother agreed: "When I go to school the first day, hey . . . they say 'Hola,' and 'I don't speak Spanish, I'm sorry' . . . 'Oh! Where are you from? . . . 'I'm from Iraq.' . . . 'Oh! You look like Spanish from Mexico.'"

As Nuha finished her story, there was some awkward silence. I did not know what to say. "I'm sorry," I fumbled. I could tell she wanted to say something else but was hesitant. Eventually the question came out:

NUHA: Mr. Ken, are there two kinds of citizens?
KEN CRANE: What do you mean?
NUHA: People like you and then people like us who come to the country?
KC: Is that the way it seems to you?
NUHA: It's different for me because of hijab.

In addition to the frightening encounter at the bus stop on the day of the December 2 attack, Nuha recounted another incident with her history teacher at the community college: "He didn't like me. I really felt it was because I was Muslim. He could see from hijab."

Nuha's story is revealing of how the increased harassment of Arabs and Muslims since 9/11 has been a gendered experience, with women who wear hijab or clothing associated with Islam bearing the brunt of public harassment, while men have experienced it more in the realm of law enforcement.[6] In a focus group with Iraqi youths conducted almost two months after the December 2 shooting, Raiya worried about what she might possibly encounter in public spaces if people actually acted on the anti-Muslim rhetoric coming so stridently from the mouths of (now) mainstream politicians:

Of course, I've seen Donald Trump and others talk the way they do on the media, and it makes me sad. It does make me scared to go out in public, because I don't know [who] agrees with them and who doesn't. And I'm scared maybe, like, I'll do something or say something or even accidental, or just they might just see me I might get angry and feel unsafe, and I don't want to make people unsafe. No one should have to feel like they are being threatened just because the way I look. And I shouldn't feel threatened going out, because, oh, maybe they are scared from the way I look.

Raiya navigated public spaces as Muslim women have done since 9/11, on a continuum between "self-discipline" and "resistance."[7] Not only did she fear personal attack, but she wondered how she might respond to an attack on her person, that she might "get angry," but did not want others to feel "unsafe." Saher Selod found that many Muslim women feel this way, that to preempt threats from others, they engage in the performance of "American values"—smiling, wearing colorful hijabs, not appearing "morose."[8] This tactic of self-discipline (cf. Foucault's internalized self-governance) amounts to a form of "self-imposed house arrest," by which Muslim women fear the potential reaction to their visible expressions of Islam by avoiding public spaces, especially after a terrorist attack anywhere in the world.[9]

Selod describes another reaction to the public space being made unsafe for Muslim women that bends toward resistance, albeit of an oblique variety. She describes a hijab-wearing Indian American woman, Zara, who after 9/11 decided to continue going to garage sales, something she loved to do with her kids: "I realized that I wanted to take a more proactive role, 'cause, you know, I can't just sit back and hide in the house."[10] She discovered that she really enjoyed engaging in conversation with random people, even about controversial foreign-policy issues like Palestine. Selod considers this a form of resistance, a claim to *belonging*: "Rather than taking off the hijab or avoiding public spaces, some Muslim women make a conscientious effort to occupy these spaces to show they *belonged*."[11]

If garage sales can be spaces where resistance is enacted, graduation speeches can be social spaces where belonging is claimed. In May 2015, Ibrahim and Layla's daughter Raiya graduated from high school, and as valedictorian, she addressed the audience: "I can't describe the years I have spent here as other than amazing. I am thankful for my days here for they have made me who I am today: a proud young Muslim woman." In the speech, Raiya invoked an apolitical high school cliché by thanking her school and family, inviting her fellow students to embrace the new possibilities of their future. She then thanked her school and family for empowering her to become a proud young Muslim woman (in the US). Raiya's speech was more than just another celebration of identity. For those who hold that Islam is a threat to Euro-American cultural hegemony, Muslim women are cultural terrorists, accepting of Islam's "subordination" of women, with its "misogynistic and anti-feminist values."[12] The hijab symbolized "the choice of Muslim American women to *reject American freedom.*"[13] Raiya, Muslim and American, embodies a counternarrative to the Trump spin on the clash of civilizations.

As with past terrorist attacks, the San Bernardino shooting immediately raised the specter of backlash against Muslims. Five days after the San Bernardino attack, candidate Trump extended his border-security proposals to include a complete ban on Muslim immigration. Less than a year later, five days after winning the 2016 election, President Trump released a statement explaining that he planned to curb refugee admissions from certain Muslim-majority countries because of their alleged cultural practices threatening to women. The two countries singled out were Iraq and Afghanistan: "In the last five years, we've admitted nearly 100,000 immigrants from Iraq and Afghanistan—in these two countries, according to Pew Research, a majority of residents say that the barbaric practice of honor killings against women are often or sometimes justified. . . . Hillary [Clinton] will bring in 620,000 new refugees in a four-year term at a lifetime cost of over $400 billion."[14] Trump's proposal, though blunt in its demagoguery, was brilliant in finding the pressure points of public fear. Drawing on Orientalist tropes of the vicious and sexually savage Arab male, Trump would not only protect our borders but preserve the United States' women as well. He had done the same for European womanhood earlier that year, when during the migration event in Europe, he observed, "Did you ever see a migration like that? . . . They're all men, and they're all strong looking guys."[15] This strategy intentionally plays on the United States' deepest fears, completing the circle of protection against both Arabs (terrorists, sexual threats, honor killers) and Mexicans (rapists).[16] To his narrative of national security, he added the protection of our women—reprising a page from a not-so-old racist playbook.

Even before Trump's immigration and refugee policy proposals were justified as protecting women, the "saving" of the Muslim woman from the medieval and repressive religion of Islam has justified colonial interventions going back well into the nineteenth century, when colonial powers "had a vested interest in portraying the Muslim woman as oppressed, . . . in need of European rescue," and has continued into justifications for the war in Afghanistan in 2001.[17] Trump's policies are directed at the domestic-internal threat of Islam, ideologically grounded in the "clash of civilizations" paradigm. Within this paradigm, Muslim women who wear hijab "symbolize an imagined cultural conflict between the West and Islam. Wearing the hijab is seen as a transgression of the cultural values of the West, a form of cultural terrorism. . . . Muslim women are assumed to support misogyny and antifeminist values that are viewed as inherently un-American."[18]

The Orientalist discourse that has painted Arabs and Muslims with the brush of incompatibility with American values, followed by the framing of Arabs and Muslims as potential threats in the War on Terror, is keenly felt in the way it has marked them with the stigma of distrust. The tangibility of this distrust was seen in Nuha's question, "Are there two kinds of citizens? . . . People like you and then people like us?" For Nuha, her new US passport was only one piece of a puzzle, which after putting together all the pieces should add up to 100 percent "American." The harassment that Hiba encountered after the San Bernardino terrorist attack was clear evidence that obtaining full belonging in the US was not going to come easily. What she experienced is a microcosm of the painful reality for Arab Americans in the post-9/11 context of suspicion. Within this microcosm, there is the added intersectionality of religion and gender, in which Arab and Muslim women experience being the nonwhite racial Other in their vulnerability to violent and hostile actions.

The dark irony here for Iraqi refugee women (and men) in the Inland Empire is in the way they named security as something they valued highly in the US. Yet for women whose religion makes them more visible targets for hate crimes, security is eroded. Even Raiya, who celebrated freedom of expression in her graduation speech, less than a year later was "scared" about how she could be perceived as threatening to others within the atmosphere of anti-Muslim rhetoric coming from the highest levels of the US polity.

Nuha learned that you can hold a US passport but still feel excluded from the experience of cultural citizenship, the sense of full acceptance and belonging, including "the right to be different."[19] As a Muslim woman, Nuha's experience of belonging was mediated by sociopolitical processes that created distinction and visibility, which exposed her to violence and led her to question the full possibility of belonging that is assumed in citizenship.[20]

Muslim women like Nuha who identify by wearing hijab are in the epicenter of the ongoing process by which Arabs and Muslims have been made into racial Others. The manner in which Muslim women face the uncertainties in public space builds on this new reality, that they are no longer seen publicly as "white." Racialization in the US is not experienced uniformly but has disproportionately targeted people of color through various technologies and practices of surveillance and policing. For Muslims and Arabs in the US, who are the primary targets in the domestic manifestation of the War on Terror, racialization is based on religion, not phenotype, argues Selod. Selod's most recent research contests the conceptualization of race as always based in some form of phenotype (primarily skin color) and argues that in the case of Muslims from Arab countries and South Asia, it is their religion that is the primary basis for their group identification, even for those whose complexions are white. Within that racialized group, as we saw in the experiences of Suha and Raiya, religious clothing (e.g., hijab) foregrounds the public identification of Otherness onto the female body. Muslim Iraqi women in the Inland Empire, like Suha and Raiya, who speak of either actual or potential violent public reactions to their religious clothing instantiate the "gendered forms of racialization."[21]

Violence drove these women from their homes in Iraq, violence perpetrated by those who believed that they did not belong. But the War on Terror, with its discourses of the Muslim threat within our borders, has in fact created both perceived and real insecurity for Muslim women in the public spaces of the US and in the Inland Empire. For Muslim women, claiming belonging in public spaces, whether bus stops, graduations, or garage sales, can never be far removed from the specter of violence. It is only within this gendered experience of the War on Terror that we can truly understand Nuha's question, "Are there two kinds of citizens?"

5

"Where Are the Americans?"

One hears more Spanish than English everywhere; I sometimes wonder where I am. South America must be empty.
—Nuha al-Radi, *Baghdad Diaries*

Ali came to the door to greet me in a gray *disdasha*, the long shirt
traditionally worn by Iraqi men. It was June in Fontana, which usually
means ninety-five degrees and bad air quality. Ali, his wife, Hiba, and
their two sons, ages twenty and eighteen, had only been in the US for
five months. Ali studied at the Art Institute in Baghdad, then taught
art at a primary school in Iraq. Hiba had been a school secretary. They
first stayed with her brother in Damascus after realizing that it was too
dangerous to stay in Baghdad in 2006. They used their savings to open
a small grocery store in the Joloromia neighborhood. The sons delivered orders by bicycle to people's apartments. After two years, they
applied to the UNHCR in Damascus for resettlement, but the onset of
the Syrian war made the grocery business difficult: prices were going
up, and it was getting harder to stock the store. They were forced to
leave what had become their Syrian home and returned to Iraq in 2012
before their UNHCR application was finalized. They were sponsored
as refugees by their cousin Ibrahim and in 2014 arrived in California.
With Ibrahim and Zaynab's help, Ali and Hiba found an apartment on
Mango Street in Fontana, a mostly Latinx working-class city of about
two hundred thousand.

We sat in the family's modest living room and made small talk: "How
are the kids?" The younger son, Khalid, was now a senior at A. B. Miller
High School. Saddiq, the oldest son, was talking outside. Then Khalid and Ali went outside. After a few minutes, a short man with a buzz
cut and dark-brown skin limped into the house with a cane, carrying a
plastic water bottle and his Bible. He sat down on the couch beside me
and introduced himself: "Hi, I'm Arthur Suarez." He shook my hand.

He gladly accepted a glass of cold water from Saddiq on that ninety-plus-degree day. "Good with a shot of tequila," he joked. "Did you grow up in Fontana?" I asked. That was all the prompt that was required: "Born in El Paso, lived there till I was five, then moved to LA, East LA, after that Watts, you know, South Central, got in with gangs, even was kicked out of school for the handicapped for dealing drugs—can you believe that?—into lockup, then back to high school, this time regular high school. I've got arthritis in my leg. Actually it's from polio. Didn't get vaccination till I was five. My parents came from Mexico. But God saved my life. I was into gangs, 18th Street gang, others." Hiba brought out fruit smoothies and chocolate cake. Arthur paused, took a sip of the smoothie, laughed, and joked again, "It's good with tequila." Ali laughed politely, then finally asked, "What is that, *takila*?" Arthur made the universal bottoms-up sign with his hands: "Spirits, liquor. Don't do that anymore—better without it."

Arthur shifted to a more serious theme: "Yesterday I was here with my wife and another woman, like Martha and Mary, talking to Khalid here about watching out for stuff at high school, like drugs and girls." Arthur opened his Bible, started reading some verses to Saddiq from the book of Revelation: "These verses are about the millennium," he said while handing out some Watchtower pamphlets. He invited Ali and family to a Jehovah's Witness evangelistic meeting to be held in Long Beach, lasting for three days: "With lots of music. You can ride with us. We go by train or sometimes with a bus." I noticed that the title of the pamphlets was *One World Government*. I asked him what he thought about the United Nations. "God is in control of the UN. Once I was in Nebraska, visiting my brother. I met some Africans. They were Muslim, from Kenya I think. One spoke French." Ali, Khalid, Saddiq, and Hiba all listened patiently and politely as he talked. He finished his smoothie and prepared to leave; the family warmly shook his hand and told him, in the Iraqi tradition of hospitality, "You are welcome, anytime."

After Arthur left, I asked the family what they thought. It turns out that he had been a regular at their door. Ali and Saddiq had even gone to the Salón del Reino meeting and met someone there who spoke Arabic: "It was okay," Saddiq shrugged. "I'd like to visit Long Beach and LA or San Diego. Can you get there by train?" I got the impression that they were not bothered by visits from Arthur, that they enjoyed a chance to practice their English with a curious guy who stopped by to visit them regularly.

Arthur is reminiscent of Sonny Arguinzoni, a Puerto Rican former gang member who "got saved" and kicked drugs. Sonny eventually founded an outreach center for drug addicts in East Los Angeles. At Alcance church in East Los Angeles, people like Sonny and Arthur are called the "Lazarus generation," referring to the biblical story of a man brought back to life. Gangbanger to born-again missionary is a common motif of urban Latinx evangelicalism.[1]

Latinx Inland Empire

When Ali and Hiba arrived from Damascus in 2014, they found a United States that they had utterly not imagined: grocery stores full of Mexican specialties like *nopales* and *pan dulce*, weekly visits from zealous evangelists. The two days of generic cultural orientation that they had received from the International Organization for Migration before departing Damascus did not include any advice on how to survive in the unique cultural universe of Southern California and lacked any description of cultural features of the region.

Like many of the Inland Empire towns, Fontana is situated along one of the most American icons, the original Route 66—"Mother Road." As chronicled by the city's native son Mike Davis, in *City of Quartz*, Fontana's settlement was fueled by the American Jeffersonian ideal of the self-sufficient landed farmer, extolled by A. B. Miller, who created Fontana Farms. Fontana originated as orchards of walnuts and oranges irrigated by streams from the surrounding San Gabriel Mountains. The influx of family farmers of citrus throughout the Inland Empire was known as the "Second Gold Rush."

Smallholder farms eventually gave way to the commercialization of orange growing in the early twentieth century. At this time, the revolution began a violent episode in Mexico's history, which coincided with the need for more labor in the California orange industry. Japanese and Chinese laborers were in short supply due to immigration laws barring their entry, which spurred the large-scale recruitment of Mexican labor. Agricultural labor migration increased the Mexican population that had already been living here for generations, since before the annexation of Mexican California by the US.

War and its subsequent detritus left its imprint on Fontana's social and economic history. During World War II, there were four thousand war-material plants in the greater Los Angeles region. Los Angeles was not prepared to handle the amount of garbage issuing from this surge in population, and the solution was to ship it by rail to Inland Empire towns like Fontana to be used as feed in large hog farms.[2] (Ibrahim would have appreciated the entrepreneurial spirit of those who made a living selling the restaurant knives and forks found in the refuse.) In 1940, the industrialist Henry Kaiser chose Fontana for the first steel mill west of the Mississippi, to manufacture material for the naval shipyards of Long Beach / San Pedro. During the mill's heyday, Fontana attracted labor from all over the US and world, outstripping available housing—even chicken coops were converted into rental units. The city's boomtown history created layers of class and ethnic differentiations—"a dissonant *bricolage* of Sunkist growers, Slovene chicken ranchers, gamblers, mobsters, over-the-road truckers, industrialized Okies, *braceros*."[3] My uncle, a steelworker aptly named Flint, put it slightly more poetically: "You would wonder at the conglomeration of people that lived there!" Uncle Flint had added to the mix by migrating to the Inland Empire from South Dakota, eventually finding work in the mill as a foreman. He was a consummate steel man, with a garage outfitted with anvils, tongs, and welders.

For all the city's historical idealism, Fontana had a dark side—the flourishing of the KKK, which murdered the black civil rights activist O'Day Short, and the subsequent police coverup. My Aunt Pauline, Uncle Flint's wife, who taught public junior high school at that time, remembered the racial tensions that arose during school desegregation. Fontana was also incubator for the Hells Angels motorcycle gang. When the steel mill was shuttered in the 1980s, the town fell into hard times, leaving the town with a look of dereliction, as Davis put it, a "junkyard of dreams."[4] Fontana followed the economic pattern of the rest of the Inland Empire and became a logistics hub. Manufacturing and agricultural jobs disappeared, to be replaced by warehouses and freight-train depots serving Southern California ports.[5] The Latinx population of the

Inland Empire continued to grow rapidly from the 1980s onward, due to both labor recruitment from Mexico and migration from Los Angeles for cheaper housing. Of Fontana's 196,069 inhabitants, 66 percent were "Hispanic," 57 percent Mexican.[6]

The rest of this chapter explores the meaning of belonging for Iraqis settling in the Latinx-dominant communities of Fontana, Rialto, San Bernardino, Riverside, and Moreno Valley. Immigrants in the US work out issues of communal belonging in a specific time and place, one that has very concrete dimensions of ethnic and racial identity, growing out of histories that are unique to that region. In chapter 4, I explored what this looked like for Iraqi women. In this chapter, I give the reader a picture of what daily experiences of exclusion and inclusion looked like for younger Iraqis, those whose present and future sense of belonging was being negotiated daily in neighborhoods, schools, and work.

Bridge People

I decided to approach the question of how Iraqis found communal belonging within the social mosaic of the Inland Empire by exploring Iraqi-Latinx interactions. I was fortunate to have as an invaluable consultant Lisa Fernandez, who had been so instrumental in the interviews with Iraqi women. Lisa had deep family roots in the Inland Empire and Mexico. She provided critical insight into how she saw the Iraqi community interacting with the Latinx population. As she participated in interviews with Iraqi adults and youth, reflecting on her own experience and family history, she became both interlocutor and researcher; her BA thesis grew out of her experiences with Iraqi families that she met at this time.

Solidarity between people divided by linguistic and cultural difference does not happen naturally but through the intentionality of people who act as bridges between communities. In recognition of that reality, the resettlement agency asked Lisa to create a new cultural-orientation workshop called "Your Latino Neighbors" for the Iraqi families in the Inland Empire. Lisa first visited the Iraqi families in their homes to offer a personal invitation for them to attend and to understand her audience. The workshop was well attended, and participants engaged with the various activities, which included presentations about the different

Latinx cultures (e.g., Mexican, Guatemalan, Salvadoran, Colombian), eating home-cooked (and halal) Mexican food prepared by Lisa's grand-mother, a *piñata* for the children, quizzes with prizes for the adults, and discussions about the similarities between Iraqi and Latinx cultures. An important factor in the workshop's success was Lisa role as the "bridge person"—who acted as a kind of cultural emissary between communities.

The creation of these types of social spaces is rare but necessary to facilitate belonging. Aihwa Ong documents how Cambodian refugees' encounters with the cultural norms of US citizenship through resettlement, social services, and medical institutions can actually hinder their political incorporation.[7] It is not enough to pay lip service to some kind of "symbolic rhetoric of inclusion," such as "we are all immigrants."[8] Acknowledging the multicultural nature of US society and supporting its local ethnic institutions (religion, self-help and advocacy groups, cultural organizations) actually lead to fuller political engagement in the long run.[9] The "Your Latino Neighbors" workshop was one small example of how resettlement agencies could approach incorporating refugees into US society by bridging them into connection with the diverse communities that they are likely to encounter.

Over the course of this phase of the research, Lisa came to see that there were many similarities between the migration narratives of Iraqis and those of Mexican and Central American ancestry:

> I was raised by my maternal grandparents, who migrated to the United States from Mexico in their youth. My maternal grandfather moved to the states from Ciudad Juarez, Chihuahua, Mexico, with his mother and three siblings after the sudden murder of his father by a business associate. My grandmother Elvira migrated to California from Fresnillo, Zacatecas, Mexico, with her mother, father, and seven siblings in search of a better life. My [grand]parents Jesse and Elvira met as young adults, quickly fell in love, and married once Jesse returned from a military draft tour in South Korea. They had four children, and the oldest daughter, Cindy, is my mother.

Lisa's family history contains striking parallels to Iraqi stories involving struggle and flight from violence. Becoming aware of this commonality, she began to reflect on what could be potential common ground between people like her and the new community of Iraqi refugees. As she listened to Iraqis tell their migration histories, she recognized in their narrative a trauma similar to that experienced by Latinx migrants:[10] "Latinos and Iraqis [both] have had migration experiences that were difficult, even traumatic. Every year hundreds of people died attempting to cross the Southern border between the USA and Mexico."[11] Lisa felt that Mexicans and Iraqis being subjected to similar treatment in their common migration experiences could lead to a form of solidarity. The violence of forced migration, with its trials of rejection, detention, and deportation, were ways that Latinxs shared commonality with Iraqis who experienced similar trauma and hardship in their long years of exile. Iraqis, like Mexicans who had crossed the southern border, suffered difficult journeys to find safe havens. For example, of the 1,011,712 asylum seekers who crossed the Mediterranean into Europe in 2015, 3,770 died trying; Iraqis were the third-largest group who attempted the crossing.[12]

As Lisa reflected on her family's migration history, she rightly observed how Mexican migration is historically linked to the history of US empire:

Parts of the United States [e.g., California] once belonged to Mexico prior to the Treaty of Guadalupe Hidalgo [in 1848]. Since that time many people from Latin America continue to immigrate to these areas of the southwestern United States. . . . Much of Latin America experiences poverty, corrupt governments and lack of education but the United States is seen as the "land of opportunity" which continues to motivate people to leave their homes or risk their lives in search of a better life.[13]

Lisa's observation about US hegemony in Latin America has a striking parallel to the relationship between the US and the Middle East. US economic and political intervention in Iraq and Mexico has in both cases led to the creation of migratory pathways. In the case of Mexico, labor migration to the US grew out of differentials of political and economic power and set the stage for decades of labor recruitment even before the Bracero arrangement starting in World War II. The US became the "land of opportunity" in part through the work of Mexican labor, recruited since the early twentieth century. The profound political and economic relationships between the US and Mexico (US land annexation and labor recruitment) initially enabled and continues to create migratory pathways. Likewise, in the United States' attempts to remake the Middle East in ways that are amenable to its interests—the Iraq War being one of the most egregious examples—the country has contributed to massive forced migration in the region. As I explained in chapter 1, the resettlement of Iraqi refugees in the US, an ostensibly humanitarian action, was justified to the American people as part and parcel of overall foreign policy toward Iraq and its neighbors, as furthering the cause in the War on Terror.

Guatemalans have been the major non-Mexican Latinx group in the Inland Empire.[14] The origins of Guatemalan migration into Mexico and northward into the US can be traced to the destabilizing impact of US foreign policy during the Cold War.[15] The outmigration from Guatemala was initiated in the 1980s by the US-backed Guatemalan dictator Rios Montt, whose genocide against indigenous and peasant populations, suspected of waging an insurgency, murdered and displaced hundreds of thousands.[16]

The hypernationalist rhetoric that emerged in the 2015–2016 presidential primary and election identified two groups—Mexicans and Muslims—as threats to US security, which fostered among those groups a heightened sense of vulnerability and fear. The proposed Muslim ban clearly drew on the post-9/11 discourse of Arabs and Muslims as the primary threats in the domestic front of the War on Terror. Likewise, the effort to portray Mexican immigrants as a threat to security and US cultural values is not new, going back at least to the 1970s with Immigration and Naturalization Service commissioner Leonard F. Chapman's warning of the "silent invasion of illegal aliens" who were "milking the U.S. taxpayer."[17] The eventual "Islamization" of the immigration debate emerged from the attempt to prevent or reduce immigrant and refugee admissions from Muslim countries, on the basis of claims that Arab and Muslim "terrorists" were sneaking in through the unmonitored doors of the refugee-resettlement program. Would Iraqis recognize in Donald Trump's pronouncement "We cannot let them [Muslims] come into this country, period," a parallel to his slogan "Build the wall"?

Lisa believed that the historical experience of Latinx who survived stigmatization and social exclusion provided potential for solidarity between the two communities: "Since Latinos are still a culture that is often associated with negative stereotypes, I am hoping that the Iraqi families living in Latino neighborhoods might be able to find comfort within these communities because both sides will know what it is like to experience intolerance."[18] In fact, the geographical isolation of Iraqis in inland Southern California has parallels for Latinxs who have settled in parts of the US like the Midwest or South, where they have found themselves to be an isolated minority population that experiences hostility from a dominant Anglo community.[19] The potential for solidarity based on similar feelings of isolation among Iraqis was expressed by this Iraqi high school student's experience: "For two months, I think, when I first came, I went to public school elementary, and I didn't speak English, like, at all. . . . But they [Latinxs] were really nice. . . . Like, there were two girls—I still remember them—they always helped me, waited for me in the morning. They were Hispanic, and they were very, very nice, very helpful."

With Iraqis being resettled in Inland Empire cities like Fontana and Moreno Valley, where some neighborhoods were 60–70 percent Latinx, I was particularly interested in how Iraqis and Latinx interacted in the public spaces of school and work. I asked Iraqi youths about their experiences at (majority-Latinx) public schools: if they saw any similarities between Latinx cultures and their own or felt any common ground through similar family histories of migration. What I found was that Iraqis offered frank opinions, both positive and negative, about the Latinx ("Mexican" and "Hispanic") community with which they interacted. The negative feelings toward Latinxs centered on language. A common reason was put forth by Mustafa, a high school senior, who described his experience soon after arriving in California from Syria: "First time I came here, I went to some store, looking for a job. . . . I thought . . . like, California, all the people's American, you know. . . . I'm looking for a job, they said, 'You speak Spanish?' . . . 'No, I'm living in California. I don't need Spanish.' He [employer] said, 'No, here, first language Spanish.' So I felt bad. Yeah, that's it . . . because I should learn Spanish. So I'm not speaking English; I'm speaking Spanish.'" During predeparture orientation, the teachers told Iraqis that learning English is essential to their success in the US. What they found in the Inland Empire was that Spanish was sometimes required for the job and was always an advantage when applying for a job. Marwan, also a senior in high school, found this reality disturbing: "Guys say, 'Learn English, English.' But when you go to work, 'No, no hablo Inglés, Español . . . Español.'"

A number of the Iraqi youths felt that Mexican immigrants were "too lazy" to learn English. Saddiq, who dropped out of university in Iraq after the 2003 invasion and was now working as a forklift driver, observed, "I don't think all the Mexican[s] are like . . . bad people. They are really nice with me. . . . But they are lazy to learn English. Maybe they just speak Spanish in school, a lot of them, not all. . . . I think they are like . . . lazy, and they don't want to learn." While Saddiq was quick to point out that Mexicans are not "bad," he embraced a common perception in the US that people of Mexican origin resist learning English. This is part of a broader claim about Mexicans who resist assimilation or engage in forms of "reverse assimilation," as claimed by pundits like Ann Coulter in *Adios, America*. It is a misconception perpetuated by movements lobbying to establish English as the official language in the US. This perception is frequently framed in comparisons with immigrant groups who have appeared to attain fluency in English more rapidly. In ESL classes, Iraqis discovered a diversity of Latinx groups, some of whom they felt were more enthusiastic toward learning English, as Saddiq did when he compared Mexicans with Colombians and Salvadorans: "I'm talking about all the Spanish, like Salvadorian, Colombian. . . . They are nice with me, but the Mexican people . . . they are lazy . . . more lazy than other people. . . . They don't speak any English; just they speak their language. But I see like from Colombia, from [El] Salvador, they speak English. . . . They want to learn [English]." Those whom I interviewed had competing views on this issue. Some felt the laziness stereotype was unfair, that there were alternative ways to understand why someone is not learning English, such as social class or educational opportunity, as Malik argued: "What about those that don't have a chance [to get to college]? Usually, they don't have a chance to learn English either." Malik suggested that people in certain occupations simply have less need to learn the language.

Among older adults and parents, there were similar negative sentiments that often came up in discussions about ESL classes. Iraqi adult learners felt it was a waste of time to go to ESL classes, where so much Spanish was spoken and the Latinx students did not interact outside their own group: "People there speak too much Spanish! Not good!" They were more pleased with classes that had fewer Spanish speakers. They also complained that they did not have enough opportunity to learn English from their neighbors. For Mohammad, life was complicated enough with a lack of fluency in English: "I don't have a problem with them—so easy to make friends. . . . And just one problem, like, the language. I try to learn Spanish. . . . It's easy language, but they don't speak English, just this problem. I came here new. I don't speak English very well. And they don't speak English, so . . ." (I should clarify that the majority of the Latinx population in the Inland Empire speaks fluent English. But there is a large first-generation, immigrant population that is predominantly Spanish speaking, and these were the people the Iraqis would naturally encounter in adult school.)

The laments we hear from Iraqis were expressions of frustration due to barriers to engagement with a Latinx-dominant community. It is important to note the distinction between tension over language as a barrier and cultural value differences. Mohammad is typical of many Iraqis who took pains to explain that they did not have any issues with the culture of "Mexicans." Apart from the issue of language, Iraqis had positive things to say about their interactions with Latinxs in the Inland Empire. They characterized Latinxs as acting more open and "free," less conservative than Iraqis in their public demeanor. A common response came from Yacoub, a Chaldean Iraqi attending a local community college: "They are people like me. . . . I don't have a problem with them." Saddiq, who had made some Colombian friends at his ESL class, elaborated on the same sentiment: "I like them. Such beautiful people. . . . And . . . when I go to my adult school, I communicate with them all the time, yeah, and I pick up the words like 'buen día,' 'hola,' 'cómo estás.' Yeah, every day, same thing . . . nice people." Saddiq's social media posts frequently showed him socializing with Latinx acquaintances he met at adult school, going to movies and to their houses for visits and parties.

Iraqis noted that there were similarities between themselves and Latinxs in culture, family values, and hospitality. They knew something of the historical contact between Spanish and Arab cultures, the Moors in Andalusia, which resulted in linguistic similarities in Spanish and Arabic. They had discovered that many of the ingredients for traditional

Iraqi dishes were used in Mexican cooking and readily available at the *tiendas* (stores that cater to Mexican tastes).

The youths spoke of Latinx friends they had made in school, with many Latinx friends following them on social media. Given these emerging friendships, some with members of the opposite sex, I asked them about the possibility of marrying someone from Latinx cultures. The dominant sentiment was that they would be open to marrying someone from those cultures since there were more similarities than differences between them: "You don't really need to adapt in the culture. They [the two cultures] are pretty much the same." (Although this perspective was not always shared by parents.) The main obstacle they anticipated would be religion, since they would be expected to marry someone from within their faith community. Even here, however, they did not see it as an open-and-shut case and cited examples where there had been mixed marriages, a Mexican man who married a Muslim Iraqi woman, an Iraqi man who married a Colombian woman. Most of those who had no objection to interreligious marriage were men, which is not surprising since a common practice in the Middle East is for women to adopt the religion of their husbands.

In sum, the barriers to Iraqis building bridges with their Latinx neighbors were fewer than the pathways toward common ground. True, they felt real frustrations about language, but this grew out of being a geographically dispersed and relatively small population within Latinx-majority neighborhoods. It also grew out of the perception of being disadvantaged in a recessionary labor market due to their lack of ability in Spanish, further complicated by prevailing stereotypes about Mexicans as "too lazy" to learn English. On the positive side, however, their frustration emerged from a desire to engage with the wider community of Spanish-speaking neighbors. More importantly, they saw no great differences in cultural values, to the point that marriage between Iraqis and Latinxs was not an unreasonable possibility; they had heard cases of it happening and working out.

On the basis of what I had heard, I still believed that the potential existed for the two groups to find common ground because of similar migration histories and hostile nativist receptions. Lisa, who had facilitated several focus groups where this issue was discussed, also came away with a sense of optimism. Unfortunately, there is little historical precedent that would support our hopes. Bridge building and solidarity between marginalized groups has been rare in the history of race relations in the US. A significant obstacle has been prevailing notions of "whiteness" that some Iraqis employed to differentiate themselves from the Mexican population, notions that they associated with being "American."

Walls

I had just finished a two-hour-long interview with Wessam and his wife, who had moved into an apartment in Moreno Valley. They lived in census tract 42622, which happens to be the Inland Empire's most diverse—44.2 percent Hispanic (ethnic Mexican), 18.2 percent white, 18 percent black, and 15.6 percent Asian and Pacific Islander.[20] As I was gathering my things to leave, Wessam dropped the question: "Mr. Crane, can I ask you, where are the Americans?"

Wessam was born in Mosul, in Northern Iraq, and had grown up in a mixed neighborhood—Christian, Kurd, Muslim—which at that time, he said, was "no problem at all." After graduating from the University of Mosul, he worked for his father's business. After the invasion, he worked for the Iraqi government and US contractors in reconstruction of infrastructure. Like the other Iraqis whom I interviewed, threats on his life began after 2003. A militia group threatened his Muslim coworker, "You must leave that job, or you will be killed." He quit his job and in 2004 fled to Syria, where he applied his management skills to distribute aid from international agencies to Iraqi refugees.

At first I did not understand Wessam's question. When I asked him to explain what he meant by "American," he elaborated, "So few white people, so many Mexicans." Wessam, who considered himself both Arab and white, was a cosmopolitan and educated person, fully aware that sectarian difference has deadly consequences. It was not the only time I was asked that kind of question, and each time it troubled me.

"Where are the Americans?" This question opened a conversation with Iraqis that explored the meaning of race within the larger project of how to find belonging in the US. What does it mean to "become American" where the US looks more Latinx than Anglo? A further complication was the recent history of the racialization of Arabs and Muslims, through which the whiteness of Arabs had transmuted into something other than white, long before Wessam arrived in the Inland Empire.

To understand both Wessam's question and the dialogue that unfolded requires that we recognize the salience of geography and history. Racial formation for Iraqis in the Inland Empire meant an encounter with layers of history that spanned Spanish colonization and subjugation of Cahuilla and Luiseño Indians within mission economies, Mexican nationhood, US annexation, the establishment of white supremacy by the Anglo capitalist class in the nineteenth century and those who would resist it in the twentieth—La Raza and the Brown Berets, then the civil rights movement, Cesar Chavez and La Huelga, the anti-immigrant politics of Prop 187, into the second decade of the twenty-first century with the border securitization frenzy. Each of these layers of history contained its own ever-changing understandings of race within social hierarchy.

Wendy Cheng, who studied relationships between Asians and Latinxs in the "majority-minority" communities in San Gabriel, fifty miles to the west of the Inland Empire, found that the formation of racial identity unfolds differently according to region, "since race is not constructed or experienced uniformly."[21] Like Cheng, Perla M. Guerrero, in her research on Vietnamese, Cuban, and Mexican migration in Arkansas, recognized that using the black/white, and Anglo/Hispanic binaries to frame intergroup relations would not allow for the nuances and comparisons of identity formed in specific places.[22] What I have attempted to do here is to be open to a geographically specific racial formation, in order to see Iraqi encounters in Latinx neighborhoods in a fresh way, not to assume they necessarily align with previously observed patterns. To begin, however, it is necessary to describe some of the historical processes of racial formation that are germane to Arab Americans, both in the US and in the West more generally.

Ta'Nehisi Coates reminds us that "race is the child of racism, not the father," that phenotype is used to signify "deeper attributes, which are indelible," which can be organizing principles in the building of the racial hierarchy of society.[23] There is a much longer history of the racial thinking about Arabs that preceded US hegemony in the Middle East and 9/11, conceptualized by Edward Said as Orientalism, the European view of the Arab male mentality as aggressive sexuality, untrustworthiness, revenge seeking, and bloodthirsty and Arab women as sexually mysterious yet submissive and sequestered.[24] Thus, it was not a stretch to speak of an entire country as belonging to an "axis of evil" and of "strange, sullen, wild-eyed insurgents."[25] Nor was it so strange to see Arab bodies in Abu Ghraib prison or detained in Guantanamo Bay, where they had been preceded by Haitian and Cuban (many of them Afro-Cuban) asylum seekers, detained there in the 1980s.[26]

The racial overtones of Orientalism, however, have been an impediment to Arab Americans in the US historically self-identifying as "white," although it is possible that their being predominantly Christians has made it somewhat easier.[27] The self-identified whiteness of Arabs and other nationalities from the Middle East and West Asia such as Iranians, which has been the status quo for decades, began rapidly to shift after the Iran hostage crisis, the oil embargoes by Arab countries in the 1970s, and the Arab bloc's vigorous resistance to pro-Israel US interests in the Middle East.[28] The "social space" in which Arabs had to negotiate their membership in US society became increasingly mediated by the geopolitical context of the Middle East, including a hegemonic US foreign policy that engaged in military interventions in Lebanon (1982) and Iraq (1991 and 2003). This means that Arabs, in ways not required of other immigrants, have come to realize that they must continually prove their loyalty and right to belong, further increasing the complexity of achieving acceptance and belonging (i.e., cultural citizenship) in the US.[29]

As the theater of two wars waged by the US and allies, the country of Iraq did not engender goodwill in the minds of most Americans, and as a result, Iraqi nationals were subjected to enhanced scrutiny. Iraqis had been required to register after arrival in the US, from 1991 to 1993. Post-9/11, Iraqis (on nonimmigrant visas) were one of the first groups subjected to port of entry special registration.[30]

Catalyzed by 9/11 and the ensuing War on Terror, the passage of the Patriot Act subjected Muslims, Arab and South Asian immigrants and citizens, to public harassment and government scrutiny that included special registrations, FBI interviews, paid informants and sting operations, and arrests and detentions of thousands "suspected of terrorism," on the basis of their Middle Eastern ancestry. Arab and Muslim Americans were left with a profound sense of "homeland insecurity," raising the question of whether the US "had ceased to be a place where members of these communities felt safe and protected."[31] This intentional pattern of racial and religious profiling, Bayoumi argues, dehistoricized Arabs to exist in the American consciousness only within this frame of potential terrorist threat.[32]

The trope of Arabs as "the potential terrorist threat," however, does not come stripped of its Orientalist and religious garments. When George W. Bush initiated the War on Terror, Nikhil Pal Singh points out, he proclaimed a new "totalitarian threat" not unlike those "who were once killed in the name of racial purity or class struggle"; but unlike fascism or secular Marxism, this new threat was characterized by "false religious purity"—a clear allusion to radical Islam.[33] Attorney General John Ashcroft's "we will defend civilization" rhetoric appealed to the "clash of civilizations" narrative, in which Islam posed a threat to Judeo-Christian values and Western democracy. As a higher proportion of newer Arab immigrants were Muslim, it further marked them with difference.

Recent research has revealed that the surveillance and profiling of Arabs, South Asians, and other nationalities from the Middle East and South Asia have disproportionately targeted Muslims and Muslim institutions.[34] Selod argues that by targeting Muslims, the securitization campaign intentionally foregrounds religion, making it the salient component in racial formation. Selod grounds her argument by paying attention to the way race making is articulated in interactions "between societal institutions and individuals": "The process by which bodies become racial in their lived realities because of biological and/or cultural traits as a result of the interaction and cooperation between ideologies, policies, laws, and social interactions that results in the denial of equal treatment in society." For Muslims, such identifiers as religious clothing have "acquired racial meaning that racializes bodies in a similar way to skin tone." Even for Muslims who do not wear religious signifiers, "their Muslim names also racialized them even if they are phenotypically white."[35] The race-making power of names and religious signifiers (hijabs for women, beards for men) is instantiated in the way even Christian Arabs (and others outside the religious binary—Sabean, Yezidi, Alawite, etc.) are largely perceived as Muslim and share in the consequences of those perceptions. Some Christian Iraqis in the Inland Empire shared with me that they experienced an Otherness even because of their names, because they sounded somehow Middle Eastern or because they were connected to an Arab country like Iraq: "I remember coming into my honors class during freshman year—full of smart kids, you know? You would think they'd be well read enough to know better. The first day I had some guy who sat behind me poke me on the shoulder, get in a conversation with me about where I was from, and then proceeded to call me a terrorist. When I denied it politely, he garnered support of other guys in the class—white guys—and kept going at it. I kept myself pretty clean-shaven for the rest of high school after that." Eric Love documents in his study of Islamophobia that anyone who looks "Middle Eastern," whether the person is Hindu, Christian, or atheist, can easily become a target of hate crimes.[36] What Aodish, a Christian, encountered in the high school classroom was actually Islamophobia, with his name, country of origin, and presumably facial hair being markers associating him with Islam.

The racial formation of Arabs took place in relatively recent history, well after the civil rights movement, meaning that they did not have to engage with the ideology and consequence of white supremacy in ways that black, Latinx, and Asian Americans did. For Arabs in the US, racial formation has not followed the white/black binary based on skin color or phenotype. Rather, it has drawn heavily on Orientalist discourses of the Arab Other, the framing of the Muslim as a terrorist, within the crucible of the War on Terror in both its geopolitical and domestic manifestations. All together, these intertwining processes have irrevocably shifted Arabs from "invisible [white] citizens to visible [Arab] subjects."[37] This reality holds whether or not Arab Americans self-identify as white on the census forms.

Having finished this exposition of how Arab Americans ceased to be white within the racial hierarchy of the US, we now return to Wessam's question. One way to understand his question is as a strategy to claim access to a majority-white US, albeit one that no longer exists in the Inland Empire. Historically, the typical pattern that is followed by nonwhite groups attempting to gain access to whiteness has been achieved by differentiating themselves from those who are nonwhite, usually from those who are furthest from white.[38] In the history of the US, blackness has been the "the key racial referent," the "'Other' against which whiteness is constructed," the valley to their mountain.[39] This was the strategy taken during the wave of European immigration in the nineteenth century, in which the Irish, arriving as a nonwhite, inferior race in the eyes of white Anglo-Saxon America, attempted to expand the circle of whiteness through blatant antagonism toward black Americans, including opposition to the abolition of slavery.[40] Immigrants from southern Europe, over time, moved up the racial hierarchy in a similar fashion, as did some non-Europeans. In the antebellum South, Chinese immigrant shopkeepers engaged in denigration of their black clientele and took on southern white manners.[41] In both cases, the Irish and Chinese, the strategy of gaining access to whiteness was not one of solidarity with other nonwhites but differentiation from them.

In California, the circle of whiteness expanded after California's annexation, as the Mexican "Ranchero" elite were begrudgingly considered white (Gente de Razon) due to their European (Iberian) ancestry and elite class standing.[42] This provisional whiteness gave them rights to vote, to hold property, and even to intermarry with Anglos. These rights, however, were denied to darker-skinned, lower-class Mestizos (mixed Indian and Spanish ancestry). Over time, the political rights and economic power of the Mexican elite were eroded through land alienation and reconfiguration of the agricultural economy from ranching to industrialized agriculture. The antipodes of whiteness during this era were not the dispossessed Mexican ranchers or the Mestizo laborers but the Chinese and, more so, the indigenous Indians, the "devils of the forest."[43]

Given that race making in the US has frequently involved struggles by new immigrants to "reposition themselves as White," the question "Where are the Americans?" can actually be seen as asserting membership in white America through a strategy of differentiation from the surrounding nonwhite Latinx population.[44] There is another way to interpret this question, in light of Wessam's self-identification as Assyrian. Chaldeans and Assyrians have used this ethnic identification in the US to distinguish themselves from Arabs, as the Arab identity has been associated with Islam and threats to national security and given that Arab Americans have fallen in the racial hierarchy.[45]

"Who Are the Americans?": Youth, Race, and Citizenship

When I asked Malik, who had just received his first US passport, what citizenship meant to him, he responded, "I don't really see a difference, because you've lived the same way; it doesn't change anything from the way I lived before." Legal citizenship for him was "just a piece of paper," less important than whether his experience in the US provided some real evidence of belonging. "I mean, it's a part of me. It's a part of who I am . . . [but] *just because you live in a place doesn't make you part of it*" (emphasis added). Malik's perspective is indicative of how an abstract notion of citizenship (based on its legal meaning) is seen in contrast to a tangible sense of belonging that grows out of being able to fully experience inclusion and to participate in the institutions of a community and country. The potential for belonging and inclusion of cultural citizenship, writes Lok Siu, only emerges out of "the lived experience of belonging."[46]

In the history of the (immigrant) United States, legal citizenship has never guaranteed full acceptance. Certainly for Arabs and South Asian Muslims, asserts Maira, "legal citizenship has not been an effective guarantee for protection under the law within the internal manifestation of the War on Terror."[47] For Arabs and Muslims in the US, religio-cultural identity, terrorism, and cultural citizenship have become linked. Being treated as "potential criminals" has a deep impact on any individual's or group's sense of national belonging. For example, in Cainkar's study of Arab communities in Chicago, she describes an Iraqi mother who told her son Usama to change his name and to say he was Jordanian or Kuwaiti, certainly not Iraqi.[48]

Being subjected to prejudice and discrimination has made Arab American youth dubious of the concept of a "social contract" assumed by citizenship.[49] And they are less likely to endorse the government or believe that they have equal opportunity.[50] They have come to feel that rights that should accrue to US citizens (freedom of religion, speech, association, equal protection) are not fully accessible to them. To understand this in terms of race making, they have lost the privileges of their former "whiteness."

Iraqi youths in the Inland Empire, both Christian and Muslim, recounted their having to deal with the constant commentary and jokes about terrorism. Some had been on the receiving end of hateful accusations from people who had lost friends or family in the Iraq War. One reported being insulted by a fellow ("Mexican") student, who told him, "Osama Bin Laden is your father." Some people might dismiss this insult as silly or sophomoric, if it were not for the fact that such insults are so ubiquitous, that so much research has reported similar accusations, and that no matter how erroneous the stereotype, people will act on it violently.[51] On this particular occasion, the slur was troubling on several counts. It clearly exposes Americans' geographical ignorance about Arabs, who are actually from many different countries, Osama Bin Laden being Saudi, not Iraqi. More sinister is how it perpetuates the myth that Iraq was involved in the 9/11 attacks, although that accusation could easily be hurled at many Arab Americans, since they are so routinely portrayed in the media as cut from the same cloth as Bin Laden.[52] The accusation is a reminder that the events of 9/11 increased Arab Americans' vulnerability to hate crimes and placed the image of the "Jihadist" and "Islamic extremist" in the crucible of public perception.[53]

Despite the various ways that Iraqi youths' cultural and national identities were questioned, they maintained a conviction that belonging in the US actually does not require one to compromise any cultural values. Their overall attitude was summed up by Raiya, a freshman at a local university: "[The US is] filled with so many cultures, and they are so open to other cultures, even being a citizen in specific, doesn't really matter. They are, like, so open to everybody, from everywhere, and the mix and match. . . . It is a society built on just mixes and matches. *So, whatever you are, wherever you have come from, you are welcome. . . . They won't treat you different*" (emphasis added). Her statement exudes a bold expression of confidence that she will take her place in US society without being forced to make any concessions in regard to her cultural or religious identity. This US imaginary is striking given that Arab Americans have been racialized precisely because they originate from specific places, that is, majority-Muslim countries of the Middle East.

Another form of expression Iraqi youths used to define their approach to cultural difference, to the "mix and match," was quoting the Arabic proverb "Mo kol asaba'ak sowa," a literal translation being, "Not all your fingers are alike."[54] This proverb was first used by youths talking about their relationship to the Latinx community. They further elaborated to me the meaning of this phrase as they applied it to their attitudes toward Latinxs at school and in the labor market, that indeed there are differences of culture and language and that these can be frustrating. When this proverb is evoked, it is saying, "Keep in mind that, even though all of us come from the same parents—Adam and Eve—everyone is going to be different, just like the fingers on your hand are not all the same; they are all different, not alike in length and shape. Neither are people all alike, yet each is important and valid.

The more dialogue I had with Iraqi youths in the Inland Empire about race, belonging, and citizenship, the more I was challenged by another question: "What and whom do you mean by 'American'?" The US is a place filled with different kinds of people, the Iraqi youths admitted, and differences arise from the various races, ethnicities, and religions; but remember, "Not all your fingers are alike." Whenever I brought up the question first posed by Wessam—"Where are the Americans?"—or versions of it such as "Who are the Americans?" the overwhelming response was that Americans could not be defined by any single race, ethnicity, religion, or nationality. Malik's response was, "It depends on what you mean by American." Their conclusion to the question was summed up with finality by Raiya: "There is no American." Those responses are quite bold coming from refugees who are expected to become compliant citizen-subjects. It was in such voices of Iraqi youth that I found grounds for hope.

It is important to remember that before arriving in the social mosaic of the Inland Empire, the Iraqis had lived in ethnically and religiously diverse societies. They had coexisted peacefully with people of other faiths and cultural traditions in neighborhoods in Baghdad, Basra, and Mosul. That changed after the invasion of 2003, in which ethnoreligious difference and political affiliations became the basis for ethnic cleansing at the neighborhood level. After fleeing Iraq, they had survived exile in other Arab countries where notions of Arab solidarity were strong, but at other times, they lived within culturally unfamiliar environments, such as Turkey and Iran.

After the Iraqi refugees arrived in the Inland Empire and despite their initial shock at finding themselves in this Latinx-dominant world, they began figuring out how to adapt to these unexpected cultural circumstances. They began working out what belonging in the US could mean within this geocultural space.[55] They did not see that the cultural differences separating them were insurmountable. Nor did finding belonging require them to participate in prejudice against others as a strategy to achieve some kind of membership in a majority-white United States.

The voices of Iraqi youths represent the future of their community, an indicator of the way formulations of racial identity will eventually play out over the long term. At this point, their solution to finding belonging did not hinge on the need to gain acceptance into any group or to differentiate themselves from any subordinated group within the racial hierarchy of the US. Within their US imaginary, as Saddiq put it, "what matters is the kind of person you are, not the color of your skin or stuff." The US is a place of mix and match: "You could be anyone, from anywhere, who believes in whatever," and you deserve "the same opportunity as everyone else."

This chapter has taken to heart Wendy Cheng's argument that race making does not happen uniformly but emerges from a particular cultural geography. I have examined the cultural spaces where group strategies of differentiation are likely to happen—those involving labor-market competition in particular. It is true that barriers to solidarity exist here, but they do not involve the denigration of other people. I find little evidence that Iraqis engage wholesale in strategies of differentiation relative to the nonwhite, Latinx population of the Inland Empire, particularly in ways that would elevate themselves at the expense of surrounding groups.

And yet the question "Where are the Americans?" cannot be altogether dismissed just because it seems to be deconstructed by a younger generation of Iraqis. It is still possible that the escalation of anti-Muslim and anti-Arab attitudes in the US will drive people either to submerge their religio-ethnic identities or to engage in animosity or differentiation from those who are at the antipode of whiteness. As 2015 unfolded in an unthinkable cascade of terror, refugee movements, and mainstreamed Islamophobia, I wondered if, and how, the US imaginary might change.

6

Belonging 2.015

Senior year and all the years before that has been one amazing adventure with you guys, and I believe we're all ready to
head off to new ones and face a whole new world. [*Cheering
and applause*]
—Raiya, graduation speech

When Raiya told the class of 2015 that they would be facing "a whole
new world," little did she know how prophetic she was. The year 2015
saw a profound shift in US and European sentiments toward refugees,
foregrounding those who were coming from the Middle East. "Refugees
haven't changed," wrote Andrew Lam in an op-ed for the *Los Angeles
Times*. "What has changed is the heart of the free world."[1]

By the end of 2015, with euphoric graduations long forgotten, Iraqi
refugees in the Inland Empire faced new realities. Globally, 2015 witnessed daily scenes of historic levels of refugees fleeing wars in Syria,
Iraq, and North Africa toward Europe. These coincided chronologically
with terrorist attacks in Paris and at home with the December 2 terrorist
shooting in San Bernardino. The threat of backlash from the San Bernardino shooting weighed heavily on Iraqis in the Inland Empire.

With the Republican presidential primaries heating up, candidates
seized on the terror and migration events to single out refugees from
Syria and Iraq as existential threats. To fully understand how this came
about, we must examine how these terror and migration events became
contextual frames for the ensuing national debates about refugee policy
during the lead-up to the presidential election.

The first of these migration events preceded those happening in
Europe and involved the large movement of Central American unaccompanied minors crossing the US-Mexico border in 2014. The political volatility of these crossings was witnessed on July 3, 2014, when two
buses carrying Central American children to the Immigration and Cus-

toms Enforcement (ICE) processing facility in Murrieta, a small town in southern Riverside County, were blocked by angry protestors shouting, "Go back home!" The movement of young asylum seekers from Central America into Mexico and northward into the US in 2014 was not new. Twenty thousand had crossed in 2013. Between October 2013 and September 2014, over sixty thousand unaccompanied alien minors (UAM) from Honduras, Guatemala, and El Salvador crossed the US-Mexico border.[2] Fleeing gang, political, and structural violence, they had traveled north through Mexico, many riding the perilous freight trains—La Bestia. After crossing, they either were apprehended or surrendered themselves to the authorities. Their arrival was seen by political groups advocating for greater border security as just the latest threat posed by a "porous" southern border, through which "floods" of migrants manage to stream. The ensuing debate culminated in a congressional attempt to roll back protections against human trafficking for migrant children from Central America, opening the door to fast-track their deportation. More broadly, it generated a national debate about who deserves refugee protections in the US.

The Obama administration faced significant criticism of its handling of Central American asylum seekers from congressional Republicans, who claimed his policies had encouraged parents to send, or bring with them, children into the country without fear of deportation. Groups that had been advocating greater border security wasted no time. The reports of possibly fifty to sixty thousand UAMs from Central America at the southern border added to the already trenchant rhetoric of crisis. Governor Rick Perry of Texas requested that the National Guard be stationed at the border (one wonders why the presence of children would warrant such a measure).[3] The Murrieta protests demonstrate the level of fear that brown children can evoke.

The "flood" of Central American children crossing the US-Mexico border in 2014 was followed in 2015 by dramatic migration events in the Middle East and Europe. As the Syrian civil war escalated, Turkey eclipsed Pakistan as the largest refugee-hosting country in the world, giving temporary protection to two million Syrians. Turkey became the major departure point for refugees attempting to reach Europe via Greece's Aegean coast and onward through the Balkans toward western Europe. A photograph of the dead toddler Aylan Kurdi, lying on the beach on the Greek island of Kos, sparked a humanitarian outpouring and call to action when it went viral. In response, many European countries pledged to accept greater numbers of refugees fleeing wars in Syria, Iraq, and Afghanistan. Germany coordinated with other EU countries to allow passage through the Balkans and Austria to Germany.[4]

During the fall of 2015, the world's attention was riveted to scenes of refugees determinedly moving through the Balkans toward western Europe, revealing what had already begun with Iraqis fleeing the 2003 war: refugees with determined rather than hopeless faces, unwilling to wait in camps or under the bombs, refusing to be kept at arm's length, foiling and protesting attempts to be "managed" at border crossings, demonstrating a stark departure from the narrative of the docile, disoriented, and submissive refugee.

This intrepid refugee narrative signaled that patience waiting for the world to act had run out, and thus the exodus toward Europe began in earnest. By May 2015, 125,942 refugees had already applied for asylum in Germany, compared to 54,956 the previous year.[5] As the epic migration through the Balkans into Germany unfolded in late summer of 2015, the German government at municipal and state levels scrambled to cope with what swelled to nearly a million asylum seekers arriving by the end of the year.[6]

Chancellor Angela Merkel's government had taken a political risk. Both the chancellor and the interior minister assured the German people, "We can handle it" (wir schaffen dass). In fact, despite the hand-wringing by politicians and the rhetoric of crisis with which the media described the refugee movements, there was much evidence that Germany, the EU country that absorbed the largest number, was actually "handling it." Throughout Germany, there emerged stories of people's Wilkommenskulture (culture of welcome) toward refugees arriving in train stations and their Hilfsbereitschaft (mobilization of support) toward refugees. Communities large and small stepped up to demonstrate their welcoming spirit, often at some sacrifice, giving up community centers and school gyms in order to house refugees.

The backlash to the chancellor's refugee policy (Flüchtlingspolitik) began during the high-water mark of refugee arrivals in 2015. Opposition parties raised concerns about possible "undocumented" refugees in the country.[7] The international press initially lauded Merkel as "Chancellor of the Free World" for her leadership in the migrant "crisis," and she was *Time* magazine's person of the year.[8] She was seen as instrumental in giving hope to Syrians who were desperate for a better life and in proposing a European plan for coping with this unprecedented influx of asylum seekers. That plan, however, sparked a politically divisive debate: the twenty-eight EU states could not agree on any kind of formula for distributing the refugees more equally by country. Some countries like Poland and Hungary flat out refused, meaning that Sweden and Germany continued to take a disproportionate share, and Greece and Italy struggled to cope with the processing and housing of asylum seekers who continued to land on their shores. There was also failure to reach consensus on what to do with refugees who were rescued from sinking boats in the Mediterranean.

During this time, Germany saw the troubling emergence of an anti-immigrant movement called PEGIDA, which staged weekly demonstrations in Dresden and Leipzig.[9] Strangely enough, this movement was based in the eastern part of the country, which, due to its former isolation behind the Iron Curtain, was home to relatively few immigrants. This movement warned that Muslim refugees bring Islamic values that are incompatible with a Christian European society. This ideology had for decades found voice and political power in right-wing, anti-immigrant parties in Italy (Berlusconi's Northern League) and France (Marine Le Pen's National Front/Rally). Unlike the anti-immigrant parties in France and Italy, however, PEGIDA held no political seats in the legislature.[10] More alarming, however, were cases of attacks on reception centers in Germany, for which no political organization has admitted responsibility, although neo-Nazi fringe groups had perpetrated similar deadly attacks in the past.[11]

The way migration events of 2015 played out in the political arenas of Europe was watched with intense interest by political parties in the US gearing up for the presidential primaries. As with the controversy over the Central American migrant children, the events that unfolded in Europe were seized on by pundits, political interest groups, and politicians urging tougher border control and reduced legal immigration admissions (including refugees). Commentators such as James Poulos claimed that this wave of refugees posed a "near-existential threat" to the EU.[12] When Donald Trump's campaign manager, Steve Bannon, saw refugees (many of them Muslim) moving stridently into the heart of Europe, he saw it as an existential crisis of a more fundamental nature: "civilization jihad personified."[13] Refugees from Muslim countries were the newest and greatest threat to Western democracies, and the tropes finding greatest traction in the presidential election were "stealth jihad" and "fifth column."

Both the social construction of the "crisis along the southwest border" and a Europe disorganized and in a reactionary political mood "caused" by a large influx of asylum seekers set the political stage for what came next in the US political theater. When the Obama administration announced that it planned to admit ten thousand Syrians for resettlement in 2016 (a minuscule number in comparison to Germany's response), it immediately provoked a visceral response from the Republican primary hopefuls.[14] Candidate Trump immediately tweeted, "Refugees from Syria are now pouring into our great country. Who knows who they are—some could be ISIS. Is our president insane?" (@realDonaldTrump, November 17, 2015). Thirty state governors (all Republican but one) followed with declarations that they would block any attempts to have Syrian refugees resettled in their states.[15]

Adding to this cascade of events was a series of terrorist attacks that happened simultaneous to European refugee movements: the November 2015 terrorist attacks in Paris, followed by the December 2 attack in San Bernardino, California. Terrorism and migration were quickly conflated into talking points of the Republican hopefuls. Candidates' and governors' stated objection to admitting refugees from Arab countries like Syria was the terrorist threat that they allegedly posed.

Fourteen years after 9/11, the anti-immigrant discourse in the US had largely been driven by the projection of public fear onto the US southern border.[16] After the terrorist attacks, the campaign talking points shifted to immigrants from the Middle East. Five days after San Bernardino, candidate Trump in a foreign-policy speech used the shooting to argue for a complete ban on Muslim immigration: "The struggle against radical Islam also *takes place in our homeland*. There are scores of recent migrants inside our borders charged with terrorism. For every case known to the public, there are dozens more. We must stop importing extremism through senseless immigration policies. A pause for reassessment will help us to prevent the next San Bernardino or worse."[17] Though blatantly untrue, it was effective messaging. Trump's statement was an eerie echo of former attorney general Ashcroft's speech after 9/11, in which Ashcroft argued for the need to watch out vigilantly for the "terrorists among us . . . plotting, planning and waiting to kill Americans again."[18] Ashcroft's claims were an attempt to justify the aggressive measures that he set into motion, later institutionalized by the Patriot Act, which were overwhelmingly directed at Muslims and those of Arab and West and South Asian ancestry. While thousands were interviewed, detained, and surveilled, there was no single conviction of terrorist activity.[19]

Ashcroft's antiterrorism policies had violated the rights of thousands of Americans of Arab descent and were largely ineffective, leading instead to thousands of Arab and South Asian Americans feeling less secure of their place within the polity. Nevertheless, candidate Trump picked up Ashcroft's script, calling US attention to the threat posed by "scores of recent immigrants" (read: Arab, Muslim, or anyone who looks Middle Eastern). Conflating terrorism with refugee movements was effective in manufacturing fear of the Arab–Middle Eastern refugee Other.

Candidate Trump's statement that "the struggle against radical Islam also takes place in our homeland" called for a surge on the War on Terror's domestic front. The first objects of that escalation were refugees from Iraq and Syria, being named as threats in the House legislation and later in executive orders from the White House that expanded to Muslim immigrants and refugees from the Middle East and North Africa. This statement as well as others clearly conflated terrorism with Islam. When the French government proposed closing certain mosques suspected of spreading extremist ideas, Trump said, "Well you're going to have to watch and study the mosques, because a lot of talk is going on at the mosques." He "would hate to do it but it's something you're going to have to strongly consider."[20]

The anti-Muslim and anti-Arab elements of the Trump platform simply continued a historical pattern of racist discourse and suppression directed toward people of Arab and Middle Eastern and South Asian ancestry that predated the attacks of 9/11.[21] What we saw in 2015 was the explicit naming of the religio-cultural threat posed to the US by the Middle Eastern immigrant/refugee. The hypernationalist rhetoric used by Trump and other candidates highlighted a fear of the undermining of US and Christian values by Muslims. As Bayoumi has observed, it is not only the racial profiling of the security state that Arabs and Muslims must fear: "Now, they have racial profiling *and* inflamed populist fear and anger to worry about."[22]

Whether these moves were based on Trump's own convictions or came from the ideologues within his campaign who pushed cultural-threat narratives, it was clear that his campaign identified as part of its base the anti-Muslim and anti-immigrant groups within the religious and alt-right.[23] These elements were being cultivated by the people in his campaign, presumably by individuals such as Steve Bannon. During his tenure with Breitbart News, Bannon was among those who had espoused the latest iterations of the "clash of civilizations" ideology: "civilization jihad." When Bannon became Trump's campaign manager, there was a greater opening to naming Arab and Muslim refugees as a "fifth column" within Trump's platform. With Bannon in the driver's seat of the campaign, those who espoused the "fifth column" narrative now had greater influence on Trump's platform. One such group was the Center for Security Policy. Quotations from Frank Gaffney, the center's director, appeared in candidate Trump's platform proposing the ban on Muslim immigrants, including references to refugees from Syria, Iraq, and Afghanistan. Gaffney had already issued a call for a restriction on Muslim immigration, including refugee admissions, back in 2015, in the foreword to a booklet authored by Ann Corcoran of Refugee Resettlement Watch titled *Refugee Resettlement and the Hijra to America*.[24] Gaffney argued for a halt to all immigration of Muslims to the US because of their "potential for subversion." He espoused the conspiracy that Muslim immigrants were part of a new *hijra*, that is, "a deliberate strategy to gradually establish an Islamic regime in the U.S. and Europe." Their presence, he maintained, posed the likelihood of "terrifying violence, from a *Fifth Column* in our country—fueled by rising numbers of [Muslim] immigrants, *many of whom are brought here legally as refugees*."[25]

Refugees from Muslim-majority countries indeed figured prominently in US refugee-resettlement programs, especially after the passage of the Iraqi Refugee Crisis Act in 2008. Of the the 69,920 refugees accepted by the US in 2015, 35 percent came from the Muslim-majority countries of the Near East and South Asia. Of the top three sending countries—Burma (18,386), Iraq (12,676), and Somalia (8,858)—two were majority-Muslim states.[26] The fallacy of Gaffney's argument is that none of these individuals was involved in any terrorist plot. Yet in direct opposition to the Obama administration's very modest plan to increase the number of Syrian refugees in its resettlement program to ten thousand, the Republican-controlled House of Representatives passed the American Security Against Foreign Enemies Act (HR 4038), naming Iraqis and Syrians as nationalities that needed much-higher levels of scrutiny.[27] Although the bill died in the Senate by a noncloture vote, the passage of HR 4038 by the House revealed just how powerful, and mainstreamed, the "fifth column" narrative had become in US political discourse on refugee policy.

The power of this highly organized and well-funded coalition of conservative political and religious organizations and immigrant-reform lobbyists had reached a high-water mark of influence in refugee policy. In 2015, this movement foregrounded an anti-Muslim discourse in the presidential primary, in which race and religion were used by political movements to categorize refugees from the Middle East and West and South Asia as serious security threats as well as incompatible with Euro-American culture and its Judeo-Christian foundations.[28] Through a perverse alchemy of fear and hypernationalism, refugees from Iraq, many who had put their lives on the line for the coalition, had now been named as a disloyal "fifth column."

Belonging and the Inner War on Terror

The preceding section has emphasized the full magnitude of the the seismic sociopolitical shifts that unfolded in 2015 and how these might have shaped the Iraqi refugee experience of belonging. At this time in my fieldwork, I became concerned about how Iraqis would find belonging in a US society that was openly revealing its white-nationalist discourses, which had previously been marginalized to the subaltern spaces that trafficked in stealth-jihadist theories.

Discussions about the events of 2015 with older adults were surprisingly subdued. Most were green-card holders working hard toward citizenship. They seemed reluctant to say anything critical about any candidate's statements directed at people like them, Iraqis and Muslims, or about the opposition to the resettlement of fellow Arab (Iraqi and Syrian) refugees. Their commentary could be summarized this way: "If these actions (a ban on Muslim immigration, governors' letters against resettlement of Syrian refugees) contributed to security, that's fine."

Saher Selod, in her research with Muslim Americans after 9/11, found that most of the men she interviewed "felt silenced for some time after 9/11 out of fear of being associated with terrorism." They experienced feeling "muzzled" when it came to talking about religion or politics, fearing that "their religious association along with their views on foreign policy, such as the invasion of Iraq, . . . could result in them being seen as supporting terrorism." Selod argues that the perception of Muslims as "incapable of being loyal to the US . . . strips them of their national identity as Americans and makes them feel they are not valued members of society, *something that citizenship should afford.*"[29]

Given the history of the way Iraqis in particular were hyperscrutinized by law enforcement after the Gulf War, 9/11, and the Iraq War, it is entirely possible that this form of self-censorship was in response to worries about the possible repercussions of criticizing the US government, just as Arabs and Muslims were afraid of openly sharing their political views after 9/11.[30] And could they be absolutely sure that the person asking the questions was not some kind of informant? Several men told me that they had Iraqi friends in states that had been approached by the FBI to become informants. They would joke with me about being under surveillance, saying (into their phones), "Just kidding," if they proffered an opinion that might be construed as critical of the US.

For this reason, I felt it was necessary to call together the youths who had shared their reflections and opinions so candidly in a previous focus group, in the hope that they would not feel similarly "muzzled" by fear of speaking openly about politics, religion, and their experiences since the terrorist attack of December 2, 2015. I wanted to find out if their faith in the US as a space to express cultural, political, and religious identity "without fear of judgment" had been eroded by the way political candidates were exploiting domestic and global events to stigmatize Muslims and Arab refugees. Had it dampened Raiya's feeling of "new beginnings and exciting possibilities"? What forms of activism might emerge as they engaged with what "the years to come hold"? Most of all, I wanted to know how the events of 2015 had shaped their pathway to finding belonging in the US.

The 2016 focus group convened in February, almost exactly a year after the 2015 group. A set of prompts were created to shed light on how the youths—so intensely involved in the process of finding their place in US society—perceived and experienced messages in the public sphere intended to make them (Muslims and/or Arabs) and people like them feel that they did not belong. To that end, they were shown a specific series of statements and news stories: candidate Donald J. Trump's response to the San Bernardino shooting, calling for a "total and complete shutdown of Muslims entering the United States until our country's representatives can figure out what is going on" (issued on December 7, 2015, five days after the shooting); the *Press Enterprise* story of a Muslim student at UC Riverside who sensed fear from fellow students when he prayed openly in the library;[31] the mosque bombing in nearby Indio.[32] They were asked to give their reaction to these events, and we reminded them of what they had said in the previous focus group, that "America is so open to everybody, from everywhere; whatever you are, wherever you come from, you are welcome; they won't treat you differently."

The Iraqi youths employed multiple strategies in confronting the disturbing ways in which their various group identities (Arab, refugee, Iraqi, Muslim) were being profiled in the public arena. One strategy they devised was to become interrogators of the media and its role in evoking public fear, how it perpetuated negative stereotypes of Arabs. The other strategy was in calling attention to a counternarrative: the proactive and positive ways that the local Muslim and Middle Eastern community was reaching out across cultural and religious barriers to mobilize against hate.

The youths admitted being alarmed at the way presidential candidates used hate speech or made inflammatory statements at their rallies, with crowds of supporters listening to them and cheering them on, as when candidate Trump vilified Mexican immigrants. They acknowledged these events as real, not fabricated. They identified the relationship between the public's fear as generated by what was being portrayed in the media and how the media could influence thinking and "play with emotions." Rana, a Christian, observed that media can play an important role in developing fear-based negative perceptions of those who are culturally and religiously different. Drawing on school experiences in Iraq, she observed,

As Christians, we were with Muslims in public schools. We didn't have any issue. I mean, even if we have issues, it won't be like as big that would reach killing. You know what I mean? . . . So, when you tell someone this person is coming to kill you, you'll be afraid. You'll hate that person. You don't know them. They might be very good. They might be very nice. They might be very welcoming. But when you play on the emotions of people and making them afraid of a group or of people, then you will have, like, "Okay, there is a boundary. Please don't come close."

Rana called for a "clear mind," suggesting the need to think critically about what was being reported. People should find out for themselves what other groups of people are like, not just believe what is reported in the media. This statement accepts the media's power to shape public sentiment and identifies the "ideological work performed by images and story lines."[33] Arab Americans view the media as a "center of power hostile to their community," because it has not represented them in a neutral fashion.[34] Even when the media attempts to give a more balanced view by juxtaposing good Muslims with bad Muslims, this frequently defines Muslims as only good insofar as they "prove allegiance to the U.S. nation."[35]

Youths were also critical of social media, which allows people to say things that they would not necessarily say to someone's face, since "you are hiding behind a screen." Social media increases the freedom people have to say something that might get them "punched in the face" in a public setting or subjected to public censure. Bloggers, the youths noted, can choose whether to simply ignore or to acknowledge their audience.

As mentioned earlier, the presidential campaign rhetoric that had emerged by February 2016 was unprecedented in the way that hypernationalistic, anti-immigrant, and anti-Muslim voices were mainstreamed by frontrunners in the Republican primary. When shown quotations from candidate Trump calling for a ban on Muslim immigration or lines from governors' letters saying that no Syrian refugees would be allowed in their states, Iraqi youths expressed some doubt as to the credibility of these politicians who mouth such extreme positions. They found the explicitly anti-Muslim and antirefugee statements almost inconceivable, so contradictory were they to fundamental "American" values. They called out such statements as "un-American," because they were so utterly inconsistent, in their minds, with the quintessentially American values of freedom, equal treatment under the law, and protection of basic human rights. In response to the governors' letters about preventing Syrian refugees from being resettled in their states, Malik said, "But . . . they are saying they'll ban Syrian refugees. That's just . . . I see that's going against what America . . . how it started. It started by refugees coming from other countries, and they kind of were security threats." He then proceeded to make the argument for the US to live up to its protection of human rights, that "humans have a right live wherever they want; . . . it is just a simple human right, that they'll pursue happiness. And they can't pursue that in a country full of war, so they come here."

Malik's statement in defense of freedom of mobility is similar to what Nahid Afrose Kabir found in his research on young American Muslims, who criticized the Patriot Act for being "un-American" because of the restrictions that it places on people's freedom.[36] The way Malik articulated his response, "*humans have a right*," suggested a more universal application to all religious or ethnic groups in the US, not just Muslims, Arabs, or Iraqis but also, for example, Honduran refugees.

Despite the youths' incredulity at the extreme exclusionary rhetoric ubiquitous in the coverage of the Republican candidates, they (and especially the Muslims) could not dismiss its effect on them altogether. They admitted that their attitudes had changed somewhat as they became more aware of what they termed "hatred" explicitly directed toward them, particularly after the December 2, 2015, shooting. At this point, the conversation shifted, and something emerged that had been absent in earlier years: fear. The US was still a place of freedom and rights but also a site of fear. Raiya recalled the days after the shooting: "I was actually afraid to go to school, and people were like, 'You guys be careful. Don't walk alone.' Like, I was actually afraid to go back to school. San Bernardino, I pass by it to get to school, you know?"

After the San Bernardino attack, fears of being profiled were echoed in many press reports from Muslim students at local universities and high schools in the Inland Empire. They palpably felt the heightened level of scrutiny and were ridiculed and harassed by other students.[37] Raiya was quick to balance this sense of fear by acknowledging the overwhelming support she felt from non-Arab or non-Muslim peers who expressed a great deal of concern for her safety:

When I look at the media and the news and what people share on Facebook or Instagram or whatever, my attitude has changed a bit, and that
now there are more people who are explicit in their hatred, . . . who are
explicit in their hatred towards Islam. But then when I go and look at
people, . . . when I go on my college campus, like, people everywhere
from, . . . like, even, like, no matter what color or race, I had after, like,
everything that's happened and after even the San Bernardino shooting
and the Paris attacks, I never [had] anyone come say anything rude or
anything mean, . . . anything that in any way discriminates me. Instead, I
had people come to me, like, "Are you okay? Has anybody bothered you?"

She remembered how right after the shooting, a neighbor made her
family a batch of cookies, and a random man in a parking lot told them
that he did not agree with Trump. She pointed out that Muslim centers in San Bernardino raised $100,000 to aid the shooting victims. One
high school student in the focus group reported that a Muslim student
club was quickly formed at his school: "It's out of nowhere. . . . It just
came up, . . . posted all over the school saying, 'Any question about
Islam, just come, . . . ask anything you have.'" He felt that this was helpful for Muslim students to support one another, but it was also a way
to build bridges with others: "People started asking questions, and you
can't really hate a religion or you can't really hate the popular religions
because the ones I know, they all support peace."

While reports of Arab and Muslim youths experiencing fear and
threats were common in the Inland Empire, equally widespread were
reports of support and solidarity from non-Arab and non-Muslim students.[38] For Arab Americans and Muslims in the post-9/11 context, such
responses are not only a demonstration of the true, peaceful, nature of
Islam but also a matter of survival. Cainkar argues that as people under
increased government surveillance since 9/11, Arab Americans and Muslims "are suspect and they know it"; they know that they need to engage
proactively with the wider community at times like this, for even while
they are engaged, they are "an exposed community . . . [whose] civil
liberties are not abstract matters of principle but vital issues of personal
and community interest."[39] In an atmosphere of intense hostility, these
positive interpersonal relationships form important buffers: "layers of
noise between the dominant national discourse of Arab and Muslim

American culpability for the 9/11 attacks and the public interpretation of these discourses."[40]

The consensus in the focus group was that the positive "counterreactions" were more significant and bigger than the negative provocations of politicians who were capitalizing on tragic events for political gain. By identifying with the heightened level of proactive organizing, Iraqi youths had found another way to cope with the backlash and fear toward Islam. Pointing out the positive way in which Arab and Muslim organizations were countering scrutiny and criticism suggested that they believed that these mobilizations throughout the Inland Empire were an effective means to mitigate both the local backlash from the shooting and the hateful political rhetoric at the national level.

Finding Belonging in the Post-2015 US

At the start of the focus group in February 2016, youths were asked, "If you could have lunch with any person, present or past, who would it be?" People chosen included Paul the Apostle, the prophet Ibrahim (father of Ishmael), Frederick Douglass, Martin Luther King Jr., Abraham Lincoln, and Gandhi. Did these choices indicate a growing awareness that belonging in the US would only come about with struggle, that they were not willing to watch passively as they saw future rights and freedom compromised? The naming of these people, some of whom so clearly embody the best of the United States' ideals, left me struck by how tenaciously these youths still clung to US ideals, made ever more elusive by the events of 2015.

The Iraqi youths clearly idealized the US as a place that nurtured, protected, and celebrated the right for anyone to belong and to express their personal and communal identity, and they confidently saw their membership in that United States unquestionably theirs to claim. As the geopolitical situation for Muslims and Arabs and refugees, both locally and globally, radically shifted in fall of 2015 in Europe and the US, I seriously wondered whether their US imaginary could survive the onslaught that was coming. Did they still feel welcome and accepted, really?

I found several entry points to probe the youths' feelings about the current climate of belonging by asking them how they understood the meaning of the word "welcome" in the context of experiencing a sense of belonging in the US.[41] Did they think that "welcome" for immigrants to the US was the same as, similar to, or different from "acceptance"? They began by differentiating between these two concepts: acceptance is much more difficult to extend to the outsider or newcomer; welcome, on the other hand, is like being allowed in the door to the house or country, required by rules of hospitality. Welcome does not require a "good relationship"; there is no positive or genuine "good feeling" associated with it; the host (society) reluctantly lets you in the door and merely tolerates you. Acceptance can be absent even when welcome is extended. By contrast, acceptance goes beyond mere tolerance of difference or reluctantly extending hospitality.

The real meaning of acceptance as the youths' saw it could best be summarized by Malik: "[Acceptance is when] you are okay with whatever they do. You are okay with how and what they are and exactly the way they are." True acceptance means that you do not wish that the person were a different religion or had lighter skin. It is exactly what the young German refugees in Nuremberg meant in the film *Angekommen* when each one said, in both their native language and in German, "We have arrived and are accepted."[42] Real acceptance, then, for these Iraqi youths in the Inland Empire, asserts "the right to be different," without compromising the felt sense of communal *belonging*.[43] Following their logic, belonging in the US does not depend on gaining membership into either a dominant race or religion. To the contrary, the very meaning of the US is expressed by drawing on "the mix and match" of national origins, cultures, races, and religions.

Iraqi youths were forced to grapple with contradictions within their US imaginary—the US as a space of expression: "Whatever you are, wherever you have come from, you are welcome; they won't treat you different"—now made glaringly apparent by the events of 2015. The US has systematically denied this space of expression to racial, ethnic, religious, and sexual identity groups that are deemed inferior or culturally threatening. Now these youths were the targets of exclusion. Were they naive to think that they, as Iraqi refugees and Arab Americans, could simply claim the same national belonging as anyone else without a struggle?

Iraqi refugee youths responded to the tensions within the US imaginary with a modality of engagement that is familiar in the history of the immigrant US, in which immigrants fight for social inclusion and eventually earn a place of belonging, not as assimilated citizen-subjects but as ethnic and religious communities that maintain distinctiveness and have proved their worth. The immigrant first generation, often silent in the face of hostility, is followed by the mobilization of the second generation around ethnic institutions (religious, political, social) that are vehicles to participating in US political life.[44]

Bayoumi wrote about his own response to the contradictions in the US imaginary in *This Muslim American Life*. Drawing on the historian Rogers Smith, he noted that "for over 80 percent of the U.S. history, American laws declared most people legally ineligible to become full U.S. citizens solely because of their race, original nationality, or gender."[45] The Bill of Rights spoke not of the rights of "citizens" but of the rights of "the people," and Bayoumi believed that as a US citizen (his previous passport was Canadian), he could fight for the rights of all "the people" of the US, not just those who had rights by virtue of citizenship.[46]

In the Iraqi youths' strategies of dealing with the events of 2015, they followed a pattern of "dissenting citizenship."[47] Instead of retreating from ethnoreligious involvement, they engaged in even stronger expressions of group identity.[48] Participation in ethnoreligious institutions became more vital even as they became targets of hostility on the basis of those aspects of identity.[49] For the Muslim youths in the focus group, the Islamic centers and student organizations were vehicles of positive engagement with a suspicious or hostile society, an opportunity to show the true side of Islam by raising money for the shooting victims and refugees, an opportunity to educate those who were ignorant that "Islam isn't intended to support that idea of killing people," as Malik pointed out. It is on this base that these youths' still hopeful and optimistic sense of membership in the US polity is grounded.

Conclusion

The people in flight from the terror behind—strange things
happen to them, some bitterly cruel and some so beautiful
that the faith is refired forever.
—John Steinbeck, *The Grapes of Wrath*

The dominant refugee narrative is preoccupied with two ends of a
trajectory, one being the violence and ensuing loss of belonging, the
other being fruits of the successful struggle, being the worthy refugee—
valedictorian, the Nobel Prize winner, cardiac surgeon. We hear less
about the long interim, the reclamation of belonging in daily life. If Iraqi
lives have taught us anything worthwhile about belonging, it is that it is
truly consummated by deliberate as well as unselfconscious actions of
the refugees themselves. They are propelled along the pathway toward
membership and belonging by the simple desires that most of us share:
to live in peace, to see children grow up to survive the passage through
youth culture, to care for our parents, to explore our life goals without
sacrificing family obligations. While Iraqi families were being named by
politicians as potential enemies for the second or third time, they went
about celebrating milestones familiar to most Americans: proms, graduations, college acceptances, weddings. They went about confronting the
hardships familiar to most Americans: divorce, unemployment, illness,
fear, loneliness.

In the preceding chapters, we have seen that the path toward belonging that unfolded for Iraqi refugees in the Inland Empire took many
turns and rarely overtly political ones. They laid claim to membership
and belonging in small, oblique, pedestrian, yet profoundly human
ways—a Grand Slam breakfast at Denny's, a camping trip to Lake Crow-
ley. This truth came home to me when I watched Yousef's son's vlog of
his family vacation in San Diego. During the family's tour of the aircraft
carrier USS *Midway*, Hasan described how much he was enjoying seeing

this amazing ship, but in the weapons control room, there was a map of Baghdad, with bombing targets marked out.[1] Studying the map, Hasan remembered during the bombing in April 2003, "We all got together at my grandfather's house with no electricity, no water, no nothing except our clothes on and some leftovers. I was so scared hearing all these bombs and many other scary sounds. So, yeah, I felt bad remembering all this stuff; and then I completed having my fun time in beautiful San Diego." Belonging is enacted on a family vacation, in the performance of acts of leisure, with which the remembrance of the US bombing missions on his hometown coexists, seamlessly yet uncomfortably. There is something both hopeful and troubling about how belonging is achieved at all levels—economic, cultural, political—appearing utterly delinked from what Nikhil Pal Singh terms "the contradictions of the American empire, long peace and continuously undeclared war whose toll of violence has been excluded from the balance sheet of moral, political, and material cost and benefit."[2] The fallout from the empire's domestic front of the War on Terror was impossible to ignore after 2015.

In 2008, a portal to belonging was opened to Iraqis seeking asylum in the US. An act of Congress, the Refugee Crisis in Iraq Act (S1651), named them as deserving of refugee status, based on their demonstrated loyalty as allies or their vulnerabilities as religious minorities or war widows. Then, in 2015, this designation was de facto revoked by the American Security against Foreign Enemies Act (HR4030), which named them (and Syrians) as the United States' newest threat. By the end of 2015, a terrible truth could not be ignored, that the War on Terror had followed them to the US. It was after 2015 that Nuha, on the verge of her citizenship swearing-in ceremony, asked me if there are two kinds of citizenship, one for people like her (hijab-wearing Muslim women), the other for people like me (born in the United States, white, non-Arab, male). A political movement in the US, with inroads in the highest levels of government, sees her as the embodiment of "stealth jihad," of "sharia creep." For Nuha, as well as for Raiya (that "proud young Muslim woman"), the United States' spaces of expression remain but are never entirely safe, constricted and bounded by the daily fear that someone will act on the belief that they—Nuha and Raiya—pose an existential threat.

For the security state to sustain itself, it needs an object of fear, which the fear industry will readily provide. It is within this political ecosystem that Iraqis have had to perform additional work to claim belonging with the US polity. The removal of the "welcome mat" for certain types of refugees reveals how both internal and external manifestations of the War on Terror feed off one another in symbiosis and grow out of the same sociopolitical conditions, in which the subjugation and racialization of groups in US history and geopolitical interventions have worked in tandem.[3] The interdiction in 1939 of the passenger ship *St. Louis* and its Jewish asylum seekers and the denial of Haitian refugees in the 1980s are other examples of the interplay between racializing groups and foreign policy.

The fallout from the inner manifestations of the War on Terror, the weight of the security state, racialization, and Islamophobia, are clearly problematic for those who are on the path toward reclaiming belonging. Much of the recent research on Arab and Muslim Americans has described the eroding effect on belonging of these manifestations: fear of expressing political or religious opinions, women's fear of harassment in public spaces because they are identified as Muslim, dealing with surveillance and profiling. It is hard not to receive the message that your worthiness to belong in the US is—at least in the view of some Americans, including those at the highest levels of government—suspect.

What has the Iraqi experience taught us about the pathways and possibilities of belonging, the encounters with exclusion, and the daily tactics of inclusion? Iraqis arrived to a sociopolitical ecosystem in which the language of terror had come to structure the public imaginary of Arabs and Muslims, keeping their "human dimensions" obscured in the "shadows."[4] Yet it is precisely in the human dimensions that belonging is articulated. This is why I have been intentional throughout this book to draw the reader to those human dimensions—family, work, friendship, religion—to demonstrate that Iraqis' lives are not defined by the the displacement of the Iraq War or by the background noise of Islamophobia and anti-Arab sentiment swirling around them.

Family is a complicated project, a very human dimension. Iraqi refugee families struggled with some of the same issues faced by Arab Americans for generations, in an arena with its own version of the culture wars. When Dera talked about "keeping certain stuff," she walked along a tightrope between being a supporter or denier of "authentic" Arab culture. Youths, whose lives were rapidly evolving as both Iraqi and

American, were quick to see the traditional Iraqi family's weaknesses in its static form. They had embraced a US imaginary that included values of freedom of expression and the need for trust and negotiation in contrast to rigid authority. They were quick, however, to affirm many of the values that their parents espoused. Being the 1.5 generation makes them bridge people.

Conversations between women from different faith communities reveal common fears that the freedom in US culture might derail their children's lives. These conversations poignantly acknowledged the lasting trauma of the Iraq War, as well as their disappointments about the present: unemployment and feelings of isolation. They hinted that the small kinship groups around them were not enough. The women wanted fuller participation outside the confines of family, and yet language seemed an insurmountable hurdle. ESL classes provided a glimmer of hope as Iraqi women found a great deal of commonality with their fellow students, particularly Latinx women.

The way in which refugees go about reestablishing belonging is the inverse of how they lost it. Finding belonging within any society is an act of "becoming"; it is ontological rather than teleological; it does not depend on the *telos* of assimilation in the narrow sense of becoming fully American (or German or Australian). In this manner, belonging comes from being able to engage with the world in ways that allow for understanding and empathy for others and being able to fight for what you need. I saw evidence of this form of belonging among Iraqi youths, from the way they took inspiration from people of good faith—Muslim, Christian, Jewish, Arab, non-Arab, white, Latinx, black—who mobilized to deal positively with the tragedy of the December terrorist attack in San Bernardino.

Hannah Arendt writes, "The fundamental deprivation of human rights is manifested first and above all in the deprivation of a place in the world which makes opinions significant and actions effective."[5] Meaningful belonging requires more than a right to reside in a country. It requires a right to take action. Michel Angier writes that in active engagement, refugees "can find a new social place, a humanity in collective action, the only condition by which they can shed their identity as victims."[6] For Iraqi youths who witnessed the backlash from the terror of December 2, even as terrifying and damaging as it was, it was dwarfed by the positive outpouring of support for the victims and their families and by the wider community's concern for those who were potential targets of Islamophobic backlash. I believe this is what grounded their sense of possibility for present and future belonging. It is what grounds mine.

Sometime around the year 2011, the Iraqi story gradually faded from the public eye, eclipsed by the horror and mass displacement of the Syrian war. It was briefly revived during the genocide against the Yezidi people in Northern Iraq. Since the humanitarian attention span can only handle one crisis at a time, Iraqi refugees stopped making the news, but their story did not end simply because the world stopped caring.

This book is the summation of a project of sustained listening. In listening, I saw the myriad ordinary ways in which Iraqi people reclaimed their lost belonging in the Inland Empire. I saw their concerns shift over time. It began with economic survival, then turned to finding cultural (more than legal) citizenship in a United States that saw them initially as the "axis of evil," reluctantly welcomed them, then named them again as a "threat to the security of the United States."[7] For this reason, I give the final word to Hiba, who after a long discussion one evening about the "Muslim ban," ended it with these words: "All I want is to be with my family and that we live in peace."

Is this too much to ask?

ACKNOWLEDGMENTS

I feel a great debt of gratitude for the multitude of people who have supported me on this decade-long journey. I begin, like so many statements of appreciation, with my mother, who was present at the beginning of the project but passed away before its completion. Betty Jean grew up on a farm in Holtville, very close to the Mexican border. She remembers neighboring farmers from around the world, some from Japan, and turbaned Sikh men from the Punjab who had come to California's Imperial Valley, where land was cheap and the Hoover Dam provided precious Colorado River water to transform a desert into farmland. My grandfather was a hard worker and a hard drinker, and one night returning home from the bar in El Centro, he missed a turn and drove into the irritation canal. In my mother's version of the story, a farm hand (a Bracero?) pulled him out of the ditch to save him from drowning. I would like to thank that unnamed man who helped avert further tragedy in my family history.

My professional life has proceeded to weave in and out of interactions with the displaced. My research with refugees began in the early 1980s when I was a graduate student in public administration at the Monterey (now Middlebury) Institute of International Studies. Professor Steve Garrett, a political scientist, tasked me with interviews of eastern European émigrés teaching obscure yet strategic languages like Czech and Polish at the Defense Language Institute. He was writing about the potential influences of the refugees from behind the Iron Curtain on Cold War foreign policy. I regret that I never had a chance to thank him for that opportunity, which started me on the path leading to this present project.

Between Monterey and the Iraqis in the Inland Empire were a series of detours, which bear mentioning for their formative influence on my development as an ethnographer. The first was my work with the displaced Sudanese in 1986. During my work in Sudan, I was inspired and befriended by many remarkable Sudanese. One of the most memorable was Hassan al Mirghani, commonly known as Sheikh Hassan. He tirelessly used his authority as the de facto mayor of his village to mobilize support for the Hawaweer pastoralists who had been displaced during the drought and economic crisis of the mid-1980s. He was one of the prime movers behind the project that allowed them to return to the *wadi* to reestablish their traditional pastoralist life but with a more diversified agro-pastoralist economy. Unfortunately, he passed away before he saw this project realized.

After returning to the US, my doctoral research deviated greatly from its Middle East and African focus and shifted toward Mexican migration to the rural midwestern US. I could not have completed my research without the financial support of the Julian Samora Research Institute at Michigan State University and the guiding hand of the sociologist-demographer Jorge Chapa. Chapa, along with his coinvestigator the anthropologist Ann Millard, had assembled an extraordinary team of doctoral students as well as faculty collaborators at other universities (e.g., Rogelio Saenz). Millard mentored me in ethnographic methods, which included fieldwork in churches and social service organizations assisting the migrant farmworker population, as well as unstructured interviews and focus groups. Millard's influence on my methodological orientation was profound. This explains several aspects of my work that the reader may wonder about, namely, my disciplinary loyalties. I call myself a hybrid, a product of a sociology department that valued ethnography, with my fieldwork mentored by an anthropologist.

By this time, Alejandro Portes and Rubén Rumbaut had published their first round of findings from the Children of Immigrants Longitudinal Study (CILS), the most comprehensive work on the second generation to date. Rumbaut was one of my important mentors during that time, and I feel fortunate to have been at the convergence of these two important lines of research, the JSRI study and CILS. That influence has continued to push me toward understanding how families cope, change, and transform in migration. It helps explain why there is a great deal of interest on Iraqi youths. My doctoral focus on youths of the second generation eventually found its way back into my research with the Iraqi refugee 1.5 generation.

I should mention and thank other methodological mentors, such as the sociologist/ethnographer Steve Gold, who chaired my doctoral committee. Gold's exemplary ethnographic writing on Vietnamese, Russian Jewish, and Arab refugee communities has been an inspiration and model for my current work.

While I was teaching at Ancilla College near Plymouth, Indiana, I became involved with people from a small town in Mexico, Santiago Capitiro, a rancho in the state of Guanajuato. Part of "Capy Ranch" had moved to Plymouth. I joined with people in Plymouth and Capitiro who desired to form a sister-city relationship between their cities. Several visits to Capitiro revealed similarities to villages in Sudan and Kenya affected by migration: strong ties between communities, circular rather than linear migration, the impact of remittances in local inequality, the effect of migration on family structures.

After returning to my natal land of California in 2008 to teach at a small faith-based liberal arts university in southeastern California, the decision to pursue a study of the emerging Iraqi refugee community in the Inland Empire finally coalesced during a trip in 2010 to Washington, DC. With a small grant from the College of Arts and Sciences to look at the broad issue of forced migration (including human trafficking), I traveled to Washington, DC, to tap several contacts, including the director of InterAction, an alliance of NGOs involved in development, advocacy, and international work. Sam Worthington, an old chum from my Monterey days, gave me an office to work from and permission to say, "Sam Worthington suggested I get in touch." From my base at InterAction, I set out to interview the players in the refugee-resettlement firmament. In my meetings with many dedicated people involved with refugee advocacy, the people who had the most profound impact were people from the List Project to Resettle Iraqi Allies.

Once the research began to focus more sharply, I was enabled in critical ways by certain people who provided access to the Iraqi refugee families in the Inland Empire. I will start with the CEO / executive vice president of Catholic Charities of San Bernardino / Riverside Counties, Ken Sawa, and My Hahn Luu, director of immigration programs and services. Ken and My Hahn, after appropriate background research, trusted me to conduct research with their resettlement population. They continued to be available for monthly ongoing discussions about the findings. Staff member Oras Mohammad was also helpful. Hilda Cruz, Justice for Immigrants coordinator for the Catholic Diocese of San Bernardino, kept me informed of the asylum situation of Central Americans in Southern California.

Having thanked those who have been instrumental in shaping who I am as an ethnographer and "social anthropologist" and enabling the ethnographic fieldwork to begin, I turn now to those have helped me over the past eight years. I could not have done this without the help of so many people. First I would like to thank my student research assistants, Emily Gifford (global studies) and Laura Kosch, now Ameen (sociology), who worked on the tedious but critical side of the data, transcribing hours of interviews, careful to spell out my every stammer ("um," "ahhhh," "I mean"). Laura's senior project provided some insight into how Arab–non-Arab mixed couples were being perceived in society. Several students developed interviewing skills enough to assist in conducting interviews in people's homes. Julie Carver (global studies) conducted a critical interview with two women whose stories would otherwise not have made it into this book. Lisa Fernandez was a huge support during the two years that she assisted in the project. Lisa was a natural-born ethnographer. More than a skilled interviewer, Lisa's empathy and compassion was palpable to the women. Like Julie, her interviews with women gave voice to those who would have otherwise remained silent. Lisa's insight into race-making processes of the Inland Empire was articulated in her senior thesis and provided some insights for chapter 5. Now that Lisa has finished her master's in women, gender, and sexuality studies, I believe that she will continue her advocacy and get involved in her own research. Sandra Beshir (sociology) brought her fluency in Arabic into the effort by translating YouTube vlogs from Arabic to English. Her senior thesis provided some critical insight into how a younger generation of Arab Christians understand their place within the inner dimension of the War on Terror.

I want to add a note of special thanks to Brandon Agcaoili (global studies / politics) and Diane Castellon (political science). Brandon facilitated a focus group and helped set up the *Force Migration Stories* blog. He wrote several moving pieces, one on the Lhotshampa refugees from Bhutan. Diane conducted interviews with organizations working with

Central American children who migrated through Mexico. Her work helped us better understand the way the Central American migration played into the framing of refugee policy beginning in 2015. Both Diane and Brandon brought their work into the classroom and contributed to a course that we taught on forced migration.

Having the resources to hire student assistants and translators, to travel to fieldwork sites, and to have release time from teaching was made possible by the generous financial support from La Sierra University. Tremendous support from the College of Arts and Sciences came in the form of three research grants, with the wholehearted support of the deans of the College of Arts and Sciences, Adeny Schmidt and April Summitt. Both Adeny and April were on board from the get-go. April's support for an ad hoc sabbatical during spring quarter of 2019 was a game changer. I should mention also the Shrillo family, whose fellowship funded fieldwork in Germany and Istanbul.

My colleagues in the Department of History, Politics, and Sociology were sources of constant encouragement. They also stepped in during my sabbaticals and absences, covering courses and chair duties. I want to give special thanks to Dr. Andrew Howe (history), without whose assuming chair duties during my 2019 sabbatical it would not have been possible. I was also inspired and supported by fellow scholars in the department who gave me constant encouragement, including the late Lisa Kohlmeier, Eric Vega, Won Yoon, Alicia Gutierrez-Romine, and Katherine Koh.

There are several people outside the department I would like to mention, including Carlos Parra of the Department of World Languages, who was a sounding board on issues of immigration and asylum and expert in finding the best cafés in which to parse out these topics. Several other individuals served as door openers for me. Dr. Larry Geraty (former president of La Sierra University) and Anees Haddad (professor of sociology, retired) introduced me to several Seventh-Day Adventist Iraqi families. Suha Huffacker recommended that I bring Eva Aisha George into the project, and Eva turned out to be indispensable. Because her father was Assyrian, she could translate both Arabic and Neo-Aramaic. Suha, whose mother was Iraqi and father Egyptian, was an informal cultural consultant for me. I often told her about what I was learning, and she filled in some of the cultural nuance.

Several people need to be recognized who read portions of this manuscript, beginning with my unofficial editor, Kris Lovekin, a former journalist for the *Press Enterprise* who gave important editorial comments on my introduction. Another important reader and reviewer has been Susan Ossman, Department of Anthropology, University of California, Riverside. Dr. Ossman, a writer I admire tremendously, read and commented on what eventually became chapters 1 and 6. Amanda Lucia, Department of Religious Studies, also at University of California, Riverside, gave helpful comments on the religious communities section of chapter 3. David Sandell, Department of Anthropology and Sociology, Texas Christian University, another writer whose work I admire, read earlier versions of the introduction and chapter 5. David was another mentor in ethnography, and I was fortunate once to accompany him on his fieldwork in Guanajuato, Mexico, where I learned a thing or two. Ruth Burke, professor of German at California State University, San Bernardino, translated several interviews from German to English and gave helpful suggestions on chapter 6.

I want to think the editors at the *Journal of Conflict Transformation and Security*, David Curran and Alpaslan Özerdem, who published the article "'The Country Chooses You': Discourses of Mobility and Immobility among Iraqi Refugees," which formed the basis of chapter 1. Their suggestions took off some of the rough edges before it was added to the current manuscript.

Selin Yildiz-Nielson and Sherry Mackey, cofounders of the local NGO Glocally Connected, provided real-time updates on what was happening in refugee resettlement in the Inland Empire. Their program with Afghan refugee women I consider a model for what is needed and possible to support refugees. Selin collaborated with me on writing a chapter on refugees in the Middle East that was used in a global studies course.

One of the people who stayed with this project from early on was Sassan Khyder. Sassan's story is a window on what was in store for those million refugees who made it to Germany in 2015, what they encountered in the complicated process of "integration," in which German discourses of *Refugeepolitik* encompassed extreme measures of generosity and fears of a jihadist "fifth column." The different points along Sassan's migratory project and intellectual journey helped formulate my concept of refugee belonging outlined in both the introduction and chapter 6.

These concepts were keenly illustrated with his poetry, some of which he has generously offered for use in this book. I should mention several other people in Germany who generously explained how the asylum, resettlement, and integration process worked in that country: Horst Rolly of Friedensau Seminary, Thomas Langwald of BAMF, Annette Naeser of Refugio, Dagmar Gerhard and Haiveen Al-Isso of Fortbildung für Betreuerinnen und Betreuer, Phillip Schafer, Monica Steinhauser of Pro-Asyl, Anna Büllesbach of the UNHCR suboffice in Nuremberg, Yvonne Preusse of Caritas Nuremberg, and Klaus Schreiner of GTZ.

My trips to Istanbul included meetings with several individuals whose research on refugees in Turkey has be invaluable. These included the sociologist and demographer Ahmet Içduygu of Koç University, Department of Humanities and Social Sciences, and Gökay Özerim, Department of International Relations, Yasar University (Izmir). Deniz Karci, a doctoral student at Koç University, was a valuable resource person, having worked in all phases of the resettlement operation, including processing resettlement cases for ICMC in UAE, Yemen, and India. Furthermore, she had helped with refugee cultural orientation in Istanbul and had visited resettlement sites in the US.

It has to be said that eight years of fieldwork would have not been possible without the welcoming spirit of the Iraqi people in the Inland Empire. They took care of me very well, and they cooked for me the best fish in the world (*masgouf*). This book is a testament to their power to break open new pathways of belonging.

Finally, I thank three people whose presence in my life has so fundamentally enabled me. My wife, Rebecca Waring-Crane, a much better writer than I, gave me a vision of the possible in the art of writing. I want to thank her also for not tolerating my whining; she simply believed. To my daughter, Justin, with whom I spent many hours in the coffee houses of Los Angeles, writing together and ruminating about Angeleno culture. To my son, Graeme, whose love of books and mysticism led us poking through the bookstores along Sunset Boulevard.

Yes, indeed, we belong to each other.

METHODOLOGICAL APPENDIX

Everything is complicated and questions simplify what is only comprehensible through intimacy and experience. Nor are people's lives free from blame and guilt and wrongdoing, and what might be intended as simple curiosity may feel like a demand for a confession. You don't know what you might release by asking a stupid question. It was best to leave people to their silences.
—Abdulrazak Gurnah, *Gravel Heart*

Fieldwork Practices

Following the principles of established ethnographic work with refugee populations, I focused on "processes and relationships" that were most salient to survival for Iraqi refugees at various points from exile to resettlement.[1] Their migration stories referenced experiences of various points on a migratory continuum, beginning with displacement from the violence and insecurity that prevailed during the postinvasion occupation, sojourns into neighboring countries, arrival in the Inland Empire of California, economic survival during and after the Great Recession, fallout from the terrorist attack in 2015, and reactions to the exclusionary politics beginning with the presidential primary in 2015–2016.

At this point, I need to clarify to a fuller extent the fieldwork challenges that I faced. Every ethnographer has a peculiar set of characteristics that emanate from oneself, and I have tried as much as possible to be aware of how I, with my status characteristics, influence the questions that I have chosen to ask and the answers given by my interlocutors. This is not to focus on my limitations, which are real; rather, it is to help the reader (and the author) understand the intersubjective silences of each encounter.

To begin, my gender usually dictated the terms of the interviews. In order to maintain propriety, there would always need to be a male family member present whenever I visited an Iraqi home (this was true regardless of the faith tradition). It became clear to me that I would need to have cultural guides who could enter the world of women without a male mediator present who inevitably filtered or shaped the narrative. Whatever success I was able to achieve in hearing women was due to two key individuals. The first was my translator, Eva Aisha George, who helped to conduct several interviews with women without men present. She served as both translator and cultural guide, interpreting the nuanced meaning of certain Arabic words and explaining behavior she observed during interviews and focus groups.

One case bears mentioning here, because it illustrates the cultural inertia that this tactic had to overcome. I asked Eva and a student research assistant, Julie, to interview Suha and her sister Janeen. I knew that if I was present, the father would have to be present, and he was notorious for dominating the conversation. Their strategy was to tell the father that this was only to involve the women. Julie recounted the scene of the interview:

As we sat down to begin the interview, Aodish [the father] stayed around, kept asking if he should sit and stay. As Eva and I began to tell him "no, no," and shooing with our hands, his daughter began to laugh and join in. We began to pass jokes back and forth, making each other laugh. During this time, their father tried to come into the conversation; as he pulled up a chair, both Janeen and Suha started laughing, waving their hands at him saying, "no, no." Eva and I mimicked them, and he laughed and walked out again. . . . Then she [Janeen] switched to her ex-husband. After a year of marriage [in the US], her husband came to her and said that their marriage certificate was not approved, as cousins were not allowed to marry in the US. He bought her a one-way ticket to Syria and said that he would join her in just two days and they would get married in Syria, where it was legal to marry your cousin, then come back to the States. He convinced her to leave everything—including all her jewelry. He got her on the plane. When she arrived in Syria, she had to use a payphone to call her brother to have him come pick her up. When two days had passed, she called her ex-husband asking when he would be coming to Syria. His response on the phone was, "I do not know who you are." . . . She collapsed and spent three months in the hospital—her family stayed in Syria so she could travel with them to the US. She then brought out [to show us] every document she had—including her forged signature on the divorce documents. She even stated that she contacted their priest in San Diego—where she had lived for a year in the States with her ex-husband—and he offered his help if she found a lawyer to take on her case to receive her belongings back.

Julie wrote that they followed protocol by ending the interview when Janeen looked distressed from telling the story. Eva and Julie were able to establish a comfort level, a more relaxed rapport, and trust with Suha and Janeen. The result was that Janeen shared very private accounts of her divorce, revealing the patriarchal hierarchy that had tolerated her ex-husband's intrigues, deceit, and theft of her jewelry. Had I or other men been part of that interview, such candidness would not have been possible.

The other person who was critical in giving women greater voice in this study was Lisa Fernandez. Although still an undergraduate major-ing in sociology, Lisa proved herself a natural ethnographer. She quickly learned the cultural dynamics in both Muslim and Chaldean Iraqi fami-lies. She always exuded acceptance and calm. Religious culture did not matter: if Shi'a women gathered separately in a room, she would join them and engage in their conversations. She was very skilled at put-ting people at ease and very comfortable visiting their homes. Lisa con-ducted interviews with several women, facilitated the focus group for Iraqi women (translated by Eva), and facilitated one of the focus groups with the youths. Admittedly, the voices of Iraqi women in this study are not as full as they could be, but without the participation of Eva and Lisa, they would have been greatly diminished.

As an outsider to the culture, not fluent in Arabic, I felt that I did not comprehend some of the nuances of their life histories. Refugees are aware of the need for their claims to surmount the prevailing suspicion that most asylum accounts are bogus. Hence, refugee narratives must, out of necessity, narrowly conform to the questions posed by officials trying to determine their legitimacy. The crafting of effective narratives illustrates what Didier Fassin means by the "vanishing truth of refugees," that the refugee narrative is multilayered, offering official versions that will be most efficacious for receiving refugee status, while giving other audiences more nuanced accounts of events and motivations.[2]

I believe this dynamic is what was going on behind the scenes with Majid and Miriam (see chapter 1). On my way to their house during a heat wave in September 2011, I stopped to buy them a watermelon to bring as a gift. I arrived at sundown; the thermometer said 101 degrees, and they wanted me to sit down with them at the table to eat. Majid said they were eating late because they had to wait for the sun to set; it was Ramadan. "The hard thing about Ramadan," he said, "not drinking water; no food is bad only at the beginning." I sat down, and they served me some traditional *iftar* snacks like dates, later fried potato fritters. As he was telling me this, I looked at the Virgin Mary on their wall with the sacred pierced heart. I asked, "Majid, do Christians fast in Iraq?" He responded, "Hey, it's not just Muslim; it's tradition for [all] Iraqis. . . . But they [Christians] fast only fifteen days during Ramadan." He mentioned that it had something to do with "Yousef and Maryam" (Joseph and Mary) during the month of November. He told me about the time US soldiers searched his parents' house in Baghdad. They had a picture of the Virgin Mary in their house, since they were Catholic: "There was this American soldier searching the house, saw the picture of Maryam, he said, 'Hey, we have one in our house too.'" I met up with Miriam, Fairuz, and Musa again, four years later, at the reenactment of the martyrdom of Hussein at an Islamic school. Miriam was wearing what the other Shi'a women wore: a black robe and hijab. Majid was not with them that day, but Miriam said Majid was doing well, now working full-time installing windshields, and that I should call him.

At the time when I was visiting and attempting to help Majid and Miriam, there were parts of their lives that remained a mystery to me. The case manager at the resettlement agency told me that Majid had been an officer in the Iraqi army. Majid never mentioned that part of his life and for good reason: such information could have disqualified him from asylum in the US. I was curious, though, why he maintained the fiction about being Christian, when Christians fasting during Ramadan is unheard of, and it is rare for Christians to give their children traditionally Muslim names.[3] Had it strengthened his asylum application? I found out that the elusive "cousin" who sponsored him owned a liquor store and had sponsored a Christian Iraqi whom I knew. When I asked Zaker about Majid, his immediate response was, "You mean that Muslim guy?" I asked Majid if he knew Zaker; he said that he did and that the aunts and the cousin were "one big family."

The inevitable friendships that I developed with people like Majid are the occupational hazard of the ethnographer. I felt that confronting him on the inconsistencies that were obvious in his posing as Christian would have been seen by him as an accusation of lying. I decided to leave the matter in mystery, since I did not want it to cause a rift in our relationship. I will never know how they crafted their appeal for asylum. I can only speculate that Majid and Miriam posed as Christians because it was safer than being Shi'a in a Sunni region of Iraq, where he worked.

In my approach in ethnographic work with refugees, I found the principle set forth by the scholar, philosopher, and rabbi Abraham Joshua Heschel to be useful. In his study of the prophets of Israel, Heschel articulated an approach to research grounded in phenomenology that I have come to embrace: "Explanation, when regarded as the only goal of inquiry, becomes a substitute for understanding. Imperceptibly it becomes the beginning rather than the end of perception."[4] My role is not to be a detective but to receive the refugee narrative as given to me, in all its open-endedness.

A total of fifty Iraqi refugees participated in this study. Forty-three of those lived in the Inland Empire, seven in neighboring Orange County. I included the Orange County subset because they were attending school and working in the Inland Empire. Three people in Washington, DC, and six in Germany were also interviewed. Chapter 2 draws on data from all Iraqi refugees interviewed, since it deals with a more universal experience of finding safe haven in surrounding countries and Europe. Chapters 2–6 draw on data only from the California population, as they concern that group of Iraqis in the Inland Empire. All participants lived in Iraq before fleeing the post-2003 civil war, with the exception of one who had been living in Cyprus, who applied for asylum while visiting relatives in the US on a tourist visa. Most lived from three to five years in Syria or Jordan before arriving in the US; thirty-two lived in one or both of those countries for more than five years before being admitted as refugees to the US.

The study population was religiously diverse: sixteen were Muslim (Shi'a and Sunni), and thirty-four were Christian, including Chaldean, Syrian Orthodox, Armenian Orthodox, Baptist, and Seventh-Day Adventist. The religious proportions of the fifty are the inverse of what they are in the Iraq, where Muslims are the vast majority.[5] Although they all identified as Iraqi, they were not all Arabs but represented several "ethnicities," including Kurdish, Armenian, and Assyrian.[6]

The study population was further defined by the parameters of the Iraq War (2003–2011), having left Iraq from 2008 to 2014. In that sense, they reflect the more recent Iraqi migration to the US, 75 percent of whom are foreign born, who came to the US as refugees following the wars of 1991 and 2003.[7] Additional characteristics of the study population, including age distribution, family structure, ethnicity, religion, education, and occupation, are found in table A.1 and in chapters 2–6.

TABLE A.1. Study Population (N = 50)

Characteristic	Number
Age	
18–24	14
25–49	21
50+	15
Gender	
Female	21
Male	29
Marital status	
Married	29
Single	21
Religion	
Muslim	16
Christian	34
Country of first asylum	
Syria	16
Jordan	25
Turkey	4
Lebanon	1
None	4[a]
Length of time in country of first asylum	
< 1 year	7
1–5 years	11
More than 5 years	32

a. Either SIV and left from Iraq or applied for asylum when already in the US.

TABLE A.1. (cont.)

Characteristic	Number
Occupation in Iraq	
Professional	16
Skilled/trade	13
Student	11
Retired or not employed	10
Employment status in Inland Empire	
Employed full-time in profession in which they trained	3
Employed full-time in different profession	1
Employed part-time, unemployed, or retired	29
Stay-at-home parent	3
Student	14
Education level (Iraq)	
University degree	17
Postsecondary certificate	7
Secondary only	21
Primary only	5

In November 2010, I contacted the resettlement agency designated by the US Refugee Admissions Program for Riverside and San Bernardino Counties. The CEO and director of the agency's Immigration Programs and Services agreed to cooperate in this study, eventually providing demographic profiles and introductions to four client families. Once I established a relationship with the resettlement agency, regular contact was maintained through quarterly meetings with the refugee and immigration services coordinator and the CEO. I participated with the agency through volunteering to help with small collaborative projects such as airport pickups, medical clearances at local clinics, cultural orientations or ESL training, and hosting citizenship courses. Another set of families was contacted through Iraqi students and staff on the campus of La Sierra University, where I taught, which I described in the introduction.

The two sites of first contact—resettlement agency and university—became the nucleus of a convenience sample, which eventually snowballed into fifty individuals. Over time, I developed and maintained the essential ethnographic routines that focused on building closer relationships with a core group of six families who became my primary research consultants. This method is implicit in ethnographic work, as information of a more honest and sensitive nature is only revealed as trust is built and a certain comfort level is achieved. This pattern of fieldwork took place from the winter of 2011 until the end of 2018. This longitudinal approach allowed me to observe changes that were happening in the families' lives: getting and quitting jobs, graduating from high school, going to college, and in some cases, moving away to other cities.

While the fieldwork for this book was conducted with Iraqis in the Inland Empire, I should mention two short fieldwork diversions to destinations outside the US. A desire to gain insight into the experience of the global Iraqi diaspora led me to Germany, where relatives of Ibrahim had settled, whom I visited and interviewed three times over three years. My interviews also included eight people who worked in refugee advocacy and asylum processing. My fieldwork in Germany coincided with the momentous migration event of 2015, which helped me understand how this was exploited by the Islamophobia industry to inspire anti-Arab refugee policy during the presidential primaries and election (see chapter 6).

In order to better understand something about the Iraqi experience of exile, I traveled twice to Istanbul to talk to people who coordinated processing and predeparture clearances for refugees going to the US. The Refugee Services Center in Istanbul was run by the International Catholic Migration Commission (ICMC) under contract with the USRAP to process asylum applications, coordinate health screening and security interviews, and conduct cultural orientation before departure. Since Catholic Charities is part of the ICMC and they are related players in the resettlement arena, I asked the CEO of Catholic Charities in the Inland Empire for an introduction to the administrators at the ICMC processing center in Istanbul.[8]

While in Istanbul, I interviewed administrators at two NGOs that dealt with refugee assistance for those who were applying to UNHCR and the Turkish government for protection status, waiting for a decision, or dealing with rejected asylum applications and trying to decide what to do next. I was also able to identify Turkish researchers at several universities whose writing and consultation were extremely valuable in cross-checking my own findings. During the approximately six weeks and three trips to Istanbul, I was able to interview a total of fourteen administrators, social service professionals and NGO support staff, and researchers, all involved in various aspects of refugee-resettlement processing, asylum, survival, and advocacy. The role that Turkey played in the Iraqi refugee crisis is described in chapter 1.

Interviewing Methods

Life-history interviews have been used effectively in ethnographies of refugee experiences dealing with economic survival and host-community reactions and in constructing narratives of how individuals negotiate a variety of institutions.[9] Within anthropology, the life-history interview has been a frequent ethnographic tool to provide "a more intimate and personal" revelation of "how people perceive, react to, and contribute to changes that affect their lives."[10] It is considered "an effective way to get the voices of previously silent people on to the historical record."[11]

The life-history interview framework was divided into four parts. The first set of questions dealt with family history and economic and cultural life before the 2003 invasion. It included an important question about the composition of the neighborhood where the interviewees' lived and the nature of intergroup relationships, since the events post-2003 led to crucial changes in communal relations at the meso-level and eventually to ethnic cleansing at the neighborhood level. The second set of questions dealt with the context of departure: events surrounding the decision to leave Iraq. The third part mapped the time spent in countries of first asylum and their interactions with the organizational players in refugee protection and resettlement. This fourth part followed the journey to the US, focusing on interviewees' experience and the adjustments they were required to make, feelings of well-being, what they missed or appreciated in their new society, and their relationships within communities of settlement. Interviews in Germany were used for purposes of comparison in formulating concepts of acceptance and belonging.

Interviews were mostly conducted at people's homes. When the level of proficiency was deemed adequate, the interviews were conducted in English. Or translators were used to conduct interviews in Arabic or Chaldean Neo-Aramaic. Recorded interviews were then professionally transcribed and translated into English. The translator was an Iraqi woman who arrived in 2012 and applied for asylum. She held a bachelor's degree in English from the University of Baghdad and had done professional translation work for companies in Cyprus for eleven years.

Focus Groups

Focus groups proved to be a vital methodological tool in endeavoring to understand Iraqi youths. Most importantly, they provided a space for youths to express opinions free of the constraining gaze of parents. By providing "multiple lines of communication," focus groups can be less intimidating than one-on-one interviews. In the company of peers of similar background, the focus groups provide a safe place to share ideas and opinions.[12] I have found focus groups to be effective in this regard, including in my research at the Julian Samora Research Institute, where we designed and facilitated focus groups with Latinx youths in churches and high schools.[13] Focus groups for this study were facilitated by student research assistants in order to further lessen the potentially distracting presence of any older authority figure.

Two focus groups were conducted from 2015 and 2016, both about one year apart, on the La Sierra University campus. Within those groups, nine youths participated, ranging in age from sixteen to twenty-five (all minors had permission from parents). They were religiously diverse: five were Muslim, and four were Christian (Chaldean and Seventh-Day Adventist), with five males and four females. Focus-group participants were recruited from families that had already been interviewed at least once. An invitation was mailed to each family explaining the purpose and nature of the interview. This was followed by a phone call and in some cases a home visit. At the beginning of the focus group, lunch was provided, and gift cards from Target were given as tokens of appreciation.

The facilitator and translator posed questions in both English and Arabic, and discussion could be in both English and Arabic. Roughly one-third of the time the discussion shifted to Arabic. When that happened, the translator give brief summaries to the facilitator of what was being said. The entire interview was recorded with an H2 Zoom digital recorder and then transcribed. This was done by the same person who translated during the interview, and she was able to differentiate the various voices. Arabic portions were translated into English, and those portions were identified as Arabic translations.

The questions posed in the first focus group (February 2015) were designed to evoke more general discussions of life in the US. (The specific questions are described in more detail in chapter 3.) The youths were given a series of prompt questions to describe their feelings toward (mostly Latinx) friends at school, the aspects of Iraqi language and culture they felt were important to keep, and relationships with parents.

The second focus group was conducted in February 2016, after which a number of political events at both the international and domestic levels formed a dramatically different context than existed for the earlier focus groups. This second focus group was designed to gauge the youths' feeling of belonging and acceptance in the US in light of the local backlash from the terrorist attack of December 2, 2015, and the exclusionary politics at the national level. They were asked to react to CNN news clips that reported on the House of Representatives vote to restrict future refugees from Syria and Iraq and candidate Donald Trump's statement that Muslim immigration to the United States should be restricted. All (including Muslim and Christian) were asked how they felt they were being perceived in their communities after the shooting. Their responses are fully described in chapter 6.

Focus groups can present a challenge to analyze, since the conversations can go in many directions and there is a dense amount of material to make sense of. I was fortunate to have as a collaborator Becky Galvez-Nelson, an assistant professor of social work at La Sierra University, who taught the research methods sequence for the Social Work Department. In addition to her academic qualifications, Galvez-Nelson had extensive experience as a clinician working with youths. She read the transcripts and identified what she thought were the main points of consensus or divergence surrounding the prompts. We compared our observations and came to conclusions based on our combined notes.

Institutional Review Board protocols required by the university were followed, and informed consent was obtained before formal interviews and focus groups. Those who were under the age of eighteen were granted written permission to participate by one of their parents.

Qualitative Data Analysis

My method in the analysis of transcripts of life history, focus-group interviews, NGO staff interviews, and field notes was to identify emerging patterns, which in turn guided further, more focused lines of inquiry. Because of the manageable number of participants, I decided not to use qualitative data analysis software. Several of the variables are compiled in table A.1, such as years in countries of first asylum, religion, age, and employment status in the Inland Empire.

Using principles of grounded theory, I looked for themes that continued to reemerge with a fair level of consistency in the data, which persisted longitudinally over several years.[14] Two interrelated themes were dominant in the first half of the study. The first centered around the strategies of accessing social capital in translocal networks after leaving Iraq, which enabled economic survival in countries of asylum and steered the Iraqis toward communities of settlement. The second was the deep concern about vulnerability, economic survival, financial struggle, frustration with agency services, finding employment, and fears of permanent downward mobility. (An example of permanent downward mobility would be an engineer or schoolteacher who cannot move past a temporary period of employment as an Uber driver.) These two constructs emerged consistently in their narratives and I felt could be best explained by an approach that acknowledged the role of social capital in migration: an openness to the role of human agency and capability and building connections beyond ethnoreligious groups. With employment scarce and government support limited, this seemed a logical place to "ground" the study, at least in the beginning.

The third theme that was most salient in grounding the line of inquiry concerned the youths who arrived with their parents. The majority of children in the study were born in Iraq and had lived with their families through the post-2003 exile in surrounding countries. Immigrant children who arrive between the ages of sixteen and twenty-five are considered the 1.5 generation (in social science parlance, the second generation consists of those who are born in the US, while the first generation consists of those who arrive as older adults).[15] What emerged throughout the interviews and focus groups was the confidence that the 1.5 generation felt as members of an idealized US society that nurtured, protected, and celebrated the right to expressions of personal and communal identity. I saw this as material that could be explored in more depth in a focus group with the youths.

The fourth theme to emerge concerned the response of Iraqis to the San Bernardino terrorist shooting and the exclusionist rhetoric directed at Arab refugees and Muslims during the Republican presidential primary. By the time of these events, most of the Iraqis participating in the study were on the verge of achieving legal citizenship. This theme of finding belonging served to ground the final two years of ethnographic work (2015–2016), which included follow-up interviews with the youths who had participated in focus groups, with some who had not been focus-group participants, and with parents. These follow-up interviews were meant to gauge the effect of explicit intolerance toward Arab refugees and Muslims in national politics on their sense of belonging. The second focus group, like the first, provided a more fine-grained look at their changing feelings toward finding belonging in US society.

To summarize, the guiding questions and theoretical frames of my research evolved over time. They began as very general and descriptive means to understand the Iraqi refugee experience, focusing primarily on an emerging Iraqi refugee community in California. It utilized a multisited ethnographic method, anchored in California's Inland Empire but encompassing organizational and geographical sites that spanned a set of processes and relationships in Turkey, Germany, and Washington, DC. From 2015 to 2017, what guided my inquiry was how Iraqis were claiming belonging in a country engaged in the domestic implementation of the War on Terror.

What emerged in the final phase of analysis and ethnographic writing was that the Iraqi refugees' experience, at its core, was about having their basis of national and cultural belonging in Iraq removed (gradually or suddenly), compelling them to leave their country for what was presumed to be a temporary period. During this period of exile, they experienced provisional belonging hinged on Arab solidarity and social capital in surrounding countries, followed by a more permanent possibility of belonging in a country of resettlement. In the US, they discovered that some elements of belonging, such as what is found in employment, are tentative and elusive. Even for those who were relatively successful in reestablishing a viable form of livelihood and becoming US citizens, the full rights of belonging that accrue to citizenship were being rhetorically questioned in Islamophobic discourses and in the War on Terror's implementation relative to Arab and Muslim people residing in the US.

NOTES

PREFACE

1. Ong, *Buddha Is Hiding*, 17.
2. It was never entirely clear if the message was meant for our clients or to bolster our own sagging morale as funding was gradually being cut.
3. Nayeri, "Ungrateful Refugee," 149.
4. The last US troops left Iraq in December 2011.
5. Rumbaut, "Portraits, Patterns, and Predictors," 143.
6. Crane et al., *Baseline Study*.
7. The institute is named for Julian Samora, the first Mexican American to receive a doctorate in sociology.
8. Crane, *Latino Churches*; Crane and Millard, "To Be with My People."
9. Manganaro, "Textual Play, Power, and Cultural Critique," 35.
10. Additional characteristics of the study population, including age distribution, family structure, ethnicity, religion, education, and occupation, are found in the appendix.
11. Fuller description of fieldwork and interviewing methods can be found in the appendix.
12. Heschel, *Prophets*, x.

INTRODUCTION

1. The "axis of evil" was identified in George W. Bush's State of the Union Address in 2002 as Iraq, North Korea, and Iran.
2. Arendt, *Origins of Totalitarianism*, 296.
3. Arendt, 294.
4. Rosaldo, "Cultural Citizenship, Inequality, and Multiculturalism," 37 (emphasis added).
5. Maira, "Citizenship, Dissent, Empire," 23.
6. Malkki, "Refugees to Exiles."
7. DeSoto, *Empire*, xii.
8. For another study that has focused on smaller, ethnically isolated urban populations, see Maira, "Citizenship, Dissent, Empire."
9. I define "Arab Americans" as people living in the United States who trace their ancestry to Arab regions of the Middle East and North Africa and who tend to self-identify as Arab, rather than, for example, Kurdish or Armenian. I use "Arab"

to refer to those who are residing in the country temporarily (students, tourists, consultants), who do not identify as residents of the United States in a permanent manner. It should be noted that while the majority of the population of Iraq is Arab, many who have immigrated to the United States do not consider them-selves Arab but rather Kurdish, Armenian, or Chaldean. For example, half of the participants in this study identified as Chaldean rather than Arab.

10. The term "fifth column" is attributed to General Emilio Modal Vidal, who during the Spanish Civil War claimed that his "fifth column" of sympathizers had already infiltrated Madrid and was undermining its defenses. Britannica, "Fifth Column."

11. The dramatic reduction in refugee admissions after the election of Donald Trump affected many non-Muslim Iraqis such as the Yezidis, a religious minority whose ancestral land had been overrun by the Islamic State in 2014.

12. Biehl and Locke, "Deleuze and the Anthropology of Becoming," 318.

CHAPTER 1. BELONGING AND DISPLACEMENT

1. *Oxford English Dictionary*, 2nd ed., s.v. "crisis," 605.

2. Because of the ongoing political instability of Iraq and civil rights abuses tolerated under the Patriot Act, all names of individuals are pseudonyms.

3. Works that have provided similar accounts include Amos, *Eclipse of the Sunnis*; Sassoon, *Iraqi Refugees*; Chatelard, "What Visibility Conceals"; Chatty, *Displace-ment and Dispossession*; Huddleston, *Out of Iraq*; and van Kesteren, *Baghdad Calling*.

4. See, e.g., Bennis and Halliday, "Iraq." Although medical supplies were theoreti-cally exempt, the bureaucratic processes to approve medical equipment (anything that could potentially have a military use, e.g., ambulances, was suspect) meant that the importation time frame was unpredictable and slow.

5. See, e.g., Wimmer, *Ethnic Boundary Making*. The strategy of terrorizing whole groups by attacking their collective symbols has a long history and has been com-mon practice in other regions, such as during the "troubles" of Northern Ireland.

6. Sassoon, *Iraqi Refugees*.

7. Van Kesteren, *Baghdad Calling*, 3.

8. For a brief elaboration on Assyrian and Chaldean communities in Iraq, see chap-ter 3.

9. Attacks against Christian churches continued after the peak of violence in 2006. In the spring of 2008, Paulus Rahho, the archbishop of the Chaldean church in Mosul, the spiritual capital for Christians in Iraq, was kidnapped and killed by Al Qaeda (Amos, *Eclipse of the Sunnis*). This was followed two years later by the attack on Our Lady of Deliverance Chaldean Catholic Church in Baghdad on October 31, 2010, which killed fifty-eight parishioners and two priests.

10. Van Kesteren, *Baghdad Calling*, 5.

11. Sassoon, *Iraqi Refugees*.

12. Gifford, "Iraqi Refugee Perceptions of Urban Violence."

13. Gifford, 16.

14. Stansfield, "Iraq." It is not in the purview of this book to fully document the com-
    plex drivers of social fragmentation and insecurity that preexisted the invasion.
    According to Nabil Al-Tiriti, the occupation ignored the complexity of the grow-
    ing division within Iraqi society: "outbreaks of sectarian violence have erupted
    in highly specific occasions . . . when long-term shifts such as dwindling natural
    resource or mass migration or changes in social identity are inflamed by deliber-
    ate and short-term policy choices" ("There Go the Neighborhoods," 24).
15. There are more comprehensive and detailed accounts to which the reader can
    refer that chronicle and analyze the effect of Hussein's regime on the communal
    tensions within Iraqi society, the mismanagement of the reconstruction, and the
    failure of the occupying forces to provide security, all of which contributed to
    the violent fragmentation of Iraqi society after 2003. See, e.g., Amos, *Eclipse of
    the Sunnis*; Sassoon, *Iraqi Refugees*; Chandrasekaran, *Imperial Life in the Emerald
    City*; Stiglitz and Bilmes, *Three Billion Dollar War*; Shadid, *Night Draws Near*;
    Stansfield, "Iraq"; Filkins, *Forever War*.
16. UNHCR, "UNHCR Country Operations Profile—Jordan"; UNHCR, "UNHCR
    Country Operations Profile—Syrian Arab Republic"; Harper, "Iraq's Refugees."
17. Sassoon, *Iraqi Refugees*.
18. Chatty and Mansour, "Unlocking Protracted Displacement."
19. Van Kesteren, *Baghdad Calling*.
20. Chatelard, "What Visibility Conceals," 28, 38.
21. Massey, "New Immigration and Ethnicity"; Cornelius, "Structural Embedded-
    ness."
22. Coleman, "Social Capital"; Granovetter, "Strength of Weak Ties."
23. Monsutti, *War and Migration*.
24. UNICEF, *Iraq's Children*.
25. Sassoon, *Iraqi Refugees*.
26. Amos, *Eclipse of the Sunnis*.
27. Harper, "Iraq's Refugees." Harper's article includes data from a survey done by
    UNHCR of Iraqi refugees in Syria: 77 percent reported being affected by air and
    rocket attacks, 80 percent had witnessed a shooting, 68 percent had experienced
    harassment or interrogation by militias.
28. Throughout the Hussein era, Iraqis had been welcome in Baathist-governed Syria.
    As the number of refugees increased, visa requirements for Iraqis seeking safe
    haven in Syria were put into place.
29. See UNHCR, "Surviving in the City."
30. Al-Zabadani was the first city to fall to the Free Syrian Army in 2011.
31. Amman was commonly referred to as "Iraq's second capital."
32. Sassoon, *Iraqi Refugees*.
33. Sassoon; Migration Policy Institute, "Top 10 Migration Issues of 2008."
34. Migration Policy Institute, "Top 10 Migration Issues of 2008."
35. The EU eventually launched a formal resettlement program to accommodate ten
    thousand Iraqis beginning in 2008.

36. Içduygu's research describes how in 1991, Turkey allowed temporary safe haven for half a million Kurdish Iraqis fleeing Saddam Hussein's brutal chemical-weapon attacks on Kurdish civilians (*Irregular Migration in Turkey*). The vast majority returned to Iraq after a no-fly safe zone north of Erbil was established in Iraqi Kurdistan by UN Security Council Resolution 688, calling for Iraq to end repression of its own population. A residual population remained and subsequently constituted "a bridge-head for more Iraqis to enter Turkey, or to use the country as a transit area towards the West" (Içduygu, 22); between 1995 and 2001 a total of 77,643 Iraqis were arrested by the Turkish authorities as "irregular migrants" (Içduygu, 29).

37. Interview with directors of refugee support organization in Istanbul, September 5, 2011.

38. Australia had supported the US invasion of Iraq and contributed personnel and equipment from 2003 to 2008 (Molan, "Australia in Iraq 2002–2010"); Migration Policy Institute, "Top 10 Migration Issues of 2008."

39. For the situation of Iraqi refugees being held in detention facilities in Indonesia, see the documentary *Between the Devil and the Deep Blue Sea*, by Jessie Taylor, Dave Schmidt, and Kris Kamen. The Australian journalist Jessie Taylor wrote a companion article to the film based on firsthand observation of the detention facilities and interviews with asylum seekers (see "Behind Australian Doors"), with photography by Dave Schmidt.

40. Jessie Taylor, telephone interview by the author, March 23, 2011.

41. Aljazeera, "Scores Missing after Indian Ocean Sinking."

42. Victoria Martin-Iverson, telephone interview by the author, March 28, 2011. Martin-Iverson helped found the Refugee Rights Action Network in Australia.

43. Depending on which political party was in power, asylum seekers would be sent for "offshore processing" to Australian-built camps on Papua New Guinea to wait for resettlement possibilities in Europe or North America ("Wrong Solution").

44. Migration Policy Institute, "Top 10 Migration Issues of 2008."

45. Hein, "Refugees, Immigrants, and the State."

46. Baker and North, *1975 Refugees*, 6.

47. Tripp, *History of Iraq*.

48. International Organization for Migration, *World Migration Report 2011*.

49. US Department of Homeland Security, "Yearbook of Immigration Statistics 2004."

50. Amos described situations in which these criteria continued to be applied even after the passage of the Refugee Crisis in Iraq Act (*Eclipse of the Sunnis*).

51. Talal, "Global Poverty."

52. Micinski, "Refugee Policy as Foreign Policy."

53. List Project to Resettle Our Iraqi Allies, "Tragedy on the Horizon."

54. List Project to Resettle Our Iraqi Allies.

55. Refugee Crisis in Iraq Act, S. 1651, 110th Cong. (2007–2008). The bill was introduced in the Senate on June 19, 2007.

56. Author interview with ICMC officials, November 12, 2010. See also Amos, *Eclipse of the Sunnis.*
57. US Department of Homeland Security, "Refugees and Asylees: 2015."
58. Author interview with ICMC officials, September 6, 2011.
59. Ong, *Buddha Is Hiding*, 8, citing Foucault, "On Governmentality."
60. Refugee Crisis in Iraq Act.
61. This calculation is based on "Refugees and Asylees" flow reports published by DHS in 2015, 2013, 2012, 2011, and 2009. The total does not include those who applied for asylum while in the US on student or tourist visas.

CHAPTER 2. WORK, AUTONOMY, BELONGING

1. Sandell, *Open Your Heart*, 32.
2. Ong, *Buddha Is Hiding*.
3. Ong, 15 (emphasis added).
4. Ong, 16.
5. Ong, 17.
6. Biehl and Locke, "Deleuze and the Anthropology of Becoming," 323.
7. Biehl and Locke, 332.
8. Mills, *Sociological Imagination*, 15.
9. Agamben, *Homo Sacer*, 4.
10. Deleuze, *Two Regimes of Madness*, quoted in Biehl and Locke, "Deleuze and the Anthropology of Becoming," 322.
11. Monsutti, "States, Sovereignties and Refugees?"
12. Semple, "War-Scarred Iraqi Refugees Find More Misery in America."
13. Olson, "Families Fleeing Violence of War."
14. Budget cutbacks during this time made ESL classes less accessible through the normal venues: adult school and community colleges. The Georgetown Law Center reported the same problem throughout the country. The researchers identified the issues of both accessibility and appropriateness, a need for more "intensive English classes during the initial resettlement period . . . with expanded schedules (i.e., day, night, and weekend classes) to accommodate those with time restrictions due to work or childcare" (Hauck et al., "Factors Influencing the Acculturation of Burmese, Bhutanese, and Iraqi Refugees," 341).
15. Hanna, "No Refuge for Iraqi Refugees."
16. Georgetown University Law Center, *Refugee Crisis in America*; US Senate Committee on Foreign Relations, *Abandoned upon Arrival*; Hanna, "No Refuge for Iraqi Refugees."
17. Yako and Biswas, "We Came to This Country"; Hauck et al., "Factors Influencing the Acculturation of Burmese, Bhutanese, and Iraqi Refugees"; Habeeb-Silva, "Resettlement Challenges for Refugees in the United States."
18. Hauck et al., "Factors Influencing the Acculturation of Burmese, Bhutanese, and Iraqi Refugees."

19. Baker and North, *1975 Refugees.*
20. Rumbaut, "Portraits, Patterns, and Predictors," 151.
21. Yako and Biswas, "We Came to This Country."
22. Yako and Biswas.
23. Office of Refugee Resettlement, *Annual Report to Congress.*
24. Rumbaut, "Portraits, Patterns, and Predictors," 151.
25. Van Selm, "Refugee Resettlement." This follows a pattern seen throughout resettlement countries (EU, Canada, Australia, US) in which asylum applications favor the most vulnerable. Fassin's ethnographic work in France looks at how European countries have created "subsidiary" categories to supplement the narrow criteria of the refugee convention, such as victims of gender-based violence, widows, victims of torture, and people with serious health problems and disabilities (*Humanitarian Reasoning*).
26. Baker and North, *1975 Refugees,* 134.
27. Maira, "Citizenship, Dissent, Empire," 26.
28. Ong, *Buddha Is Hiding,* 16.
29. Ong, 17.
30. Bellah et al., *Habits of the Heart,* 22.
31. Maira, "Citizenship, Dissent, Empire," 27; Ong, "Cultural Citizenship as Subject-Making," quoted in Maira, 27.
32. Ong, *Buddha Is Hiding,* 16.
33. Bellah et al., *Habits of the Heart,* 22.

CHAPTER 3. "JUST TRUST US"

1. See, for example, the documentary about the "lost boys" of Sudan, *God Grew Tired of Us.*
2. Portes and Rumbaut, *Legacies,* 150.
3. Naber, *Arab America,* 5.
4. Portes and Rumbaut, *Legacies.*
5. Rumbaut, "Crucible Within."
6. Bayoumi, *How Does It Feel to Be a Problem?*; Naber, *Arab America*
7. Portes and Rumbaut, *Immigrant America.* Some recent research on Mexican families, however, suggests that powerful abiding norms of respect (*respeto*) may moderate this tension. See Nieri et al., "Reconsidering the 'Acculturation Gap' Narrative."
8. Portes and Rumbaut, *Immigrant America.*
9. Zehr, "U.S. Bringing Iraqi Students and Educators to America."
10. Naber, *Arab America,* 12.
11. Bayoumi, *How Does It Feel to Be a Problem?,* 120.
12. Naber, *Arab America,* 64.
13. Portes and Rumbaut, *Immigrant America.*
14. Bankston and Zhou, *Growing Up American.*

15. Stevens-Arroyo, Goris, and Keysar, *PARAL Study*; Crane and Millard, "To Be with My People."

16. Crane, *Latino Churches*.

17. Crane and Millard, "To Be with My People."

18. Ebaugh and Chavetz, *Religion and the New Immigrants*, 13 (emphasis added).

19. Rosaldo, "Cultural Citizenship, Inequality, and Multiculturalism," 37 (emphasis added).

20. Handlin, *Uprooted*.

21. Williams, *Religions of Immigrants from India and Pakistan*, 12.

22. Warner, "Work in Progress," 1045.

23. I was fortunate to have the doctor mentioned in this account sitting next to me and translating the entire proceedings.

24. Arbaeen Walk, "How the Walk Works" (translated as "forty days' walk," as it is taking place forty days after the martyrdom: *arbaeen* is "forty" in Arabic).

25. Dearborn.org, "March for Justice."

26. Granovetter, "Strength of Weak Ties."

27. Ghori, "Tension Rising for Inland Muslims"; Sheridan, "Police Chief Reluctantly Accepts Hero Role."

28. Hanoosh, *Chaldeans*. The Assyrian International News Agency claims that it designates both the geographical center for Christianity in Iraq and the Assyrian origins in the ancient Assyrian empire ("Assyrians: Frequently Asked Questions").

29. In what is probably the definitive work on the history of the Chaldeans, the historian Yasmeen Hanoosh untangles the origins of the ethnoreligious identifications of Chaldeans and Assyrians (*Chaldeans*). How Chaldeans identify themselves, as in all forms of situational ethnicity, is in constant flux and has different meanings depending on where communities are situated—Northern or urban Iraq, in Chaldean diasporas of Europe, Australia, and North America. Hanoosh understands Chaldean identities holistically through the lenses of ancient Middle Eastern history, contemporary Iraqi politics, and transnational diasporic communities.

30. Many of the Iraqi Seventh-Day Adventists attended a small Arabic-speaking congregation in the nearby town of Loma Linda.

31. Hanoosh, *Chaldeans*, 81–87.

32. Land, *Historical Dictionary of the Seventh-Day Adventists*.

33. Hanoosh, *Chaldeans*, 4.

34. Bates and Rassam, *Peoples and Cultures of the Middle East*.

35. Sassoon, *Iraqi Refugees*, 26.

36. United States Commission on International Religious Freedom, "USCIRF Annual Report 2013."

37. Ufheil-Somer, "Iraqi Christians."

38. Hanoosh, *Chaldeans*.

39. Hanoosh. For comparison with other diasporic religious communities, see Levitt, *God Needs No Passport*.

40. Appadurai, *Fear of Small Numbers*; Anderson, *Imagined Communities*.
41. Naber, *Arab America*.
42. Pyke, "Normal American Family."
43. Naber, *Arab America*.
44. Bellah et al., *Habits of the Heart*.
45. Foucault, "Technologies of the Self."
46. MacLeod, *Ain't No Makin It*.
47. Baker and Amaney, "Values and Cultural Membership."
48. Wardi, *Understanding Iraq*, 82.
49. Wardi, 83.
50. Barth, *Ethnic Groups and Boundaries*.
51. Naber, *Arab America*, 66 (emphasis in original).
52. UNHCR, *Angekommen—We Have Arrived*, 39.
53. Naber, *Arab America*, 7.
54. Naber, 8 (emphasis added).

CHAPTER 4. TWO KINDS OF CITIZENS
1. St. Claire, Botelho, and Ellis, "San Bernardino Shooter Tashfeen Malik"
2. CNBC, "FBI Investigating California Massacre as 'Act of Terrorism.'"
3. Ghori, "Tension Rising for Inland Muslims."
4. Rahman, "Muslim Women Who Wear Hijabs," quoted in Selod, *Forever Suspect*, 11.
5. Abdelkader, *When Islamophobia Turns Violent*, cited in Selod, *Forever Suspect*, 10.
6. Selod, *Forever Suspect*; Cainkar, *Homeland Insecurity*.
7. Selod, *Forever Suspect*, 100.
8. Selod, 100.
9. Foucault, *Discipline and Punish*, cited in Selod, *Forever Suspect*, 100.
10. Selod, *Forever Suspect*, 102.
11. Selod, 102 (emphasis added).
12. Abu-Lughod, *Do Muslim Women Need Saving?*, quoted in Selod, *Forever Suspect*, 11.
13. Cainkar, *Homeland Insecurity*, 6
14. Trump, "Immigration Policy."
15. Finnegan, "Trump and the Refugees."
16. In 2018 and 2019, President Trump mischaracterized the migrant "caravans" from Central America as a male phalanx, while in fact the group was mostly populated by mothers and children.
17. Abu-Lughod, *Do Muslim Women Need Saving?*; Haddad, *Emergence of Muslim American Feminisms*, 135.
18. Selod, *Forever Suspect*, 11.
19. Rosaldo, "Cultural Citizenship, Inequality, and Multiculturalism," quoted in Ong, *Buddha Is Hiding*, 5.

20. Baker and Shryock, "Citizenship and Crisis."
21. Selod, *Forever Suspect*, 24.

CHAPTER 5. "WHERE ARE THE AMERICANS?"
1. León, "Born Again in East Los Angeles."
2. Patterson, *From Acorns to Warehouses*.
3. Davis, *City of Quartz*, 398–399 (emphasis added).
4. Davis, 373.
5. Patterson, *From Acorns to Warehouses*.
6. US Census Bureau, "Data Finder for Riverside, San Bernardino, Fontana, Moreno Valley."
7. Ong, *Buddha Is Hiding*.
8. Bloemraad, *Becoming a Citizen*, 244.
9. Bloemraad, 244.
10. A carefully documented example is Urrea, *Devil's Highway*.
11. Fernandez, "Your Latino Neighbors," 6.
12. Crawley et al., "Understanding the Dynamics."
13. Fernandez, "Your Latino Neighbors," 9.
14. There is a Guatemalan consulate in San Bernardino, an indicator of the significant presence of Guatemalans in the Inland Empire.
15. Reimers, *Still the Golden Door*.
16. Menchu, *I, Rigoberta Menchú*.
17. Massey, Durand, and Pren, "Why Border Enforcement Backfired," 1561.
18. Fernandez, "Your Latino Neighbors," 6.
19. Chapa and Millard, *Apple Pie and Enchiladas*.
20. US Census Bureau, "Data Finder for Riverside, San Bernardino, Fontana, Moreno Valley."
21. Cheng, *Changs Next Door to the Díazes*, 10.
22. Guerrero, *Nuevo South*.
23. Coates, *Between the World and Me*, 7.
24. Said, *Orientalism*; Abu-Lughod, *Do Muslim Women Need Saving?*
25. West, *No True Glory*, quoted in Singh, *Race and America's Long War*, 16.
26. Campisi, *Escape to Miami*.
27. Jen'nan Read points out that Arabs are commonly perceived to be Muslim even though the majority of Arabs in the US are Christian, approximately 65 percent ("Multiple Identities among Arab Americans"). See also similar findings in Cainkar, *Homeland Insecurity*.
28. Said, *Covering Islam*. See also Tehranian, *Whitewashed*.
29. Baker and Shryock, "Citizenship and Crisis."
30. In the following, I rely on Cainkar's book *Homeland Insecurity* for her extensive detailing of the measures implemented toward Arab and Muslim populations in the US.

31. Cainkar, *Homeland Insecurity*, 3. See also Baker and Shryock, "Citizenship and Crisis"; Maira, *9/11 Generation*; Selod, *Forever Suspect*.

32. Bayoumi, *This Muslim American Life*.

33. Singh, *Race and America's Long War*, 13.

34. Selod, *Forever Suspect*.

35. Selod, 23.

36. E. Love, *Islamophobia and Racism in America*.

37. Jamal and Naber, *Race and Arab Americans before and after 9/11*.

38. Warren and Twine, "White Americans, the New Minority?"

39. Warren and Twine, 215; Coates, "Between the World and Me."

40. Takaki, *Different Mirror*.

41. Warren and Twine, "White Americans, the New Minority?"

42. Almaguer, *Racial Fault Lines*.

43. Almaguer, 108.

44. Warren and Twine, "White Americans, the New Minority?," 208.

45. For racial differentiation among Chaldeans in the US, see Hanoosh, *Chaldeans*.

46. Siu, "Diasporic Cultural Citizenship," quoted in Maira, *Missing*, 82.

47. Maira, 83.

48. Cainkar, *Homeland Insecurity*.

49. Wray-Lake, Syvertsen, and Flanagan, "Contested Citizenship and Social Exclusion."

50. Flanagan et al., "Ethnic Awareness, Prejudice, and Civic Commitments."

51. See, e.g., Bayoumi, *This Muslim American Life*.

52. Alsultany, *Arabs and Muslims in the Media*.

53. Selod, *Forever Suspect*.

54. According to the translator Eva George, this saying can apply to people's character but also to situations and circumstances. You find variants of this saying throughout the Arab world.

55. There are initiatives in other places of Southern California, like Latino Muslim Unity in Orange County, that have attempted to intentionally "unite Muslims and Latinos through community building and healing projects," utilizing a "taco truck at every mosque" (Latino Muslim Unity, "About").

CHAPTER 6. BELONGING 2.015

1. Lam, "Refugees Then, Trespassers Now."

2. US Customs and Border Protection, "United States Border Patrol Southwest."

3. Olivo, "Deployed by Gov. Rick Perry."

4. Germany later put into effect temporary border controls when the flow became much greater than expected in late summer and autumn of 2015.

5. Bundes Amt für Migranten und Flüchtlinger, *Asylgeschäftsstatistik für den Monat Dezember 2015*.

6. Bundes Amt für Migranten und Flüchtlinger. The top five nations of origin were, in order of the number of refugees, Syria, Albania, Kosovo, Afghanistan, and Iraq.

7. Neumann, "Die Herkunft vieler Flüchtlinge ist ungeklärt." Neumann's article cites a researcher at the University of Bremen who estimated that as many as one hundred thousand unregistered asylum seekers could be in the country.

8. "Angela Merkel, Chancellor of the Free World."

9. PEGIDA stands for Patriotische Europäer gegen die Islamisierung des Abendlandes, or Patriotic Europeans against the Islamization of the Occident German.

10. That changed with the emergence the AfD (Alternativ für Deutschland) party, which gained legislative seats in 2016.

11. Hassan and Chu, "Germany's Embrace of Refugees Spurs Backlash."

12. Poulos, "Obama Bungled US Response to the Arab Spring."

13. Green, *Devil's Bargain*, 207.

14. Beaumont, "Ben Carson Says 'No' to Syrian Refugees in U.S."

15. Fantz and Brumfield, "More than Half the Nation's Governor's Say Syrians Not Welcome."

16. See, e.g., Massey, Durand, and Pren, "Why Border Enforcement Backfired."

17. Trump, "Donald J. Trump Statement" (emphasis added).

18. Quoted in Cainkar, *Homeland Insecurity*, 110.

19. Bayoumi provides an excellent description of one the more notorious sting operations, directed at a mentally unstable suspect (*This Muslim American Life*).

20. Kopan, "Donald Trump: Syrian Refugees a 'Trojan Horse.'"

21. Jamal and Naber, *Race and Arab Americans before and after 9/11*; Maira, "Citizenship, Dissent, Empire."

22. Bayoumi, *This Muslim American Life*, 139.

23. See Malley and Finer, "Long Shadow of 9/11."

24. *Refugee Resettlement Watch* is a blog site devoted to opposition to USRAP which scours the web for any news of refugees involved in nefarious activities, with particular focus on Muslims.

25. Corcoran, *Refugee Resettlement and the Hijra to America*, 7 (emphasis added).

26. It should be noted that those who are seeking asylum from Muslim-majority countries are not ipso facto Muslim (US Department of Homeland Security, "Refugees and Asylees 2015").

27. American Security Against Foreign Enemies Act (American SAFE Act) of 2015, HR 4038, 114th Cong., 1st sess. Introduced in the House on November 17, 2015. HR 4038 identified as security risks refugees from Syria and Iraq, adding layers of additional screening from twelve additional oversight committees. It would have essentially shut down the admission of refugees from those countries.

28. See Lean, *Islamophobia Industry*. Lean's book carefully details the movement's recent history, traced to the activists Pamela Geller and Robert Spencer, who mobilized opposition to the Park51 Islamic Center in Manhattan, due to its proximity to Ground Zero. After the election of Barack Obama, the president's middle name (Hussein) and Muslim heritage provided further grist for the conspiracy mill.

29. Selod, *Forever Suspect*, 72, 74 (emphasis added).

30. See, e.g., Selod; Cainkar, *Homeland Insecurity*.

31. Ghori, "Religious Leaders Call for Unity."
32. KESQ, "Palm Desert Man Sentenced to Six Years."
33. Alsultany, *Arabs and Muslims in the Media*, 14.
34. Stockton, "Civil Liberties," 215.
35. Mamdani, *Good Muslim, Bad Muslim*, quoted in Alsultany, *Arabs and Muslims in the Media*, 14.
36. Kabir, *Young American Muslims*, 28.
37. Ghori, "Tension Rising for Inland Muslims."
38. See, e.g., C. Love, "Inland Muslims Face Both Hatred and Compassion"; Yarbrough, "Prom Queen like No Other."
39. Cainkar, *Homeland Insecurity*, 216.
40. Cainkar, 5.
41. Words such as "welcome" and "acceptance" and "belonging" were translated into Arabic during the interview to ensure that the meaning was understood.
42. UNHCR, "*Angekommen—We Have Arrived.*"
43. Rosaldo, "Cultural Citizenship, Inequality, and Multiculturalism," quoted in Ong, *Buddha Is Hiding*, 5.
44. Portes and Rumbaut, *Immigrant America*.
45. Smith, *Civic Ideals*, quoted in Bayoumi, *This Muslim American Life*, 126.
46. Bayoumi, 127.
47. Maira identified this pattern among Muslim youths in her research on the "9/11 generation" (*9/11 Generation*).
48. Kabir, *Young American Muslims*.
49. See, e.g., Flanagan et al., "Ethnic Awareness, Prejudice, and Civic Commitments"; Ewing and Hoyler, "Being Muslim and American."

CONCLUSION

1. The *Midway* was utilized during the first Gulf War, not the 2003 war, so it would not have been used to bomb Iraq in 2003; but other aircraft carriers like it were utilized in 2003.
2. Singh, *Race and America's Long War*, xi.
3. Singh.
4. Bayoumi, *This Muslim American Life*, 5.
5. Arendt, *Origins of Totalitarianism*, 296.
6. Angier, *On the Margins of the World*, 6.
7. American Security Against Foreign Enemies Act (American SAFE Act) of 2015.

METHODOLOGICAL APPENDIX

1. Malkki, *Purity and Exile*, 1.
2. Fassin, *Humanitarian Reasoning*.
3. Whenever I shared the case of Majid and Miriam (without divulging their real names) with people who I felt might have some insight, I was assured that they were most likely not Christians. But one individual knew of a case in which a

Christian couple, unable to have children, prayed to a saint at a Muslim shrine and named their child after the saint after making a vow.

4. Heschel, *Prophets*, x.

5. Baker and Shryock, "Citizenship and Crisis."

6. In my attempt to focus on the commonalities of the refugee experience, I did not fully explore the differences based on all of the ethnoreligious groupings. In the case of Armenian Iraqis, I felt that my sample was too small to say anything definitive about their experience relative to the others, with the exception of mentioning their ancestral origins in Ottoman Turkey.

7. For demographic profiles of Arab Americans by national origin, see E. Love, *Islamophobia and Racism in America*.

8. The ICMC, in a contract with the State Department, processed 6,140 of the 18,000 Iraqis resettled in the US in 2010, over one-third of the total admissions from Iraq. These included mobile and satellite operations in places where the US government could not operate at the time, such as Beirut, Lebanon.

9. See Gold, *Refugee Communities*; Cainkar, *Homeland Insecurity*; Selod, *Forever Suspect*; Naber, *Arab America*; Fassin, *Humanitarian Reasoning*; and Kenworthy, "Asylum's Asylum."

10. Kottak, *Anthropology*, appendix, 22–23.

11. Angrosino, *Doing Ethnographic and Observational Research*, 38.

12. See, e.g., Madriz, "Focus Groups in Feminist Research"; Hollander, "Social Contexts of Focus Groups."

13. Crane and Millard, "To Be with My People."

14. See Charmaz, "Grounded Theory"; Strauss, *Qualitative Analysis for Social Scientists*.

15. See Portes and Rumbaut, *Immigrant America*.

BIBLIOGRAPHY

Abdelkader, Engy. *When Islamophobia Turns Violent: The 2016 U.S. Presidential Elections*. Washington, DC: Bridge Initiative, Georgetown University Center for Muslim-Christian Understanding, 2016. http://bridge.georgetown.edu.

Abu-Lughod, Lila. *Do Muslim Women Need Saving?* Cambridge, MA: Harvard University Press, 2013.

Agamben, Giorgio. *Homo Sacer: Sovereign Power and Bare Life*. Translated by Daniel Heller-Roazen. Stanford, CA: Stanford University Press, 1998.

Aljazeera. "Scores Missing after Indian Ocean Sinking." June 22, 2012. www.aljazeera.com.

Almaguer, Tomás. *Racial Fault Lines: The Historical Origins of White Supremacy in California*. Berkeley: University of California Press, 2009.

Alsultany, Evelyn. *Arabs and Muslims in the Media: Race and Representation after 9/11*. New York: NYU Press, 2012.

Amara, Lamea Abbas. "San Diego (on a Rainy Day)." In *The Poetry of Arab Women*, edited by Natalie Handal, 79. New York: Interlink, 2001.

Amos, Deborah. *Eclipse of the Sunnis: Power, Exile, and Upheaval in the Middle East*. New York: Public Affairs, 2010.

Anderson, Benedict. *Imagined Communities: Reflections on the Origins and Spread of Nationalism*. New York: Verso, 1983.

"Angela Merkel, Chancellor of the Free World." *Time*, December 21, 2016.

Angier, Michel. *On the Margins of the World: The Refugee Experience Today*. Cambridge: Cambridge University Press, 2008.

Angrosino, Michael. *Doing Ethnographic and Observational Research*. Newberry Park, CA: Sage, 2007.

Appadurai, Arjun. *Fear of Small Numbers: An Essay on the Geography of Anger*. Durham, NC: Duke University Press, 2006.

Arango, Tim. "Amiriya Bomb Shelter: America's Legacy in Iraq." March 2, 2016. https://gulfnews.com.

Arbaeen Walk. "How the Walk Works." Accessed October 16, 2019. www.arbaeenwalk.com.

Arendt, Hannah. *The Origins of Totalitarianism*. Orlando, FL: Harcourt, 1985.

———. "We Refugees." In *Altogether Elsewhere: Writers in Exile*, edited by Marc Robinson, 110–119. Boston: Faber and Faber, 1994.

Assyrian International News Agency. "Assyrians: Frequently Asked Questions." Accessed April 21, 2018. www.aina.org.

Baker, Reginald P., and David S. North. *The 1975 Refugees: Their First Five Years.* Washington, DC: New Transcentury Foundation, 1984.

Baker, William, and Jamal Amaney. "Values and Cultural Membership." In *Citizenship and Crisis: Arab Detroit after 9/11,* edited by Detroit Arab American Study Team, 134–164. New York: Russell Sage Foundation, 2009.

Baker, William, and Andrew Shryock. "Citizenship and Crisis." In *Citizenship and Crisis: Arab Detroit after 9/11,* edited by Detroit Arab American Study Team, 3–32. New York: Russell Sage Foundation, 2009.

Banerjee, Paula. Plenary address to the annual meeting of the International Association for the Study of Forced Migration, Poznan, Poland, July 14, 2016.

Bankston, Carl I., III, and Min Zhou. *Growing Up American.* New York: Russell Sage Foundation, 1998.

Barth, Fredrick. *Ethnic Groups and Boundaries: The Social Organization of Culture Difference.* Long Grove, IL: Waveland, 1998.

Bates, Daniel G., and Amal Rassam. *Peoples and Cultures of the Middle East.* Upper Saddle River, NJ: Prentice Hall, 2001.

Bauman, Zygmunt. *Strangers at Our Door.* Cambridge, UK: Polity, 2016.

Bayoumi, Moustafa. *How Does It Feel to Be a Problem? Being Young and Arab in America.* New York: Penguin, 2008.

———. *This Muslim American Life: Dispatches from the War on Terror.* New York: NYU Press, 2015.

Beaumont, Thomas. "Ben Carson Says 'No' to Syrian Refugees in U.S." *Washington Times,* October 2, 2015. www.washingtontimes.com.

Bellah, Robert, Richard Madsen, William M. Sullivan, Ann Swidler, and Steven M. Tipton. *Habits of the Heart.* Berkeley: University of California Press, 1996.

Bennis, Phyllis, and Denis J. Halliday. "Iraq: The Impact of Sanctions and U.S. Policy." In *Iraq under Siege: The Deadly Impact of Sanctions and War,* edited by Anthony Arnove, 35–46. Cambridge, MA: South End, 2000.

Berger, J. M. "Author Says New Zealand Massacre Points to a Global Resurgence of 'Extremism.'" Interview by Terry Gross. *Fresh Air,* NPR, March 25, 2019.

Berry, J. W. "Globalisation and Acculturation." *International Journal of Intercultural Relations* 32 (2008): 320–330.

Bettis, Rita. "The Iraqi Refugee Crisis: Whose Problem Is It?" *Transnational Law and Contemporary Problems* 19 (2010): 261–277.

Between the Devil and the Deep Blue Sea. Directed by David Schmidt. 2011.

Biehl, João, and Peter Locke. "Deleuze and the Anthropology of Becoming." *Current Anthropology* 51, no. 3 (2010): 317–351.

Bloemraad, Irene. *Becoming a Citizen: Incorporating Immigrants and Refugees in the United States and Canada.* Berkeley: University of California Press, 2006.

Britannica. "Fifth Column." Accessed March 23, 2018. http//:brittanica.com.

Bundes Amt für Migranten und Flüchtlinger. *Asylgeschäftsstatistic für den Monat Dezember 2015.* Nuremberg, Germany: BAMF, 2015.

Bush, George W. "State of the Union." January 29, 2002. https://georgewbush-white-house.archives.gov.

Cainkar, Louise. *Homeland Insecurity: The Arab American and Muslim American Experience after 9/11*. New York: Russell Sage Foundation, 2008.

Campisi, Elizabeth. *Escape to Miami: An Oral History of the Cuban Rafter Crisis*. Oxford: Oxford University Press, 2016.

Carling, Jorgen. "Migration in the Age of Involuntary Immobility: Theoretical Reflections and Cape Verdean Experiences." *Journal of Ethnic and Migration Studies* 28, no. 1 (2002): 5–42.

Castles, Stephen, Hein de Haas, and Mark J. Miller. *The Age of Migration: International Population Movements in the Modern World*. 5th ed. New York: Guilford, 2014.

Chandrasekaran, Rajiv. *Imperial Life in the Emerald City*. New York: Vintage Books, 2006.

Chapa, Jorge, and Ann V. Millard, eds. *Apple Pie and Enchiladas: Latino Newcomers in the Rural Midwest*. Austin: University of Texas Press, 2004.

Chapa, Jorge, Rogelio Saenz, Refugio I. Rochín, and Eileen Diaz McConnell. "Latinos and the Changing Demographic Fabric of the Rural Midwest." In *Apple Pie and Enchiladas: Latino Newcomers in the Rural Midwest*, edited by Ann V. Millard and Jorge Chapa, 47–74. Austin: University of Texas Press, 2004.

Charmaz, Kathy. "Grounded Theory: Objectivist and Constructivist Methods. In *Handbook of Qualitative Research*, edited by Norman K. Denzin and Yvonna S. Lincoln, 509–536. Thousand Oaks, CA: Sage, 2000.

Chatelard, Géraldine. "What Visibility Conceals: Re-embedding Refugee Migration from Iraq." In *Dispossession and Displacement: Forced Migration in the Middle East and North Africa*, edited by Dawn Chatty and Bill Finlayson, 17–44. Oxford: Oxford University Press, 2010.

Chatty, Dawn. *Displacement and Dispossession in the Middle East*. Cambridge: Cambridge University Press, 2010.

Chatty, Dawn, and Nisrine Mansour. "Unlocking Protracted Displacement of Refugees and IDPs: Somali and Iraqi Displacements and Policy Responses." Podcast from Refugee Studies Centre and United Nations High Commissioner for Refugees at UNHCR London, March 6, 2012. http://forcedmigration.org.

Cheng, Wendy. *Changs Next Door to the Díazes: Remapping Race in Suburban California*. Minneapolis: University of Minnesota Press, 2013.

CNBC. "FBI Investigating California Massacre as 'Act of Terrorism.'" December 4, 2015. http://cnbc.com.

Coates, Ta'Nehisi. *Between the World and Me*. New York: Spiegel and Grau, 2015.

Coleman, James S. "Social Capital in the Creation of Human Capital." *American Journal of Sociology* 94 (1990): 95–120.

Corcoran, Ann. *Refugee Resettlement and the Hijra to America*. Washington, DC: Center for Security Policy, 2015.

Cornelius, Wayne A. "The Structural Embeddedness of Demand for Mexican Immigrant Labor: New Evidence from California." In *Crossings: Mexican Immigration in Interdisciplinary Perspectives*, edited by M. Suarez-Orozco, 114–144. Cambridge, MA: Harvard University Press, 1998.

Coulter, Ann. *Adios, America*. Washington, DC: Regnery, 2015.

Crane, Ken R. "'The Country Chooses You': Discourses of Agency, Mobility, and Immobility in the Iraqi Experience." *Journal of Conflict Transformation and Security* 7, no. 1 (2019): 8–23.

———. *Latino Churches: Faith, Family, and Ethnicity in the Second Generation*. New York: LFB Scholarly, 2003.

———. "Mexicans, Americans, and Neither: Students at Wheelerton High." In *Apple Pie and Enchiladas: Latino Newcomers in the Rural Midwest*, edited by Ann V. Millard and Jorge Chapa, 149–168. Austin: University of Texas Press, 2004.

———. "Not Racist like Our Parents: Anti-Latino Prejudice and Institutional Discrimination." In *Apple Pie and Enchiladas: Latino Newcomers in the Rural Midwest*, edited by Jorge Chapa and Ann V. Millard, 69–82. Austin: University of Texas Press, 2004.

Crane, Ken R., and Lisa Fernandez. "Iraqi Refugees in Spanish-Speaking Californian Communities." *Forced Migration Review*, February 2017, 99.

Crane, Ken R., Mohamed Iddris, Layla, Mustafa, Moawia Mohamed, and Ali Mousa Rufai. *Baseline Study of Socio-economic and Environmental Characteristics of the Um Gawaseer Project Area*. Khartoum: Adventist Development and Relief Agency, Sudan, 1995.

Crane, Ken R., and Ann V. Millard. "'To Be with My People': Latino Churches in the Rural Midwest." In *Apple Pie and Enchiladas: Latino Newcomers in the Rural Midwest*, edited by Ann V. Millard and Jorge Chapa, 172–195. Austin: University of Texas Press, 2004.

Crawley, Heaven, Franck Duvell, Katharine Jones, and Dimitris Skleparis. "Understanding the Dynamics of Migration to Greece and the EU: Drivers, Decisions and Destinations." MEDMIG Research Brief no. 2, September 2016. www.medmig.info.

Davis, Mike. *City of Quartz: Excavating the Future in Los Angeles*. New York: Vintage Books, 1992.

Dearborn.org. "March for Justice to Mark the 40th of Imam Hussain A.S. in Dearborn." October 22, 2019. https://dearborn.org.

DeFronzo, James. *The Iraq War: Origins and Consequences*. Boulder, CO: Westview, 2010.

de Haas, Hein. *Mobility and Human Development*. New York: UNDP, 2009.

Deleuze, Gilles. *Two Regimes of Madness: Texts and Interviews 1975–1995*. Los Angeles: Semiotext(e), 2006.

DeSoto, Lewis. *Empire: Photographs and Essays*. Berkeley, CA: Heyday, 2014.

Detroit Arab American Study Team, eds. *Citizenship and Crisis: Arab Detroit after 9/11*. New York: Russell Sage Foundation, 2009.

Ebaugh, Helen R., and Janet S. Chavetz. *Religion and the New Immigrants: Continuities and Adaptations in Immigrant Congregations*. Walnut Creek, CA: AltaMira, 2000.

Eurostat. "Record Number of over 1.2 Million First Time Asylum Seekers Registered in 2015." Accessed April 5, 2016. http://ec.europa.eu.

Ewing, Katherine P., ed. *Being and Belonging: Muslims in the United States since 9/11*. New York: Russell Sage Foundation, 2008.

Ewing, Katherine P., and Marguerite Hoyler. "Being Muslim and American: South Asian Muslim Youth and the War on Terror." In *Being and Belonging: Muslims in the United States since 9/11*, edited by Katherine P. Ewing, 80–104. New York: Russell Sage Foundation, 2008.

Fantz, Ben, and Ashley Brumfield. "More than Half the Nation's Governors Say Syrian's Not Welcome." CNN, November 19, 2015. www.cnn.com.

Fassin, Didier. *Humanitarian Reasoning: A Moral History of the Present*. Berkeley: University of California Press, 2012.

Fernandez, Lisa. "Your Latino Neighbors." BA thesis, La Sierra University, Riverside, CA, 2016.

Filkins, Dexter. *The Forever War*. New York: Vintage Books, 2008.

Finnegan, William. "Trump and the Refugees." *New Yorker*, October 2, 2015. www.newyorker.com.

Flanagan, Constance, Amy K. Syvertsen, Sukhdeep Gill, Leslie S. Gallay, and Patricio Cumsille. "Ethnic Awareness, Prejudice, and Civic Commitments in Four Ethnic Groups of American Adolescents." *Journal of Youth and Adolescence* 38, no. 4 (2009): 500–518. doi:10.1007/s10964-009-9394-z.

Flores-Gonzales, Nilda. *Citizens but not Americans: Race and Belonging among Latino Millennials*. New York: NYU Press, 2017.

Florido, Adrian. "A Decade after War's Start, Iraqi Refugees Are Transforming a California Town." KPBS, March 22, 2013. www.kpbs.org.

Foucault, Michel. *Discipline and Punish*. New York: Vintage Books, 1995.

———."Governmentality." In *The Foucault Effect: Studies in Governmentality*, edited by Graham Burchell, Colin Gordon, and Peter Miller, 87–104. Chicago: University of Chicago Press, 1991.

———. "Techniques of the Self: Lectures at University of Vermont, October 1982." Foucault.info. Accessed May 6, 2020. https://foucault.info.

Georgetown University Law Center. *Refugee Crisis in America: Iraqis and Their Resettlement Experience*. Washington, DC: Georgetown University, Human Rights Institute, 2009.

Ghori, Imran. "Religious Leaders Call for Unity: Representatives from Several Faiths Deliver a Plea for Peace at Mosques in Riverside and Corona." *Press Enterprise* (Riverside, CA), December 12, 2015.

———. "Tension Rising for Inland Muslims: Since the Shootings, They've Heard More Whispers and Stereotypical Comments." *Press Enterprise* (Riverside, CA), December 11, 2015.

Gifford, Lindsay. "Iraqi Refugee Perceptions of Urban Violence." Presentation at Boston University Workshop, "The Syrian Refugee Crisis and Lessons from the Iraqi Refugee Experience," Institute for Iraqi Studies, Boston, MA, 2013.

God Grew Tired of Us. Directed by Christopher D. Quin. Pace Films, 2008.

Gold, Steven J. "Arab American Reflections on Documentary Images of their Community: A Photo-Elicitation Study." *Visual Studies* 30, no. 3 (2015): 228–243.

———. *The Israeli Diaspora*. New York: Routledge, 2002.

———. *Refugee Communities: A Comparative Field Study*. Thousand Oaks, CA: Sage, 1992.

Granovetter, Mark. "The Strength of Weak Ties: A Network Theory Revisited." *Sociological Theory* 1 (1983): 201–233.

Green, John. *Devil's Bargain: Steve Bannon, Donald Trump, and the Storming of the Presidency*. London: Penguin, 2017.

Guerrero, Perla M. *Nuevo South: Latinas/os, Asians, and the Remaking of Place*. Austin: University of Texas Press, 2017.

Gurnah, Adbulrazak. *Gravel Heart*. New York: Bloomsbury, 2017.

Habeeb-Silva, Rebecca. "Resettlement Challenges for Refugees in the United States." Master's thesis, Department of Social Work, California State University, San Bernardino, 2016.

Haddad, Yvonne Y. *The Emergence of Muslim American Feminisms*. Louisville, KY: Westminster John Knox Press, 2014.

Haines, David W., ed. *Refugees as Immigrants: Cambodians, Laotians, and Vietnamese in America*. Totowa, NJ: Rowman and Littlefield, 1989.

———. *Safe Haven? A History of Refugees in America*. Sterling, VA: Kumarian, 2010.

Haj, T. A. El-. "Becoming Citizens in an Era of Globalization and Transnational Migration: Re-imagining Citizenship as Critical Practice." *Theory into Practice* 48, no. 4 (2009): 274–282. doi:10.1080/00405840903192714.

Hamilton-Merrit, Jane. *Tragic Mountains: The Hmong, the Americans, and the Secret Wars for Laos, 1942–1992*. Bloomington: Indiana University Press, 1992.

Hamoudi, Haider A. *Howling in Mesopotamia*. New York: Beaufort Books, 2008.

Handlin, Oscar. *The Uprooted: The Epic Story of the Great Migrations That Made the American People*. Boston: Little, Brown, 1951.

Hanna, Thomas E. "No Refuge for Iraqi Refugees: How the United States Can Improve Its Refugee Resettlement Policies." *California Western International Law Journal* 42 (2010): 189–219.

Hanoosh, Yasmeen. "The Chaldean Church between Iraq and America." In *Minorities and the Modern Arab World*, ed. Laura Robson, 191–211. Syracuse, NY: Syracuse University Press, 2016.

———. *The Chaldeans: Politics and Identity in Iraq and the American Diaspora*. London: I. B. Taurus, 2019.

Harper, Andrew. "Iraq's Refugees: Ignored and Unwanted." *International Review of the Red Cross* 90, no. 869 (2008): 169–190.

Hassan, Amro, and Henry Chu. "Germany's Embrace of Refugees Spurs Backlash." *Los Angeles Times*, September 1, 2015.

Hauck, Fern R., Elsbeth Lo, Anne Maxwell, and P. Preston Reynolds. "Factors Influencing the Acculturation of Burmese, Bhutanese, and Iraqi Refugees into American Society: Cross-Cultural Comparisons." *Journal of Immigrant and Refugee Studies* 12 (2014): 331–352. doi:10.1080/15562948.2013.848007.

Hein, Jeremy. "Refugees, Immigrants, and the State." *Annual Review of Sociology* 19 (1999): 43–59.

Heschel, Abraham Joshua. *The Prophets*. New York: Harper and Row, 1962.

Hollander, Jocelyn. "The Social Contexts of Focus Groups." *Journal of Contemporary Ethnography* 33, no. 5 (2004): 602–637.

Hondagneu-Sotelo, Pierrette, and Ernestine Avila. "'I'm Here, but I'm There': The Meanings of Latina Transnational Motherhood." *Gender and Society* 11, no. 5 (1997): 548–571.

Howell, Sally. "Muslims as Moving Targets: External Scrutiny and Internal Critique in Detroit's Mosques." In *Arab Detroit 9/11: Life in the Terror Decade*, edited by Nabeel Abraham, Sally Howell, and Andrew Shryock, 151–185. Detroit: Wayne State University Press, 2011. ProQuest Ebook Central.

Huddleston, Elizabeth. *Out of Iraq: True Stories of Iraqis Forced to Flee Their Country*. Self-published, 2013.

Husing, John E. "Inland Empire 2012 Forecast." *Inland Empire Quarterly Economic Report* 24, no. 2 (2012). http://sanbag.ca.gov.

Içduygu, Ahmet. *Irregular Migration in Turkey*. IOM Migration Research Series, Report No. 12. Geneva: IOM, 2003.

International Catholic Migration Commission. *Restoring Dignity, Inspiring Change*. Geneva: ICMC Headquarters, 2010.

International Catholic Migration Commission and International Rescue Committee. *10,000 Refugees from Iraq: A Report of Joint Resettlement in the European Union*. Brussels: ICMC and IRC, 2010.

International Organization for Migration. *World Migration Report 2011*. Geneva: International Organization for Migration, 2011. https://publications.iom.int.

International Rescue Committee. *In Dire Straits: Iraqi Refugees in the United States*. New York: IRC, 2009.

Jamal, Amaney A., and Nadine C. Naber. *Race and Arab Americans before and after 9/11: From Invisible Citizens to Visible Subjects*. Syracuse, NY: Syracuse University Press, 2008.

Jendian, Matthew J. *Becoming American, Remaining Ethnic: The Case of Armenian Americans in Central California*. New York: LFB Scholarly, 2008.

Jubany, Olga. *Screening Asylum in a Culture of Disbelief: Truths, Denials, and Skeptical Borders*. New York: Palgrave Macmillan, 2017.

Kabir, Nahid Afrose. *Muslim Americans: Debating the Notions of American and Un-American*. London: Routledge, 2017.

———. *Young American Muslims: Dynamics of Identity*. Edinburgh: Edinburgh University Press, 2013.

Kenworthy, Nora. "Asylum's Asylum: Undocumented Immigrants, Belonging, and the Space of Exception at a State Psychiatric Center." *Human Organization* 71, no. 2 (2012): 123–134.

KESQ. "Palm Desert Man Sentenced to Six Years for Firebombing Coachella Mosque." February 29, 2016. www.kesq.com.

Kibria, Nazli. *Family Tightrope: The Changing Lives of Vietnamese Americans*. Princeton, NJ: Princeton University Press, 1995.

Kopan, Tal. "Donald Trump: Syrian Refugees a 'Trojan Horse.'" CNN, November 16, 2015. www.cnn.com.

Kottak, Conrad. *Anthropology: The Exploration of Human Diversity*. 12th ed. Boston: McGraw-Hill Higher Education, 2008.

Krogstad, Jens Manuel, and Jynnah Radford. "Key Facts about Refugees to the US." Pew Research Center, January 30, 2017. http://pewresearch.org.

Kurien, Prema. "Becoming American by Becoming Hindu: Indian Americans Take Their Place at the Multicultural Table." In *Gatherings in Diaspora: Religious Communities and the New Immigration*, edited by R. Stephen Warner and Judith G. Wittner, 37–70. Philadelphia: Temple University Press, 1998.

Lam, Andrew. "Refugees Then, Trespassers Now." *Los Angeles Times*, November 8, 2015.

Land, Gary. *Historical Dictionary of Seventh-Day Adventists*. Lanham, MD: Scarecrow, 2005.

Latino Muslim Unity. "About." Accessed December 3, 2019. www.latinoandmuslimunity.org.

Lattimer, Mark. "In 20 Years There Will Be No More Christians in Iraq." *Guardian*, October 2, 2006.

Lean, Nathan. *The Islamophobia Industry: How the Right Manufactures Fear of Muslims*. London: Pluto, 2014.

León, Luís D. "Born Again in East Los Angeles: The Congregation as Border Space." In *Gatherings in Diaspora: Religious Communities and the New Immigration*, edited by R. Stephen Warner and Judith G. Wittner, 163–196. Philadelphia: Temple University Press, 1998.

Levitt, Peggy. *God Needs No Passport*. New York: New Press, 2009.

Light, Ivan H., and Steven J. Gold. *Ethnic Economies*. Bingley, UK: Emerald Group, 2000.

Lipca, Michael. "Muslims and Islam: Key Findings in the U.S. and around the World." Pew Research Center, August 9, 2017. https://pewresearch.org.

List Project to Resettle Our Iraqi Allies. "Timeline of Events." Accessed September 30, 2018. http://thelistproject.org.

———. "Tragedy on the Horizon: A History of Just and Unjust Withdrawal." Accessed December 3, 2010. http://thelistproject.org.

Love, Carl. "Inland Muslims Face Both Hatred and Compassion." *Press Enterprise* (Riverside, CA), January 3, 2016. www.pe.com.

Love, Eric. *Islamophobia and Racism in America*. New York: NYU Press, 2017.

MacLeod, Jay. *Ain't No Makin' It*. Boulder, CO: Westview, 1995.

Madriz, Esther. "Focus Groups in Feminist Research." In *Handbook of Qualitative Research*, edited by Norman K. Denzin and Yvonna S. Lincoln, 2nd ed., 835–850. Thousand Oaks, CA: Sage, 2000.

Maira, Sunaina M. "Citizenship, Dissent, Empire: South Asian Muslim Immigrant Youth." In *Being and Belonging: Muslims in the United States since 9/11*, edited by Katherine P. Ewing, 15–46. New York: Russell Sage Foundation, 2008.

———. "Fighting with Rights and Forging Alliances: Youth Politics in the War on Terror." In *The War of My Generation: Representation and Reality*, edited by David Kieran, 60–82. Austin: University of Texas Press, 2015.

———. *Missing: Youth, Citizenship and Empire after 9/11*. Durham NC: Duke University Press, 2009.

———. *The 9/11 Generation: Youth, Rights, and Solidarity in the War on Terror*. New York: NYU Press, 2016.

Malaika, Nazik Al-. "New Year." In *Fifteen Iraqi Poets*, edited by Mikhail Dunya. New York: New Directions, 2013.

Malkki, Liisa H. *Purity and Exile: Violence, Memory, and National Cosmology among Hutu Refugees in Tanzania*. Chicago: University of Chicago Press, 1995.

———. "Refugees to Exiles: From Refugee Studies to the Natural Order of Things." *Annual Review of Anthropology* 24 (1995): 495–528.

Malley, Robert, and Jon Finer. "The Long Shadow of 9/11: How Counterterrorism Warps U.S. Foreign Policy." *Foreign Affairs*, July–August 2018.

Mama, Amina. "Asylum and Making of Home Terrain." In *Losing Place: Refugee Populations and Rural Transformations in East Africa*, edited by Jonathan Bascom, 130–147. New York: Berghahn Books, 1998.

Mamdani, Mahmood. *Good Muslim, Bad Muslim: America, the Cold War, and the Roots of Terror*. New York: NYU Press, 2004.

Manganaro, Marc. "Textual Play, Power, and Cultural Critique: An Orientation to Modernist Anthropology." In *Modernist Anthropology, from Fieldwork to Text*, edited by Marc Manganaro, 3–47. Princeton, NJ: Princeton University Press, 2014.

Massey, Douglas S. "The New Immigration and Ethnicity in the United States." *Population and Development Review* 21, no. 3 (1995): 631–652.

Massey, Douglas S., Jorge Durand, and Karen A. Pren. "Why Border Enforcement Backfired." *American Journal of Sociology* 21, no. 5 (2016): 1557–1600.

Menchú, Rigoberta. *I, Rigoberta Menchú: Indian Woman in Guatemala*. New York: Verso, 2010.

Micinski, Nicholas R. "Refugee Policy as Foreign Policy: Iraqi and Afghan Refugee Resettlements to the United States." *Refugee Survey Quarterly* 37, no. 3 (2018): 253–278. doi:10.1093/rsq/hdy00.7.

Migration Policy Institute. "Refugees and Asylees in the United States." Accessed March 3, 2016. www.migrationpolicy.org.

———. "Top 10 Migration Issues of 2008." 2008. www.migrationpolicy.org.

Mills, C. Wright. *The Sociological Imagination*. Oxford: Oxford University Press, 1967.

Molan, Jim. "Australia in Iraq 2002–2010: Inconsequential, Confused, and Timid." *Interpreter* (Lowy Institute), March 10, 2017. www.lowyinstitute.org.

Monsutti, Alessandro. "States, Sovereignties and Refugees: A View from the Margins?" Refugee Studies Centre podcast, 2012. www.rsc.ox.ac.uk.

———. *War and Migration: Social Networks and Economic Strategies of the Hazaras of Afghanistan*. New York: Routledge, 2005.

Naber, Nadine. *Arab America: Gender, Cultural Politics, and Activism.* New York: NYU Press, 2012.

Nayeri, Dina. "The Ungrateful Refugee." In *The Displaced: Refugee Writers on Refugee Lives*, edited by Viet Thanh Nguyen, 145–158. New York: Abrams, 2018.

Neumann, Philipp. "Die Herkunft vieler Flüchtlinge ist ungeklärt." *Berliner Morgenpost*, July 21, 2016.

Nguyen, Viet Thanh, ed. *The Displaced: Refugee Writers on Refugee Lives.* New York: Abrams, 2018.

Nieri, Tanya, Michele Adams, Matthew Grindal, Jeffrey T. Cookston, William Fabricius, Ross D. Parke, and Delia Saenz. "Reconsidering the 'Acculturation Gap' Narrative through an Analysis of Parent-Adolescent Acculturation Differences in Mexican American Families." *Journal of Family Issues* 37, no. 14 (2014): 1919–1944.

Noorani, Ali. *There Goes the Neighborhood: How Communities Overcome Prejudice and Meet the Challenge of American Immigration.* Amherst, NY: Prometheus Books, 2017.

Office of Refugee Resettlement. *Annual Report to Congress.* Washington, DC: US Department of Health and Human Services, 2013.

Olivo, Antonio. "Deployed by Gov. Rick Perry, National Guard Adjusts to Its New Role on the Texas Border." *Washington Post*, September 1, 2014. www.washingtonpost.com.

Olson, David. "Families Fleeing Violence of War Bring Hopes for Peaceful Lives." *Press Enterprise* (Riverside, CA), February 18, 2009.

Omi, Michael, and Howard Winant. *Racial Formation in the United States.* 3rd ed. New York: Routledge, 1994.

Ong, Aihwa. *Buddha Is Hiding: Refugees, Citizenship, the New America.* Berkeley: University of California Press, 2003.

———. "Cultural Citizenship as Subject-Making: Immigrants Negotiate Racial and Cultural Boundaries in the United States." *Current Anthropology* 37, no. 5 (1996): 737–762.

On Her Shoulders. Directed by Alexandria Bombach. Amazon Digital Services, 2018.

Ossman, Susan. *Moving Matters: Paths of Serial Migration* Stanford, CA. Stanford University Press, 2013.

Patterson, Thomas C. *From Acorns to Warehouses.* New York: Routledge, 2014.

Portes, Alejandro, and Rubén G. Rumbaut. *Immigrant America: A Portrait.* 4th ed. Berkeley: University of California Press, 2014.

———. *Legacies: The Story of the New Second Generation.* Berkeley: University of California Press, 2001.

Poulos, James. "Obama Bungled US Response to the Arab Spring." *Press Enterprise* (Riverside, CA), June 5, 2016.

Pyke, Karen. "The Normal American Family as an Interpretive Structure of Family Life among Grown Children of Korean and Vietnamese Immigrants." *Journal of Marriage and Family* 62 (February 2000): 240–255.

Radi, Nuha al-. *Baghdad Diaries: A Woman's Chronicle of War and Exile*. New York: Vintage, 2003.

Rahman, Shazia. "Muslim Women Who Wear Hijabs Are Fearful of Backlash after Attacks." Interview by David Greene. *Morning Edition*, NPR, December 11, 2015. www.npr.org.

Rassam, Suha. *Christianity in Iraq*. Herefordshire, UK: Gracewing, 2005.

Read, Jen'nan G. "Multiple Identities among Arab Americans: A Tale of Two Congregations." In *Being and Belonging: Muslims in the United States since 9/11*, edited by Katherine P. Ewing, 80–104. New York: Russell Sage Foundation, 2008.

Reimers, David M. *Still the Golden Door*. New York: Columbia University Press, 1992.

Rosaldo, Renato. "Cultural Citizenship, Inequality, and Multiculturalism." In *Latino Cultural Citizenship: Claiming Identity, Space and Rights*, edited by William V. Flores and Rina Benmayor, 27–38. Boston: Beacon, 1997.

Rosenberg, Mica, and Julia Edwards Ainsley. "Immigration Hardliner Says Trump Team Preparing Plans for Wall, Mulling Muslim Registry." Reuters, November 15, 2016. http://reuters.com.

Rumbaut, Rubén G. "The Crucible Within: Ethnic Identity, Self-Esteem, and Segmented Assimilation among Children of Immigrants." *International Migration Review* 28 (1994): 748–794.

———. "Portraits, Patterns, and Predictors of the Refugee Adaptation Process: Results and Reflections from the IHARP Panel Study." In *Refugees as Immigrants: Cambodians, Laotians, and Vietnamese in America*, edited by David W. Haines, 138–182. Totowa, NJ: Rowman and Littlefield, 1989.

Said, Edward. *Covering Islam: How the Media and the Experts Determine How We See the Rest of the World*. New York: Vintage, 2015.

———. *Orientalism*. New York: Pantheon Books, 1978.

Saleh, Omar Al. "Iraqi Refugees Flee Syrian Violence." *Al Jazeera*, August 1, 2012. http://aljazeera.com.

Sandell, David. *Open Your Heart*. South Bend, IN: University of Notre Dame Press, 2015.

Sassoon, Joseph. *The Iraqi Refugees: The New Crisis in the Middle East*. New York: I. B. Tauris, 2009.

Selod, Saher. "Criminalization of Muslim American Men in the United States." In *The Immigrant Other: Lived Experiences in a Transnational World*, edited by Rich Furman, Greg Lamphear, and Douglas Epps, 62–74. New York: Columbia University Press, 2016.

———. *Forever Suspect: Racialized Surveillance of Muslim Americans in the War on Terror*. New Brunswick, NJ: Rutgers University Press, 2018.

Semple, Kirk. "War-Scarred Iraqi Refugees Find More Misery in America." *Press Enterprise* (Riverside, CA), August 16, 2009.

Shadid, Anthony. *Night Draws Near: Iraq's People in the Shadow of America's War*. New York: Picador, 2006.

Shahoian, Levon. *On the Banks of the Tigris*. London: Gomidas Institute, 2012.

Sheridan, Tom. "Police Chief Reluctantly Accepts Hero Role: The Muslim Event Also Urges Members of the Faith to Confront Extreme Ideology." *Press Enterprise* (Riverside, CA), December 27, 2015.

Singh, Nikhil Pal. *Race and America's Long War*. Oakland: University of California Press, 2017.

Siu, Lok. "Diasporic Cultural Citizenship: Chineseness and Belonging in Central America and Panama." *Social Text* 19 (2001): 7–28.

Smith, Rogers. *Civic Ideals: Conflicting Ideas of Citizenship in US History*. New Haven, CT: Yale University Press, 1999.

Stansfield, Gareth R. V. *Iraq: People, History, Politics*. Cambridge, UK: Polity, 2016.

St. Claire, Pat, Greg Botelho, and Ralph Ellis. "San Bernardino Shooter Tashfeen Malik: Who Was She?" CNN, December 8, 2015. http://cnn.com.

Stein, Barry. "The Experience of Being a Refugee: Insights from the Research." In *Refugee Mental Health in Resettlement Countries*, edited by Carolyn L. Williams and Joseph Westermeyer, 5–21. Washington, DC: Hemisphere, 1986.

Steinbeck, John. *The Grapes of Wrath*. 1939. Reprint, London: Penguin Classics, 2006.

Stevens-Arroyo, Anthony M., Anneris Goris, and Ariela Keysar. *The PARAL Study: The National Survey of Leadership in Latino Parishes and Congregations*. Brooklyn, NY: Office of Research for Religion in Society and Culture, Brooklyn College of CUNY, 2002.

Stiglitz, Joseph, and Linda J. Bilmes. *The Three Billion Dollar War*. New York: Norton, 2008.

Stockton, Ronald R. "Civil Liberties." In *Citizenship and Crisis: Arab Detroit after 9/11*, edited by Detroit Arab American Study Team, 193–226. New York: Russell Sage Foundation, 2015.

Strauss, Anselm. L. *Qualitative Analysis for Social Scientists*. Cambridge: Cambridge University Press, 1987.

Takaki, Ronald. *A Different Mirror: A History of Multi-cultural America*. New York: Little, Brown, 1993.

Talal, HRH Prince El Hassan bin. "Global Poverty, Humanitarian Need in the Middle East and Prospects for Peace in the Region." Podcast. November 21, 2007. www.forcedmigration.org.

Taylor, Jessie. "Behind Australian Doors: Examining the Condition of Asylum Seekers in Indonesia." Unpublished ms., 2009.

Tehranian, John. *Whitewashed: America's Invisible Middle Eastern Minority*. New York: NYU Press, 2009.

Thomas, William, and Florian Znaniecki. *The Polish Peasant in Europe and America: A Classic Work in Immigration History*. 1918. Reprint, Urbana: University of Illinois Press, 1996.

Tiriti, Nabil Al-. "There Go the Neighborhoods: Policy Effects Vis-à-Vis Iraqi Forced Migration." In *Dispossession and Displacement: Forced Migration in the Middle East and North Africa*, edited by Dawn Chatty and Bill Finlayson, 17–44. Oxford: Oxford University Press, 2010.

Tobin, Sarah. *The Syrian Refugee Crisis and Lessons from the Iraqi Refugee Experience.* Boston: Boston University Center for Iraqi Studies, 2013.

Tripp, Charles. *A History of Iraq.* Cambridge: Cambridge University Press, 2000.

Trump, Donald J. "Executive Order: Protecting the Nation from Foreign Terrorist Entry into the United States." January 27, 2017. https://whitehouse.gov.

———. "Immigration Policy." 2016. www.donaldjtrump.com.

———. "Statement on Preventing Muslim Immigration." December 7, 2015. www.donaldjtrump.com.

Twine, France Winddance, and Charles Gallagher. "Introduction: The Future of Whiteness: A Map of the 'Third Wave.'" *Ethnic and Racial Studies* 31, no. 1 (2008): 4–24.

Ufheil-Somer, Amanda. "Iraqi Christians: A Primer." *Middle East Report* (Middle East Research and Education Project) 267 (Summer 2013). https://merip.org.

UNHCR (United Nations High Commission for Refugees). *Angekommen—We Have Arrived: A Dialogue with Young Refugees in Germany.* Nuremberg, Germany: UNHCR, 2011.

———. "Global Focus: Iraq." Accessed April 8, 2018. http://reporting.unhcr.org.

———. "Iraqi Refugee and Asylum Seeker Statistics." 2003. http://unhcr.org.

———. "Surviving in the City: A Review of UNHCR's Operation for Iraqi Refugees in Urban Areas of Jordan, Lebanon and Syria." Geneva, 2009. http://unhcr.org.

———. "Syria Fact Sheet." Accessed April 8, 2018. http://reporting.unhcr.org.

———. "UNHCR Country Operations Profile—Jordan." 2012. http://unhcr.org.

———. "UNHCR Country Operations Profile—Syrian Arab Republic." 2012. http://unhcr.org.

UNICEF. *Iraq's Children: A Year in Their Life.* Geneva: United Nations, 2007.

United States Commission on International Religious Freedom. "USCIRF Annual Report 2013—Countries of Particular Concern: Iraq." 2013. www.refworld.org.

Urrea, Louis Alberto. *The Devil's Highway: A True Story.* New York: Black Bay Books, 2008.

US Census Bureau. "Data Finder for Riverside, San Bernardino, Fontana, Moreno Valley." Accessed August 23, 2016. http://factfinder.census.gov.

US Citizenship and Immigration Services. "Iraqi Refugee Processing Fact Sheet." 2013. http://uscis.gov.

US Customs and Border Protection. "United States Border Patrol Southwest Family Unit Subject and Unaccompanied Alien Children Apprehensions Fiscal Year 2016." 2016. www.cbp.gov.

US Department of Homeland Security. "Refugees and Asylees 2009." Office of Immigration Statistics, 2010. www.dhs.gov.

———. "Refugees and Asylees 2010." Office of Immigration Statistics, 2011. www.dhs.gov.

———. "Refugees and Asylees 2011." Office of Immigration Statistics, 2011. www.dhs.gov.

———. "Refugees and Asylees 2012." Office of Immigration Statistics, 2012. www.dhs. gov.

———. "Refugees and Asylees 2014." Office of Immigration Statistics, 2014. www.dhs. gov.

———. "Refugees and Asylees 2015." Office of Immigration Statistics, 2015. www.dhs. gov.

———. "Yearbook of Immigration Statistics 2004." 2004. www.dhs.gov.

———. "Yearbook of Immigration Statistics 2013, Table 14d." 2013. www.dhs.gov.

———. "Yearbook of Immigration Statistics 2016." 2016. www.dhs.gov.

US Department of State. "Status of Iraqi Special Immigrant Visa Programs." USDoS publication no. MERO-IQO-08-01. 2008. http://oig.state.gov.

US Senate Committee on Foreign Relations. *Abandoned upon Arrival: Implications for Refugees and Local Communities Burdened by a U.S. Resettlement System That Is Not Working.* S. Rep. No. 111-52. Washington, DC: US Government Printing Office, 2010.

van Kesteren, Geert. *Baghdad Calling.* Rotterdam: Episode, 2008.

Van Selm, Joanne. "Refugee Resettlement." In *The Oxford Handbook of Refugee and Forced Migration Studies,* edited by Elena Fiddian-Oasmiyeh, Gil Loescher, Katy Long, and Nando Sigona, 512–524. Oxford: Oxford University Press, 2014.

Wardi, Ali. *Understanding Iraq: Society, Culture and Personality.* 1965. Translated with a foreword by F. Baali. New York: Edwin Mellen, 2008.

Warner, R. Stephen. "Work in Progress toward a New Paradigm for the Sociological Study of Religion in the United States." *American Journal of Sociology* 98 (1993): 1044–1093.

Warner, R. Stephen, and Judith Wittner, eds. *Gatherings in Diaspora: Religious Communities and the New Immigration.* Philadelphia: Temple University Press, 1998.

Warren, Jonathan W., and France Winddance Twine. "White Americans, the New Minority? Non-Blacks and the Ever-Expanding Boundaries of Whiteness." *Journal of Black Studies* 28, no. 2 (1997): 200–218.

West, Bing. *No True Glory: A Frontline Account of the Battle for Fallujah.* New York: Random House, 2006.

Westermeyer, Joe. "Hmong Acculturation to the U.S.A.: An Analysis of a Complex Intervention." Presentation at 71st annual meeting of the Society for Applied Anthropology, Seattle, WA, 2011.

Williams, Raymond B. *Religions of Immigrants from India and Pakistan: New Threads in the American Tapestry.* Cambridge: Cambridge University Press, 1988.

Wimmer, Andreas. *Ethnic Boundary Making: Institutions, Power, Networks.* Oxford: Oxford University Press, 2013.

Wray-Lake, Laura, Amy K. Syvertsen, and Constance Flanagan. "Contested Citizenship and Social Exclusion: Adolescent Arab American Immigrants' Views of the Social Contract." *Applied Developmental Science* 12, no. 2 (2008): 84–92. doi:10.1080/10888690801997708.

"Wrong Solution, The." *Economist,* September 3, 2011.

Yako, Rihab M., and Bipasha Biswas. "'We Came to This Country for the Future of Our Children. We Have No Future': Acculturative Stress among Iraqi Refugees in the United States." *International Journal of Intercultural Relations* 38 (2014): 133–141.

Yarbrough, Beau. "A Prom Queen like No Other: Summit High Students Nominate a Conservative Muslim for the Honor and Her Classmates and Friends Wear Hijabs to Support Her." *Press Enterprise* (Riverside, CA), April 4, 2016.

Zehr, Mary Ann. "U.S. Bringing Iraqi Students and Educators to America." *Education Week* 24, no. 18 (2005): 1–9. http://search.proquest.com.

INDEX

Al-Askari Mosque (Iraq), xiv
Al-Khadmiya Mosque (Iraq), 9–10
American Security Against Foreign
    Enemies (SAFE) Act, 5, 114, 126,
    163n27
Amos, Deborah, 19
Angier, Michel, 128
Arab-Americans, definition of, 153n9,
    165n7
Arendt, Hannah, 1, 128
Armenian Iraqis, 16, 59, 60, 143, 144,
    154n9; Armenian Orthodox, 143; in
    study population, 165n6
Ashcroft, John, 2, 101, 112
Assyrian Iraqis, 6, 14, 58–60, 144, 159n28;
    Aramaic (neo-Aramaic, neo-Syriac)
    language, 58–61; ethnicity, 59–60; out-
    migration from Iraq, 61; transnational
    community, 61
Australia: asylum policy toward Iraqi boat
    people, 17–18, 156n43; Refugee Rights
    Action Network, 156n42; resettlement
    of Iraqi refugees, 14, 17, 18; support of
    US invasion, 156n38
autonomous self, 41

Baath Party, 12
Bannon, Steve, 111–12, 114; "civilization
    jihad" statement, 114
Bayoumi, Moustafa, 44, 48, 101, 113, 163n19
Bellah, Robert, 25, 41, 68
belonging, for refugees: citizenship and,
    23; felt sense of, 1, 6; loss in Iraq, 2,
    7–13; market norms of, 29, 41–42;

relation to religious community, 56;
    relation to work, 40; research frame,
    151
Biehl, João, 6, 30
Bureau of Population, Refugees, and
    Migration (PRM), US Department
    of State: processing centers, 22, 146.
    See also Turkey: Istanbul refugee
    agencies
Bush, George W., 1, 101

Cambodia refugees (Hmong people), xi,
    25, 29, 35, 37, 41
Catholic Charities, xv, 37, 146
Center for Security Policy, 114
Central American refugees: Donald
    Trump statement, 160n16; Guatemalan
    presence in Inland Empire, 161n14;
    protest at Murrieta ICE facility, 108–9;
    unaccompanied minors as asylum
    seekers, 108–9, 160n16
Chaldeans, 4, 6, 11, 14, 58–60, 143, 148;
    Aramaic language (neo-Aramaic,
    neo-Syriac), 58–61, 147; Arch-
    bishop Paulus Rahho, kidnapping
    of, 154n9; composition of study
    population, 143–44; ethnic identity
    in US, 103; Our Lady of Deliverance
    Church, attack on, 154n9; outmi-
    gration from Iraq, 61; parishes in
    Riverside, 32, 58–59, 61, 78; trans-
    national community, 61. *See also*
    Assyrian Iraqis
Cheng, Wendy, 99, 107

ABOUT THE AUTHOR

KEN R. CRANE is Associate Professor of Sociology and Global Studies at La Sierra University and the author of *Latino Churches: Faith, Family, and Ethnicity in the Second Generation.*